Dramatic Education . . . is a whole new way of looking at the process of education. If dramatic play is such an important factor in a child's life . . ., Dramatic Education asks that we centre the educative process upon it. We must examine our whole educational system in this light – the curricula, the syllabuses, the methods, and the philosophy upon which these are based. In all instances, we must start from acting. . . .

Richard Courtney, *Play, Drama and Thought.*

Educational Drama

A Practical Guide for Students and Teachers

Brian Peachment
Lecturer in Educational Drama,
Royal Scottish Academy of Music and Drama

MACDONALD AND EVANS

MACDONALD & EVANS LTD.
Estover, Plymouth PL6 7PZ

First published 1976

©

MACDONALD AND EVANS LIMITED
1976

ISBN: 0 7121 0552 2

Printed in Great Britain by Butler & Tanner, Ltd, Frome and London

Preface

This book is the outcome of thirteen years devoted to the theory and practice of educational drama.

It was as a general subjects teacher in a secondary school in 1962 that I first had a glimmering of the enormous potential that existed when drama was used as a tool in the learning situation. Vocabulary forms part of the staple diet of the English syllabus. But the rote learning of new words and their meanings had little appeal for the children of average ability and below when I was teaching. And yet the subject came alive by the simple expedient of putting the children into pairs, giving them each a character to play, and encouraging them to use the words we had been studying in the correct context within a dramatic situation.

My use of educational drama grew as I linked it to such subjects as religious education,* history and geography; but it was not until I attended a year's course in Drama in Education at Newcastle University Institute of Education and came under the spell of Mrs. Dorothy Heathcote that I realised fully just how valuable drama could be in the learning situation. My debt to this remarkable teacher is incalculable.

Of the many others who have helped me on my journey I would like to single out in particular my ex-pupils at South Hunsley School, who taught me what was acceptable, my ex-students at Middleton St. George College of Education, who enabled me to view the learning situation at one remove, and my present students at the Royal Scottish Academy of Music and Drama, for creating a tolerant environment in which I can think aloud.

My special thanks are due to Mr. Geoffrey Coates, who, as Education Producer with BBC Radio Durham suggested the idea of an improvised drama series exploring the problems of being a teenager in the 1970s. The series, entitled The Life and Times of Jimmy Robson, forms the basis of the scenarios in the chapter on ROSLA drama. And to Sister Julie, Headmistress of St. Charles Primary School,

* See *The Defiant Ones*, B. Peachment, Religious Education Press.

Kelvinside Gardens, Glasgow, for providing me with a class to try
out my ideas for drama as a focal point for integrated studies

April 1976   B.P.

Acknowledgments

I would like to express my grateful thanks to the following for permission to quote from copyright material:

Anthony Blond Ltd. for *Unsafe At Any Height*, John Godson.

Anthony Sheil Associates Ltd. and The Julian Bach Agency for *Soledad Brother*, George Jackson, Jonathan Cape Ltd.

Cassell & Company Ltd. for *Play, Drama and Thought*, Richard Courtney.

Tower Publications Inc. for *Survival Handbook*, Bruce Cassiday.

University of Oklahoma Press for *Red Men Calling On The Great White Father*, Katherine C. Turner.

Contents

List of Illustrations

Introduction

Educational Drama can be divided into two categories:

Drama involving research

This is drama which gives children an opportunity to seek knowledge by gathering information from varied sources (books, visits, visiting speakers, documents, films, film strips, etc.) relevant to a subject to be dramatised and then use that knowledge (as far as time and information will allow) to create a presentation of the subject chosen that is as realistic as possible. For example, if children are creating a play about the slave trade, the teacher might provide reproductions of advertisements offering slaves for sale, diagrams showing the cramped conditions on a slave ship, and photographs of the various types of irons used to secure the slaves after capture, plus relevant literary material. A study of such material pays huge dramatic dividends.

Drama using inner resources

However, the drama teacher does not have the time, the inclination, or often the resources available to produce such material for every project undertaken, therefore, much of his time will be spent drawing upon the inner resources of knowledge and experience provided by the pupils themselves. The teacher's skill lies in developing this material to maximum educational advantage.

To take an example. At the time of writing I am working with a primary seven class for three two-hour sessions. With only six hours at our disposal we have no time to spend studying literary source material.

Through discussion I found the children keen to explore a situation involving the kidnapping of a Leader of the Opposition by a group of gangsters, which, if left at that level, would, I foresaw, inevitably develop into a piece of rough and tumble chaos. I had to deepen the experience, take it beyond the realms of entertainment and create a viable atmosphere out of which meaningful learning experiences could arise. I began to probe more deeply into the motivations behind the kidnap attempt.

> "Why did they want to kidnap the Leader of the Opposition?"
> "For money."
> "Wouldn't it be simpler to rob a bank?"

Most of the children agreed that it would, especially in view of the tightened security arrangements surrounding MPs at the present time.

> "Who might want to kidnap the Leader of the Opposition in that case?"
> "People wanting to call attention to themselves."
> "Who would want to call attention to themselves in this way?"

And so we built up a picture of a vaguely middle-eastern country governed by a military junta. The majority of the population were living in poverty so that a select few could live in the lap of luxury. A country where insufficient funds were available for private housing while five-star hotels designed to woo rich foreign tourists proliferated.

Where political prisoners were forced to undertake dangerous work in munitions factories and where the freedom of the press had been silenced. The inevitable backlash occurred. A guerrilla organisation grew up engaging in acts of sabotage against the regime, but with little success. A group of dissidents tried to address a meeting of the United Nations but were ejected before they could begin. Driven to the limits of their endurance a break-away group hi-jacked a plane carrying a British Leader of the Opposition on a visit to Moscow. The pilot was forced at gun-point to bring the plane down on the runway of the airport in the guerrillas' own city. The resultant improvisation ended with a tense scene in which the hi-jackers attempted to bargain with the military: the lives of the passengers and crew for a promise to review the existing conditions. The lesson ended with a lively discussion on the theme of whether gangster methods are ever justified in an attempt to gain social justice. To which the reply was a resounding No!

And so, what originally began as "B picture" material turned into

an exploration of one of the problems currently facing the civilised
world, made all the more valuable through vicarious experiences only
possible through the medium of drama.

Educational drama should never stay at the level of superficiality
and cliché. If there is no more to educational drama than this, the
subject should be dropped from the timetable and replaced with extra
playtime – the experience would be just as valuable. Drama, if it is
to take its rightful place on a curriculum, must be an educational
tool not merely an indulgence. Children should be stretched in drama
just as much as they are in other subjects.

The scope of this book ranges from myths and legends with lower-
middle-school pupils to an outline of possible scenarios suitable for
development by fifth-year leavers, and is designed for drama students,
drama teachers, and teachers of other subjects who would like to use
drama as an aid in teaching their particular discipline. Chapter 1
offers pointers to an English teacher wishing to improvise myths and
legends studied in literature. Chapter 3 opens up possibilities for a
history teacher searching for a way in to a historical project via children's interests. While a geography teacher might consider a plane
crash as a way in to the study of a primitive tribe as outlined in
Chapter 4. Chapter 5 – Small Boys for Small Flues – deals with ways
in which drama can be used as the focal point for integrated studies,
either as a self-contained project at primary school level or in a more
limited way in the secondary school.

The book contains scenarios which can be improvised by children,
teaching points arising out of the material, and relevant factual information for the busy drama teacher who may not have the time or
the facilities for extended research. The book also shows how a drama
teacher works. How to achieve "non-directed direction." How to deploy a class of children so that there is maximum involvement and
scope for personal development. How to cope with difficult classes.
The advantages and disadvantages of group and class work, and how
to set out a drama lesson plan. All these topics are fully dealt with
under the relevant headings.

The aim of good drama teaching lies in the ability of the teacher
to stimulate his pupils to a deeper understanding of themselves and
the world around them. A drama teacher is not training children to
become actors and actresses, consequently, acting exercises as such
have not been included. The idea that children should first of all learn
the language before they can become involved in educational drama
is based on the misapprehension that educational drama, like music,
has a special language which can be taught. In the case of children
engaging in educational drama, they are in possession of that language already: they have the ability to feel, move, and speak, the

only qualifications necessary for successful play-making. Exercises should arise naturally out of the work in progress. For example, if a dramatic situation calls for a group of soldiers to march into a town and commandeer an important building the scene would first of all be improvised. And then if the soldiers found difficulty in keeping step or halting on the command of the officer in charge and only then would exercises be introduced to help the boys concerned to realise their roles. In the teaching of English, grammar is no longer taught in many schools as a subject in its own right but arises out of the children's own attempts at written expression. Giving children exercises in a vacuum can be a sterile process, they prefer to see the relevance of what they are doing.

The many and varied reasons for teaching drama in schools have been set out at length in a number of books, but basically drama is a unique tool for exploring the human condition. We are told that every teacher should be a teacher of English; ideally, every teacher should be a teacher of drama able to use it wherever appropriate. The aim of this book is to show how this is possible.

CHAPTER 1

WHAT HAPPENS NEXT?
Dramatising a Scenario

"The Goblin of Oyeyama"

Myths and legends lend themselves particularly well to dramatisation, especially with children in the upper primary and lower secondary schools. Here, in the realms of magic, monsters and heroes, are many of the literary ingredients enjoyed by children.

This chapter is an account of drama work based upon the Japanese legend of "The Goblin of Oyeyama" as discussed and improvised by a class of thirty-two mixed-ability, co-educational, second-year children in a Comprehensive school. A combination was used of group work and class work over an extended period and illustrates the main teaching points involved.

"The Goblin of Oyeyama" is characteristic of a type of myth found throughout the world, *Beowulf* perhaps being the most outstanding example. A country, or community, is threatened by a malevolent being. In a state of desperation, the leader of the people sends for a hero gifted with superhuman powers, or under the protection of a deity. After an epic struggle, good triumphs over evil and the hero either marries into the community or journeys on to seek further challenges. The following version is adapted from F. Hadland Davis, *Myths and Legends of Japan*, George G. Harrap & Co. Ltd.

The children were told the story seated in a half-circle in front of the teacher.

The Japanese city of Kyoto lay at the mercy of a band of goblins. These creatures, led by their King, Shutendoji, lived high up on the slopes of Mount Oye in a black palace from which they made periodic sorties into the city, kidnapping young people and spiriting them away to their mountain stronghold.

Enslavement, abuse and death awaited the hapless victims.

This situation reached crisis point when the Emperor's own daughter was snatched away while walking with one of her maids in the palace garden. The Emperor's advisers suggested that the only

person who could save his daughter was a courageous knight called
Raiko. Raiko was summoned to the palace and he agreed to undertake this perilous mission, selecting a party of brave knights to go with
him. Before setting out, they sought the blessings of the gods and goddesses for success in their enterprise. Then, disguised as mountain
priests, their armour and weapons concealed in innocent-looking
knapsacks, they began the ascent of Mount Oye. The mountain
proved a formidable obstacle: giant chasms yawned beneath them,
precipitous slopes towered above. At last, almost at the end of their
tether, they were confronted by five strangers who turned out to be
the gods at whose shrines they had worshipped before leaving Kyoto.
One of the gods gave Raiko a jar of magic *saké*, which, although whole-
some for men, was poison for goblins. Raiko was to persuade Shutendoji and his followers to drink it, whereupon the goblins would
become paralysed, enabling the knights to despatch them without
difficulty.

Heartened by this encounter, Raiko and his companions pressed on.
After further climbing, they came upon a girl washing blood-stained
clothing in a mountain stream. She proved to be the Emperor's
daughter. Raiko introduced himself and explained the purpose
of his journey. The Princess agreed to lead them to the goblin King.

Shutendoji, thinking them harmless mountain priests, invited them
to a meal. Raiko offered Shutendoji a drink of the magic *saké*.
Pronouncing it the finest he had ever tasted, Shutendoji asked for
more, and soon all the goblins were filling and re-filling their glasses.
Gradually overcome by paralysis they fell one by one to the floor;
the last to collapse being the goblin King himself. At a signal from
Raiko, the knights drew their swords and despatched the demons.
Raiko released the captives and, accompanied by his knights, led a
triumphant procession down the slopes of Mount Oye to friends and
relatives waiting in the city below.

Improvisation

SCENE ONE   (The final scenario can be found on pp. 15–19 (*see
also* Fig. 2.)

The key to effective classwork lies in developing a questioning tech-
nique which allows wide-ranging opportunities for action; enabling
children, through discussion, to make their own decisions based upon
the dramatic possibilities available to them. Questioning begins by
seeking a starting point for the improvisation:

Q. (Refers throughout to questions or statements by the

teacher.) Where do we begin our story? Do we start with the capture of the Princess, explain how the demons first arrived on Mount Oye, or illustrate Raiko's powers by showing him in a previous encounter with the forces of darkness?

Whatever the starting point, the opening scene must always be an exciting one to capture the children's interests and enthusiasm from the very outset. A weak beginning, a false start and children begin to lose interest in the play as a whole; a series of false starts can lead to a breakdown in discipline and a loss of confidence in the teacher. An exciting opening scene is, therefore, crucial to the success of the project.

It is decided to begin with the capture of the Princess. Basically, this need only involve two people, the Princess and the goblin King, but there are thirty-two children in the class, each with his or her specific needs and abilities to be catered for, and to employ just two children would be a sure way of losing the interest of the others who might be tempted to make up their own plays under the legs of the chairs, or out in the corridor much to the annoyance of Mr. Smith teaching maths in the next room.

Q. Where was the Princess when she was captured?
R. (Refers throughout to the response from the children.)
Walking in the palace gardens.

Locations are very important: areas must always be defined, children should always know where the action is taking place, both in the play and on the classroom floor.

Q. Was anyone with her at the time?
R. Her maid.
Q. Was anyone on hand to guard her against a possible kidnap attempt?
R. Yes, there were guards.
Q. How many?
R. Five.
Q. Apart from the guards, were the palace gardens protected in any other way?
R. There was a wall around them.

Discussion time, especially in the early stages, should, if possible, be kept to a minimum. Children are keen to begin improvising and too much discussion can kill initial enthusiasm. The teacher must always be sensitive to the first signs of boredom on the part of the children and tailor the discussion accordingly.

Q. Could we have a girl to play the Princess?

A girl volunteers. If a female volunteer is not forthcoming, choose a boy and kidnap a Prince instead. Flexibility is vital in all good drama teaching. If there is no response at all it often happens that members of the class will suggest a popular child and he, or she, can usually be persuaded to take the part. Unless someone first breaks the ice there can be no play. One is, therefore, justified in using a little gentle persuasion.

Q. Will you choose a maid to walk with you in the garden, Princess?

Always let children select the member, or members of the class they are to work with: it is much harder to refuse a friend than the teacher.

Q. Could we have a guard? (A boy volunteers.) Now, guard, would you choose four others to help you man the walls. Then with chairs, rostrums, desks, and anything else available, I would like the Princess, her maid and the five guards to make a wall around the palace gardens. Make it as high as you can and either build it right across the room, or in the form of a square. (If gaps are left in the walls there are always children who will slip through rather than climb over.)

The climbing could, of course, be mimed, but only if the children have had some experience in this medium; otherwise, dog-paddling movements to the accompaniment of nervous laughter is the usual atmosphere-destroying response. The seven children concerned set about the task of building the wall. The instructions to the "builders" must be given as quickly as possible; twenty-five other children are waiting for their instructions too. Unlike rehearsals in a theatre where actors may be kept waiting for long periods before they are called, children in the classroom must be constantly engaged in fruitful activity, otherwise they may seek alternative sources of amusement detrimental to classroom discipline. The teacher turns to the rest of the class.

Q. Could we have a goblin King?

A boy volunteers. The remainder of the class are to be his followers, helping him to kidnap the Princess.

> **Q.** What kind of creatures are you?

If no ideas are forthcoming the teacher can make some preliminary suggestions.

> **Q.** Are you animal-like, or human?
> **R.** Human.
> **Q.** Do you walk upright, or on all fours?
> **R.** We stoop . . . we have large heads . . . long spindly arms
>   . . . (ideas are coming now, thick and fast) short legs . . .
>   hunched backs.
> **Q.** What noises do you make?
> **R.** Grunts.

A word picture of the goblins begins to emerge.

> **Q.** Now close your eyes and try to imagine the creatures
>   you have been describing.

If possible, the room should be blacked-out at this point. There will usually be enough light for the "builders" to see to build the wall around the palace garden.

> **Q.** Now goblins, I would like you to move around the room
>   as large-headed, spindly-armed, short-legged, hunch-
>   backed creatures. You can grunt at your friends as you
>   pass by them.

A suitable accompaniment to this might be the long-drawn-out grunts obtainable by playing a 78 rpm record at 16 rpm, or "The Enemy God and The Dance of the Black Spirits" from the *Scythian Suite* by Prokofiev. There may be some initial embarrassment at first: nervous giggles and slowness to respond, but gradually the music and the dark-ness create an atmosphere in which inhibitions are dispersed and the imagination begins to take over.

The wall is finished. Time now for further discussion.

> **Q.** Are the guards outside, or inside the palace walls?
> **R.** Outside.
> **Q.** Goblins, how do you descend upon the palace gardens?
>   Together? Or do some of you rush ahead leaving the
>   stragglers strung out behind?

R. We keep together.
Q. Why?
R. Well, if some of us got to the wall first, the guards might be able to deal with a few of us. There's safety in numbers.

It is very important for the children to have a reason for staying together, otherwise the kidnapping would turn into a race in which the first person to get to the Princess would consider himself the winner. It must be emphasised that there are no house points, etc., for the winner; the children are not taking part in a race. Drama seeks to foster a spirit of co-operation, not competition.

Q. How do the goblins deal with the guards?
R. We paralyse them.
Q. How?
R. We raise our arms and point at them, like this. (They demonstrate.)
Q. So, guards, as soon as the goblins raise their arms and point at you you become paralysed.

This is a fortunate suggestion. A child could quite easily have suggested a fight between the two groups producing the unequal struggle of twenty-five goblins against five guards and the possibility of someone getting hurt. If the children are spoiling for a fight the teacher would have to think of an imaginative reason for dissuading them, *e.g.*

Q. You are not physically equipped to fight, goblins, with your short legs and hunched backs. You have magic powers for dealing with human beings, you don't have to tangle with them. Does a tank commander step down and fight his enemies bare-handed? No. If you have a superior advantage you use it.

If children are still unconvinced by argument and insist on fighting, then it must be arranged, and rehearsed several times in slow motion to avoid accidents.

Q. Do you paralyse the Princess?
R. No.
Q. Princess, are you going to resist, or will you be too overcome by fear to put up a struggle?
R. I'll scream and struggle.

Q. What happens to the maid?
R. We'll take her with us.
Q. When you have kidnapped the Princess and her maid,
goblins, take them once around the room and then go
back to your places.

The teacher must step in here and dictate the end of the scene; otherwise in a surge of enthusiasm the goblins might carry the screaming Princess and her maid out into the corridor causing annoyance to other teachers, or, as normally happens, enthusiasm peters out on the return journey leaving embarrassed groups of children strung out across the room. To ask the children to return to their seats creates the de-climax so necessary after a noisy movement sequence.

The children are now ready to begin improvising. The guards stand watch outside the walls, the goblins retreat to a far corner of the room.

Q. Now, goblin King, in your own time. . . .

The guards patrol the outer walls of the palace, the Princess and her maid walk in the garden; Shutendoji nods his head and the goblins advance. They paralyse the guards, climb over the wall and snatch the Princess and her maid and carry them back to their seats. The scene is short, over in seconds, but it was an enjoyable experience. The first hurdle has been overcome, time to go straight on to the next scene, there will be opportunity for polishing and shaping later if required. It is preferable to go straight through a scenario at first, however superficially, rather than break off and shape each individual scene. After a swift initial run-through, the children are in a much better position to decide upon the final form of the play.

SCENE TWO

Q. What happens next?
R. The Japanese Emperor finds out that his daughter has
been kidnapped by the goblin King.
Q. How does he find this out?
R. Another maid saw the goblins taking her away.

Again this scene need only involve two people, the maid and the Emperor. Of course, the rest of the class could play servants and guards, etc., but these are nebulous roles, unrelated to the main action of the play. A much more fruitful way of involving the children has to be found. The children discuss the Emperor's whereabouts at the time of the kidnapping. To incorporate the rest of the class, he has to be in a public place with plenty of people around him. What is known of the lives of Japanese Emperors? They were autocrats, having the power of life and death over their subjects. They seemed to spend a great deal of their time conducting summary trials; people were executed at their slightest whim. (Of course, research into the period will be necessary.)

The children now possess the clue they have been searching for. It is decided that the Emperor is attending a court of law in his role as state judge and prosecutor—this gives the children plenty of scope for characterisation. An Emperor and an Empress are chosen and sent away to set up their respective thrones.

Q. Who else might be present in a Japanese courtroom?
R. An executioner.

An executioner is chosen. He produces a piece of rolled-up newspaper as an axe and a box for the block.

Q. Who else might be there?
R. There would be guards.
Q. How many?
R. Four. Also a Lord Chamberlain.
Q. We have an executioner. Could we have someone to give a roll on the drums should an execution take place?

The drama teacher should always try to cater for individual interests. One boy is a keen drummer.

The drummer volunteers; he is given a drum and sent off to practise.

Drama is concerned very much with elementary mathematics. Eight characters have now been chosen out of a class of thirty-two—twenty-four children have still to be catered for.

Q. Divide yourselves into six groups, four in a group. One person in each group is to be the accused, the other three will be the accusers. Discuss a possible crime the accused might be guilty of: it could be something quite trivial like stealing a morsel of food, or a more serious crime such as murder. Build up a story of the crime, each accuser contributing his or her knowledge of the events that took place. Each one of you will have something to say: either you saw the crime being committed, or you discovered the accused with the stolen goods on him. Make up your own evidence. The accused is either guilty or the victim of falsely-laid information. If you are innocent, prepare your case; if guilty, are there any mitigating circumstances you can plead?

This takes very little time to prepare and the groups return with these sub-scenes carefully worked out. The teacher runs through the scene (after giving each group a number for easy reference).

Q. The Court Chamberlain will announce the arrival of the Emperor. The assembled company will make obeisance, touching the ground with their foreheads. The Emperor and Empress take their places and the accused persons come forward in order of number. The accusers outline the crime, the defendants offer their testimony and it is up to the Emperor to pronounce whatever sentence he thinks fit. He may, for example, find the accusers guilty of perjury and allow the accused to go free. If the sentence is death, the guards will step forward, seize the accused, drag him to the block and the executioner will chop off his head to a roll of drums; if the case is dismissed, the accused and accusers return and join the rest of the class. The Court Chamberlain will previously have asked each group the name of their accused and the crime for which they are standing trial, so that he can make an announcement in each case.

A girl from group One is chosen to appear at the end of the scene to announce that the Princess has been kidnapped.

Traditional Japanese music can be used throughout the scene especially for the entrance of the Emperor, the teacher taking care to turn down the volume while the children are speaking. Suitable music can be found, *e.g. Classical Music of Japan*, Polydor Special 236 516.

If one child has to speak to another during a crowd scene and it is important for the rest of the group to hear what is being said, ensure that there is a suitable distance between the children concerned. Do not let them come together as in every-day conversation. Otherwise, the rest of the class, especially if they cannot hear what is being said will feel cold-shouldered and begin to talk amongst themselves. This leads to fragmentation and a breakdown in dramatic involvement. For example, the accused and accusers should give their testimony from amongst the rest of the class, not moving forward to be close to the Emperor. If they insist on moving towards the throne, a whispered instruction to one of the guards: "Keep them back!" usually overcomes this difficulty.

Should a child "dry" in a scene use an imaginative challenge: for example, the teacher can say to one of the defendants: "Come on, girl, if you don't say anything it will look as though you are guilty, and you know what that means. . . ." If the teacher senses that a child is genuinely embarrassed, and prefers not to speak, he can take a part himself: "My Lord, Atsumori was born without the powers of speech. I have come to speak for her. She stands accused of . . ."

The children are now ready to improvise Scene Two.

SCENE THREE

> **Q.** What happens next?
> **R.** Raiko is brought in to rescue the Princess.

Again, the same problem arises: how to involve the rest of the class while the Emperor commands Raiko to rescue his daughter. One of the boys has mentioned reading a book (*An Introduction To Kendo*, R. A. Lidstone, Judo Ltd., Croydon, Surrey) about the ancient sport of Kendo—Japanese sword fighting. Could this be utilised? All is grist to the drama teacher's mill. The children discuss the possibility of Raiko being a Kendo enthusiast, practising with other knights at the same time as the Emperor learns of his daughter's disappearance. The Emperor's grief overcomes court protocol and he goes in person to command Raiko to rescue the Princess. The children each find a partner and the boy who has read the book is asked to explain something of the art of Kendo. He tells the class that each participant is equipped with a long sword with which he lunges at his opponent, wielding it with both hands like a club, at the same time screaming out threats and harassments, his voice soaring from a deep bass to a strangled falsetto. Newspapers are found, rolled up and sealed with adhesive tape to make harmless weapons. The children begin practising Kendo, making up their own pseudo-Japanese language. They find it great fun. An Emperor and a Raiko are chosen.

> **Q.** When the Emperor appears in your gymnasium, knights, what do you do? Do you continue with your exercises?
> **R.** No, we stop practising and bow down as we did in court.

The children return to practising Kendo. The teacher asks the boy playing the Emperor to join them in his own time, allowing him an opportunity to think out what he is going to say. And, as the children clash with their paper swords, the Emperor bursts in stricken with grief. From now on the scene is impromptu and Raiko responds to the situation by calling for volunteers to help him kill the goblins and rescue the Princess.

SCENE FOUR

    Q. What happens next?
    R. The knights go to pray at the temples of the gods and goddesses.

Here is an opportunity for group work. The teacher divides the class into five groups and the children are asked which shrines Raiko and his followers might go to before setting out on their journey.

    R. The shrine of the god of war ... victory ... the mountains ... the goddess of mercy. ...

The children are asked to build a shrine with chairs, tables, and rostrums, to the particular god or goddess they would like to represent, and then devise a ritual of speech and movement appropriate to their special deity. Each ritual is then shown to the rest of the class.

SCENE FIVE

Scene Five concerns Raiko's journey across the mountains to the Black Palace of the goblin King. The children "built" a wall in Scene One; now they must "construct" a mountain. Some of the boys were asked to design, with the help of the rest of the class, an obstacle course/mountain pathway of chairs, tables and rostrums, up which Raiko and his followers could scramble in their search for the Princess. The "mountain" soon took shape and the boys responsible were asked to demonstrate the route to be taken. Questions are asked concerning the journey.

    Q. What are the weather conditions like on the mountain?
    R. Very slippery. The chasms are filled with snow. The precipitous slopes are covered with thick layers of ice and one false step means death on the jagged rocks below.

The room is blacked-out, leaving sufficient light to see to climb by. One of the boys who demonstrated the route up the "mountain" is asked to play Raiko. In the initial stages, the more interchangeable the roles, the better chance the teacher has of assessing the capabilities of the children and making the right choice in the final casting.

    Q. Do climbers spread out, some scrambling ahead to get to the summit first?

R. No.

Q. Why don't they?

R. Well, you've got to keep together for safety's sake. You all help each other, especially if the going is rough.

And so with a final plea to them to help each other, especially over the more difficult sections of the climb, and a reminder that this is not an army assault course and that there are no medals for the winner, they set out to the accompaniment of a wind effects record HMV 7 FX 10. A boy flashes the hall lights on and off at intervals to create the effect of distant lightning. They heave themselves over boxes, walk along the tables, crawl under the chairs with total involvement. One can tell from their faces that they are no longer clambering over a jumble of chairs, tables and rostrums, but climbing Mount Oye itself. So enjoyable is the experience that they ask to repeat it. This time two sub-scenes have to be added: the meeting with the gods and goddesses, and Raiko's discovery of the Princess washing blood-stained clothing in a mountain stream. The children decide where these incidents will take place. The five gods and goddesses, one chosen from each of the previous group plays, the Princess and Raiko are then given a few minutes to discuss what they are going to say. In the meantime, the boys who constructed the "mountain" have one or two alterations to make and other members of the class offer suggestions. A second run-through takes place. When the scene between Raiko and the gods and goddesses is over the children playing the gods and goddesses become knights and join Raiko. Always integrate children who have dispensed with special roles into the remainder of the action.

SCENE SIX
At the Black Palace

Q. Where does the scene begin?

R. The Princess leads Raiko and his companions to the goblin's stronghold.

Q. What are the goblins doing at the time?

R. Eating.

Q. Do they get their own food, or are they waited on?

R. Some of the captured girls wait on them.

Q. Do they sit at tables?

R. No, on the floor.

Q. What about their table manners. Would your mother have them in for a meal?

R. No, their manners are terrible...they grab at their

food... fight each other for it... make horrible noises
when they eat... they are like pigs.

Entry into a large group situation, in the early stages, often proves
difficult for all concerned. The children in the group, if not carefully
primed, carry on talking and ignore the newcomers. One of the advantages of class work in drama is the sense of power and heightened
language flow achieved, even by an inhibited child, when speaking
to, or in the presence of, a class imaginatively absorbed in the action.
To allow children to talk freely while Raiko and the goblin King are
in conversation will make it difficult for those who wish to follow the
action. These children become disillusioned and begin to talk amongst
themselves until most of the class is fragmented into small huddled
groups of children discussing anything from the play to the latest pop
star. With such lowering of dramatic tension, conversation peters out
between the principal characters causing them some embarrassment.
And the scene is a failure.

It might be argued that the teacher is striving too much for a
theatrical effect: child drama should come from the child, and not
be imposed by the teacher. But this is to ignore the ease with which
freedom within a drama lesson soon degenerates into licence unless
firm control is maintained. If one of the aims of teaching drama is
the encouragement of sensitivity towards others, then part of that
sensitivity comes from giving others the right to be heard, unless the
context of the scene dictates otherwise. But the quietness must be
achieved imaginatively, never enforced by word of command.

Q. Would the goblins be quiet or noisy when Raiko arrives?
R. They would be quiet.
Q. Why?
R. Well, they wouldn't get many visitors and they'd be
interested to know who Raiko was and why he had come
to see them.

That problem is solved. If the suggestion had been that the goblins
did continue making a noise while Raiko and the King were in conversation, then to avoid the results outlined above, a method must
be found of appealing to the children's imagination with a parallel
situation which they can understand, for example:

Q. If you were having lunch at home and a group of
strangers walked in, would you go on talking among
yourselves or stop and listen to what they had to say?

Q. How would the Princess introduce Raiko?

R. She would say that he and his companions were poor mountain priests needing food and shelter for the night.

Q. Would the goblin King agree to put them up for the night?

R. Yes.

Q. Why should he? Remember, he has been kidnapping human beings to be his slaves. Might he not want to enslave Raiko and his friends as well?

R. He might be frightened of priests.

Q. Frightened of them. Why?

R. He might be frightened of what the gods might do to him if he harmed their priests.

Q. Would the rest of the goblins agree?

R. They'd have to, they couldn't go against the King.

Q. After agreeing to put Raiko and his companions up for the night, what happens then?

R. The goblin King would invite Raiko to join in the feast.

Q. When would Raiko give the goblin the magic *saké*?

R. After they'd talked for a bit.

Q. Why would they have to talk first?

R. The goblin King might get suspicious if he was given the *saké* too early.

Q. Would he be suspicious anyway?

R. He might be.

At the risk of appearing tiresome, the drama teacher must ask the most obvious questions sometimes. There must be a justifiable reason for each action, however irrational, so that the children can believe in it because it was arrived at corporately, thus enabling them to create a personally satisfying response. This needs reinforcing, especially in view of the quantity of information that one expects the children to assimilate.

Q. How could Raiko show the goblin that he had nothing to fear?

R. By drinking some of the wine himself.

Q. Is this wise?

R. Well, you told us in the story that it is safe for men but poison for goblins.

Six weeks have passed since they were told the legend, which illustrates the keenness with which children listen to a story to be dramatised and how well the facts are absorbed.

Q. The goblin King takes the wine. Does he enjoy it?

R. Yes.

Q. What does he do then?

R. He passes it round to the others.

Q. What happens then?

R. The goblins begin to feel ill, they fall to the ground, and Raiko and his knights kill them off one by one.

Q. How would the girls react, those who had been kidnapped?

R. They would be overjoyed.

Q. How would the play end?

R. With Raiko, his companions, and the girls, making their way back to Kyoto carrying the head of the goblin King.

Another Raiko is chosen, together with five companions and a Princess. The rest of the class once more become the goblins as they did in the first scene and the run-through comes to an end.

Scenario:
The Goblin of Oyeyama

CHARACTERS Princess Sanjo
                Kaguya, her maid
                Five palace guards
                Shutendoji, the goblin King
                His followers

SCENE ONE The palace garden, Kyoto

1. Princess Sanjo and her maid are walking in the palace gardens. Outside the wall the guards keep watch.

2. Shutendoji and his followers creep up to the guards, paralyse them, climb over the wall, seize the Princess and her maid and carry them away to their mountain stronghold.

    CHARACTERS Kimitaka, the Emperor
                    Empress
                    Maid
                    Executioner
                    Four guards
                    Drummer
                    Defendants
                    Accusers
                    Lord Chamberlain

SCENE TWO The Emperor's Court

Japanese names for the accused and accusers—Male: Yorimasa, Chinu, Hazoku, Hikoboshi, Ishidomaro. Female: Aya, Atsumori, Iha-Naga, Kaminari.

1. The defendants and accusers wait for the Emperor and his officials. Guards keep order.

2. The Lord Chamberlain announces the Emperor. He enters accompanied by the Empress, the executioner, and a drummer. They take their places.

```
┌─────────────────────────────────────────────────────────────┐
│       Guard        Emperor       Empress      Guard           │
│  Lord Chamberlain                                             │
│                                                               │
│                                                    Drummer    │
│                                                    Executioner│
│                                                               │
│      Defendants                                               │
│       Accusers                                                │
│                                                               │
│     Guard                              Guard                  │
└─────────────────────────────────────────────────────────────┘
```

Fig. 1. Floorplan for the Emperor's Court.

3. The Lord Chamberlain calls out the name of the first defendant and the crime for which he or she stands accused. The accusers come forward and present their evidence. The defendant speaks in his or her own defence.

4. The Emperor pronounces sentence. He can order the execution of the defendant if he finds him guilty; or the accusers if he feels that they are presenting perjured evidence. Alternatively, he can dismiss the case.

5. If he orders an execution, the guards move forward and drag the victim to the block. The executioner cuts off his head to a roll on the drums. The guards drag the body to one side.

The next defendant's name is read out, and so on until all the cases have been tried.

6. One of the maids rushes in with news that the Princess has been kidnapped by the goblins.

7. The Empress, grief-stricken, leaves the court. The Emperor follows her. There is consternation. The guards clear the court.

CHARACTERS Raiko
                        Knights
                        The Emperor

SCENE THREE A Gymnasium

1. Raiko and his knights are in pairs practising the art of Kendo.
2. The Emperor appears at the door. One by one the knights, realising the presence of the Emperor, bow in homage.
3. The Emperor bids them rise. He tells them of his daughter's disappearance and asks Raiko if he will lead an army of knights to bring her back.
4. Raiko agrees at once and selects a number of knights to accompany him.
5. The Emperor leaves and Raiko begins to make preparations.

SCENE FOUR The shrines of the Japanese deities

CHARACTERS Raiko
             Knights
             Gods
             Goddesses

1. Raiko and his companions pray at the shrines of the gods and goddesses able to help them in their enterprise. The children go into groups, of no more than eight and select a god or goddess that they think might help Raiko and his companions to rescue the Princess: Hachiman, the God of War, Kwannon, the Goddess of Mercy, etc. Decide who are going to be gods and goddesses, the rest playing the parts of Raiko and his companions.
2. Show the ritual that might have taken place at each particular shrine. End with Raiko and his companions setting out on their journey.

SCENE FIVE The slopes of Mount Oye

CHARACTERS Raiko } dressed as simple
             Knights } mountain priests
             Five gods and goddesses

1. Raiko leads the way. It is a perilous ascent. There are chasms to be negotiated—freezing death traps for the unwary—precipitous slopes to be climbed, dark gloomy forests to stumble through. The wind howls, whipping up the snow. It is bitterly cold. The god of the mountain seems to be against them.
2. They begin to weary. The strongest help the weakest until they reach the limits of their endurance.

3. Suddenly, five figures appear before them. These are the gods and goddesses at whose shrines they prayed before setting out on their journey. One of the gods hands Raiko a jar of magic *saké* and tells him that the drink is good for men, but poison for goblins. Raiko is to persuade the goblin King and his followers to drink it, and then when he and his fellow goblins are paralysed, the knights are to cut off their heads and release the captives. The gods disappear.

4. Heartened by their encounter with the gods, Raiko and his companions set off again.

CHARACTERS Raiko
Knights
The Princess

SCENE SIX A mountain stream

1. Raiko and his companions come upon a girl washing blood-stained clothing in a mountain stream.

2. She tells them that she is the Princess Sanjo, who has recently been made captive by Shutendoji.

3. Raiko introduces himself and tells her that he and his companions have come to kill the goblin King and release the prisoners.

4. The Princess offers to show them the way to the Black Palace.

CHARACTERS Shutendoji
Goblins
The captives from Kyoto

SCENE SEVEN The Black Palace

1. The goblin King and his companions are feasting and making sport of their recent captives.

CHARACTERS As for Scenes Six and Seven

SCENE EIGHT The Black Palace

1. The goblin King and his followers continue feasting.

2. The Princess introduces Raiko and his companions as wandering mountain priests in search of a night's board and lodging.

3. The goblin King is highly amused and invites them to join him.

4. He continues to humiliate the helpless captives.

5. Raiko seizes his opportunity and offers him a drink of the magic *saké*. Shutendoji drinks some of the *saké* and hands it to his followers.

They drink large quantities.
6. Slowly, one by one, they fall to the floor paralysed. The goblin King is the last to fall.
7. Raiko gives the signal and his companions reach for their weapons. They cut off the heads of the goblins one by one.
8. Raiko and his companions release the captives and lead them back down the mountain to their friends and relatives in Kyoto.

The children may now want to go back and polish their scenario or they may wish to move on to another story. It is no criticism of

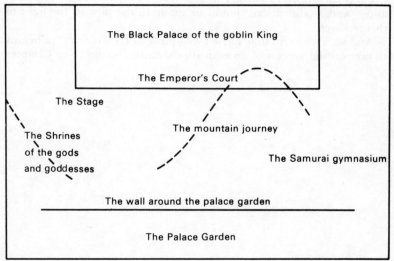

Fig. 2. Staging floorplan.

the drama teacher's methods if they do. One must expect "butterfly" drama in the early stages—children flitting from one scenario to another with no desire to return; but, with the growth of confidence and the development of their critical faculties, a time will come when the children will want to shape and polish a particular scenario, perhaps with a view to presenting it to other classes in the school. In that case, roles will have to be established and developed and the existing scenes modified in the light of further discussion. If it is the majority decision to work on this scenario, then obviously some research will have to be carried out on the period. Books and film strips on ancient Japan will have to be requested and literature perhaps obtained from the Japanese Embassy.

Answers to the following questions will have to be sought:

1. In what period does the play take place? (This will depend, of course, on which period is the best documented.)
2. What was the layout of an ancient Japanese palace?
3. How was a Japanese court constituted? What officials were present?
4. What were the powers of the Emperor? Did he attend trials?
5. What climatic conditions would be met with on Mount Oye?
6. What are the rules of Kendo?
7. What rituals took place at the ancient shrines?

Facts should be as correct as the source material assembled will allow, and modifications should be made to the play in the light of this research.

And so, a scenario that started as a piece of creative drama begins to take on the aspects of an educational drama project (*see* Chapter 5).

CHAPTER 2

MAKE A CIRCLE
Group Work

Group work is probably the most popular form of educational
drama in use today: children are placed in small groups and elect
their own chairman/producer; the teacher presents them with a
stimulus and, by means of discussion and improvisation, each group
creates a play which is presented to the rest of the class.

Contrasting with this is class work (*see* Chapter 1, The Goblin of
Oyeyama) in which the children work together on a scenario, possibly
over a lengthy period, the teacher himself acting as chairman/pro-
ducer. The end result is a polished presentation which may be shown
to other classes in the school.

There are arguments for and against both methods of approach.

Group Work

The advantages of group work may be summarised as follows:
1. The children themselves are in control of their material.
2. The children are less teacher-directed.
3. There are usually large parts for everyone.
4. Group work is a less demanding form of drama for the teacher.
5. It is a useful way of introducing drama to children.
6. Girls have much more chance of taking part in drama relevant
to their sex, especially if their drama teacher is a man.

Against these, one must set the following disadvantages:
1. Because children are in control, friction can more easily develop
between members of the group.
2. A disruptive child may prove more troublesome, and superficial
work may be offered as the best of which the children are capable
away from the direct influence of the teacher.
3. Group plays tend to be "one-off jobs"—discussed, rehearsed, and
presented within the one lesson. There is little opportunity for extending the work beyond the period in which it takes place.

4. There is little opportunity for research to improve the educational quality of the work.

5. A considerable part of each lesson is spent watching others present their improvisations. The time could be more profitably spent improving their own work.

6. The time factor. The teacher has to telescope preparation, presentation, and discussion, into a forty-minute lesson, creating an assembly-line approach to the subject.

Class Work

Several arguments can similarly be advanced in favour of class work.

1. The teacher can stimulate, challenge, and channel the interests and abilities of the children from the play stage to that approaching a work of art.

2. The teacher is in control and knows exactly what is going on at any given time.

3. A sense of power and heightened language flow can be achieved even by an inhibited child when speaking to, or in the presence of, a whole class imaginatively involved in the action, *e.g.* a rebel leader addressing a crowd of discontented peasants.

4. There is ample time for research, to extend, and develop a scenario to a high standard.

5. By swapping around the parts in the initial stages most of the children have an opportunity of playing leading roles.

Also, however, there are two disadvantages to be noted.

1. Many children have to accept small parts.

2. The drama can become too teacher-directed.

The Organisation of a Group Work Lesson

At the beginning of the lesson the children should be seated in a circle leaving one or two gaps between the chairs for exits and entrances. With young children, if any other form of seating is allowed, there is a tendency for the actors and actresses to move further and further away from the audience during the presentations, causing one child, at least, to call out from the audience, "We can't hear you!" To which the reply is invariably, "Well, you should wash your ears out then!" Although this arrangement teaches children something of the working conditions of medieval and Elizabethan actors, it does little to develop sensitivity towards others.

The children can then form their groups with no more than eight in a group; over eight and the group becomes too unwieldly for the children themselves to handle. They should be allowed to work with their friends and there should be no direction on the part of the teacher unless, as sometimes happens, a child, for one reason or another, feels rejected. Then a firm but kindly approach to a group comprising the most sympathetically disposed members of the isolate's own sex: "Would you have...in your group?" usually brings the hoped-for response, "Yes. Would you like to be a nurse/pirate...etc." If two or more isolates present themselves, let them work together as a group.

Nothing creates dramatic *ennui* amongst children more than having to endure the same type of lesson format week after week, *e.g.* when a teacher's only concept of educational drama is to read a story and then ask the children to dramatise it. Variety of mood and the ability to surprise are well-known devices used by playwrights in order to hold the attention of their audiences, the drama teacher should do likewise. The more varied the stimuli, the more stimulating the lessons.

Stimuli for group work

1. *Music.* Part of a record is played and the children are asked to imagine the music as the background to a film or television play. In groups they improvise a scene that might accompany such a sound track. Nineteenth- and twentieth-century programme music proves the most popular for this type of work, also electronic music.

Music can also be used to introduce each group play and accompany movements where there is no speech, *e.g.* soldiers moving stealthily through the jungle, walking into an ambush.

2. *Sound Effects.* Part of a sound effects record can be used as a stimulus, the children being asked to imagine the type of scene that might take place within range of the sound in question. The teacher can string a whole series of effects together creating a sound scenario which the children have to translate into action.

If there is a tape recorder available for each group the children can create their own sound effects which can then be passed on and used by other groups in turn.

3. *One-word Stimulus.* Group plays can be centred around one or more of the following characters outlined by Theophrastus (see *Menander Plays and Fragments, Theophrastus The Characters*, translated by Philip Vellacott, Penguin Books).

A flatterer, a chatterbox, a boor, a sycophant, an outcast, a liar, a bad-tempered person, someone with a grievance, a distrustful person, a boaster, one who is always causing offence, a mean person, an arrogant person, a coward, a slanderer, an authoritarian person, a slanderer, an evil person, a glutton.

4. *Styles of Comedy.* The teacher explains the meanings of the terms listed below in order to encourage children to create group plays in the following comic styles.

Farce, melodrama, black comedy, absurd comedy, surrealistic, situation, historical (*1066 And All That*), silent film, satire.

5. *Props.* Make a collection of objects that can be used as props. Try to avoid the representational if possible, a twisted stick allows far more scope for the imagination than, for example, a pistol. The teacher explains that he has assembled a number of objects on the side of the stage or outside the classroom door and that he would like the leader of each group to select one object, or a variety of objects, depending upon the number available. These objects are to form an integral part of each group play. Assembling the objects out of sight of the class prevents the children from calling out the name of the object they would like their group leader to bring back; it also introduces an element of surprise into the lesson and the eagerness with which the rest of the class wait for the return of the group leaders amply justifies the extra time involved.

6. *The Unfinished Story.* Read, or tell the children the beginning of a story ending at an exciting moment:

> "You are on a camping holiday with your friends. It is three o'clock in the morning. You wake up disturbed by a noise in the tent. Dimly through the gloom you make out a group of figures standing at the end of your sleeping bag. Your friends are still sound asleep. Who are the intruders? What do they want? Is it just a bad dream?"

The children can act out what they think happened.

Unsolved mysteries are a valuable source of material for this type of group work. The teacher tells briefly the story of the *Mary Celeste* and then asks the children in their groups to show what they think happened to the captain and the crew.

Or what happened to the inhabitants of a remote eskimo village who vanished completely without trace one day in 1930? For further examples, see Frank Edwards, *Stranger Than Science* and *Strange People*,

Lyle Stuart; Valentine Dyall, *Unsolved Mysteries*, Hutchinson; and Brian Peachment, *You be the Judge*, Edward Arnold Ltd.

7. *Photographs and Pictures*. The teacher assembles a collection of portraits. Each group leader selects a portrait, to be the leading character in the play. Or, a photograph could show several people engaged in an exciting, tragic or humorous activity. The teacher asks the children to show the events that led up to the scene on the photograph, or show the events that took place immediately following it. If there are more people on the photograph than members of the group, the children are to concentrate on the main characters; if there are more children in the group than people in the picture then they must create additional characters for themselves. Abstract paintings and surrealistic photographs give more scope for the imagination than more conventional compositions.

8. *Slides and Filmstrips*. Most school departments have a selection of slides and filmstrips which the drama teacher could borrow. The teacher projects a slide, or a series of filmstrip pictures on to the classroom wall to be used as stimuli for group work in the same way as the photographs; or, they can form an integral part of the play, *e.g.* the scene could take place in an art gallery if the slide concerned is the reproduction of a painting. Alternatively, the picture can become an integral part of the action, the children creating shadow-graphs with their bodies on the picture itself.

9. *Psychedelic Effects*. Buy a selection of vegetable colourings. Obtain two pieces of glass of similar size which will fit into the front of the film strip projector. Pour a drop from each bottle on to one of the pieces of glass, place the other piece on top of it and fit the two pieces of glass into the front of the filmstrip projector. Switch on the projector and wait for the heat of the bulb to warm up the glass. As it does so, the globules begin to move between the two pieces of glass creating interesting psychedelic effects when projected on to the wall of the classroom. As with the filmstrips, these can be used as stimuli, or incorporated into the action of the play.

10. *Audio-Visual*. The slide or filmstrip picture can be combined with relevant music or sound effects. The scene of a blitzed street could be accompanied by the sound of an air raid siren, or psychedelic effects could be accompanied by a piece of electronic music creating the stimulus for a science fiction play.

Alternatively, for older children, filmstrip and music/sound effects could be in opposition, *e.g.* a picture showing the interior of a cathedral could be accompanied by the "Meuzzin's Call to Prayer" from the *HMV History of Music in Sound*, Volume 1. "Ancient and Oriental Music."

11. *A Visitor.* A visitor whose expertise may stimulate drama could be invited to school either to give a talk and act as a consultant, or actually to take part in the play itself. For example, a shop steward would be able to add a considerable amount of local colour to a play dealing with an industrial dispute, and a coal miner could give details of conditions down the pit for a play centred around a mining tragedy. Although a working man might find it difficult to give up his time, there are often retired experts within easy reach of the school who would welcome the opportunity of working with young people.

The preceding examples are only means to an end, and there should be no cause for concern if the children reject the given stimulus and present a play of their own, providing that it conforms in other ways to the teacher's requirements.

The teacher should suggest a time limit for preparation, no more than ten minutes in a forty-minute lesson, and stick to it regardless of the fact that the leader of at least one group will explain that his group is not ready yet; they could keep the class waiting for the rest of the lesson and still not be ready.

During the "rehearsal" time the teacher visits each group in turn helping those in difficulty.

A child holds up a top hat, another a fox fur and a third a revolver.

R. How can we make a play out of these?
Q. Which do you think is the most important prop?
R. The top hat.
Q. Why?
R. I just like wearing it.
Q. Who might wear a top hat?
R. A posh bloke.
Q. So one of your characters could be a posh bloke. What about the fox fur, who might wear that?
R. A rich lady.
Q. Now what about the gun?
R. The rich man might kill the rich lady.
Q. Why?
R. Perhaps he's not rich any more and he's after her money.

They begin to discuss a scenario amongst themselves; the teacher can move on to the next group.

By asking relevant questions interspersed with suitable suggestions the teacher helps the children to overcome their difficulties. Only as a last resort should the teacher outline a possible scenario. If the children in a particular group are not in the mood for improvising, and on rare occasions this can happen for a variety of reasons (*e.g.* a child may have just been reprimanded by the headmaster), a teacher could hand out short extracts from a script, or disperse the children around the other groups where they will be less of a problem than if allowed to stay together. If one group finishes well within the ten minutes they should be encouraged to work on the weaker parts of their play, that is, if they confess to having any.

At the end of ten minutes the teacher asks the children to stop what they are doing and come back to their places in the circle of chairs.

Group drama lessons fall into two categories, the occasional and one of a series. The occasional lesson is probably a substitute lesson, a teacher is absent and the drama teacher has been asked to fill in with a period of drama. It is possible that he will not see these children again for a long while, if at all. In this case each group can be given a number depending upon the total of children in the class. When it comes to the presentations, group One is to begin, group Two will follow, and so on. The rest of the class can talk quietly amongst themselves while the members of group One create the type of set they need from the furniture available; this can be single or multiple, depending upon the number of scenes in the play. As soon as the members of group One have done this, they move quietly outside the circle; this is the signal for the audience to stop talking thereby obviating the need for tiresomely-repeated permutations on a "stop talking!" theme by the teacher. The group leader tells the audience where the scene or play takes place. This is the only information required. Girls, in particular, if not prevented, will outline the whole plot, sometimes in great detail, giving away any surprise twists that the children may have been at pains to work out. The teacher should not allow two groups of children to talk at once in a presentation, this is a common failing in the initial stages of group drama, unless this is the effect desired, otherwise it produces "tennis neck" on the part of the children in the audience as they turn from one group to another in an attempt to follow what is being said. As soon as group One has finished, the children return to their places and the members of group Two prepare to show their play. While this is happening the children in the audience discuss the play they have just seen, the discussion ending as soon as the actors in group Two are ready to begin. A suitable piece of background music can be played to cover this section of the lesson. If each group has been given a similar theme to work on, for example, ghosts, the same piece of music (*e.g. Octandre* by

Varèse) could be played throughout to cover beginnings and endings and suitable movement sequences in between, the teacher at the volume control of the tape recorder or record player, fading in and fading out as required.

If the drama teacher has the class on a permanent basis, then for variety the running order of the groups should be changed from week to week. The teacher must keep an eye on the clock and allow adequate time for presentation; sometimes the initial enthusiasm is lost if one or two groups, because of lack of time, have to present their plays at the beginning of the next lesson. Try to set a deadline for the length of each play, no longer than five minutes in a forty-minute lesson; and if a group overruns the time limit have no compunction about stopping them. A typical breakdown of a forty-minute drama lesson might be as follows:

Five minutes:	Settling down, forming groups, presenting the stimuli.
Ten minutes:	Preparation.
Twenty minutes:	Four five-minute presentations.
Five minutes:	Discussion
Forty minutes	

Because the children are, to a certain extent, working independently of the teacher, particular care must be taken to ensure that there is progression in group drama. One way of achieving this is to encourage the children to think critically during group presentations and to give them the opportunity at the end of the lesson to state their criticisms in general discussion. Educational drama covers many of the elements found in theatre—characterisation and dialogue, play construction, sets, music, sound effects, planting and style.

A. *Characterisation and dialogue*

The two most important elements in educational drama are characterisation and dialogue. If left to themselves to play characters beyond their understanding or experience, children will, in the main, tend to give cliché performances using the stock responses of actors in farces and melodramas seen on television. Ask a child to play a teacher and, even in these educationally-enlightened times, the result is a grotesque caricature that even Dickens in his wildest dreams could never have imagined in the classrooms of Dotheboys Hall.

There are, of course, those who would point out the necessity for children to play out their relationships with authority in order to come to terms with and accept reality. There is a place for these experiments—in the playground. They should find no acceptance in the drama lesson.

Dialogue, which is an integral part of characterisation, should also be given careful consideration, especially in view of the findings of the D.E.S. Drama Report* that, in the main, little attempt has in the past been made to help children to fashion their language to the characters they are portraying.

How does one help children to create character? There are several ways of doing this: the first is, of course, by means of observation. Each child should be given an exercise book in which to jot down the idiosyncrasies of friends, relatives and strangers, noting down snatches of conversation, accents and dialects, the movements of the elderly, reactions under stress, etc. In this way, the child, like the actor, builds up a character "bank" on which to draw when the need arises, taking one aspect of this person, something else from another, blending the various elements into his own interpretation of the part. This type of observation is best left to the child himself. A teacher taking a class of children to watch men digging a hole in the road could prove embarrassing to everyone concerned, even though it may prove excellent preparation for a play on railway navvies. As stimuli for role-creation, the teacher is therefore left with the source material available in the class room.

1. *Clothing and Accessories.* There should always be a dressing-up box in the drama room. Clothing helps immensely when creating a character—a torn coat reaching down to the ankles for the child playing the tramp, a piece of curtain material folded into a triangle and held in place on the head with a circle of rope, the ends flicked under the chin and over the shoulder, becomes an Arab headdress. Cowboy and Indian playsuits, rifles and pistols can be brought from home for an improvisation about the American West and girls can simulate period costumes quite effectively by wearing their mothers' cast-off dresses.

Simple props, too, help to create character: a cardboard tube becomes a telescope for a boy playing a ship's captain, a walking stick for a girl playing an old woman, although cliché interpretations are liable to creep in if every "old woman" is given a walking stick, and every "ship's captain" carries a cardboard tube. Children can be encouraged to make their own props during art and craft lessons providing this fits in with the art teacher's syllabus.

2. *Masks.* Masks are a very effective way of creating creatures of myth

* Drama Education Survey 2, H.M.S.O., 1967.

and legend, African tribesmen, Japanese samurai, etc. The mask is a very powerful symbol which helps to break down inhibitions, giving to the wearer an aura of dignity or malevolence. Again, liaison with the art department pays dividends. One can often find masks which, having served their purpose, are due to be thrown away. These can be added to the dressing-up box for future use.

3. *Percussion*. Ideally, every drama department ought to have a set of percussion instruments enough for each child in the class. The boy playing stroke on a Roman galley beats out the rhythm on a drum, a child playing an African witchdoctor can enter into the spirit of the part more effectively if he shakes a tambourine as he hovers over his patient, or "smells out" those guilty of putting a hex upon the chief of the tribe. A percussion orchestra can be formed to accompany a Red Indian or African war dance. Incidentally, if no percussion instruments are available, the effect of war drums can be created by the children tapping on the seats of chairs with their finger tips (in order to avoid breakages).

4. *Photographs*. These are also an effective way of helping children to create character. I was once at a loss to help a child realise the character of an insane person. And then I remembered a collection of photographs showing human beings in varying stages of desperation, anger, and obsession. I showed these to the boy concerned. He studied the pictures for a long time and then put them to one side. As he sat in his chair a metamorphosis took place before our eyes: his cheeks hollowed, his lips began to twitch, the mouth opened and spittle dribbled from the gaping hole. He was no longer the boy we knew; a state of insanity had temporarily overcome him. And the stimulus for this was a photograph of an American revivalist preacher caught with a sneer on his face as he castigated his audience for their godlessness. Still photographs are full of such clues to successful characterisation.

5. *Films*. Dealing as he does in such human diversity, the drama teacher has to make up his mind whether to accept an imaginative or factual approach to artistic truth. Does he, for example, allow the children to portray the Australian aborigine as an almost imaginative creation based upon often spurious information arrived at solely through discussion; or does he encourage the children to seek out as many facts as possible before committing them to action? This is, of course, the dichotomy between utilitarian and educational drama; and time is always at a premium in the group drama lesson. However, films can often come to his aid, the contents of a film can be assimilated

much more readily than the contents of a book. In the case of the Australian Aborigine, for example, there is a wealth of authentic material available.

Five Aboriginal Dances from Cape York (No. 700). 1 reel, colour, 6 minutes. An anthropological record of traditional Aboriginal dancing at Aurukun Mission Station on Cape York Peninsula in the far north of Queensland.

Tjurunga (No. 308). 2 reels, colour, 20 minutes. C. P. Mountford's colour record of the rarely-seen life and customs of some of Australia's Aborigines.

Walkabout (No. 309) 2 reels, colour, 20 minutes. A film of great anthropological interest made by C. P. Mountford, on an expedition organised by the University of Adelaide, showing the landscape of Australia's little-known interior and the way of life of its Aboriginal people.

Desert People (No. 710). 5 reels, black and white, 51 minutes. A unique anthropological record of the way of life led by the nomadic Aboriginal people of the Australian Western Desert. Available from The Film Officer, Australian News and Information Bureau, Australia House, Strand, London WC2R 3ER.

Primitive Peoples, Parts 1–3 (No. 493A 2–4). 3 sound films, black and white, 15, 12 and 9 minutes, with notes. Films illustrating the daily life of a tribe of Aborigines living in Arnhem Land in Northern Territory. Part 1 illustrates the nomadic habits of the people, and shows them making bark shelters, making fire, hunting, gathering food, and primitive cooking. Part 2 is concerned with weapons and hunting practices. The people of the tribe are shown making spears and domestic implements. There follows an account of a kangaroo hunt, in which men use primitive magic in enticing the animal. The final sequences show the feast at which the kangaroo is eaten, and a traditional dance. Part 3 shows ceremonies connected with the funeral corroboree, in which the body of the dead man is wrapped in bark and placed on a high platform; the bones are later placed in a totem pole. The film shows part of the ceremonies. Distributed by Rank Audio Visual Ltd, P.O. Box 70, Great West Road, Brentford, Middlesex.

Films are a particularly stimulating educative medium for children and a study of some of the foregoing films will help them to create the character of the Australian Aborigine in a way in which no amount of book-learning could possibly accomplish. The clips showing the Aborigine dances can be shown on the wall of the school hall or classroom, the children reproducing the movements of the natives to the music on the soundtrack. As the children become proficient in the movements of the dance, the film can be faded out while continuing with the sound track accompaniment. The children can then make up their own plays about the Australian Aborigines. The soundtrack can be taped and used to accompany any dance sequences, or the children can provide their own objects for simulating Aborigine music.

6. *Physical Experiences.* The possibilities of simulating actual physical experiences in the classroom are dependent upon the equipment and lighting available. However, as a stimulus for a nineteenth-century coal-mining tragedy, the claustrophobic conditions underground can be simulated with the minimum of equipment by getting children to crawl under a line of chairs laid out along the floor, preferably in a blacked-out room.

Children can be introduced to the idea of blindness by putting them into pairs. One partner is blindfolded while the other leads him, or her, around the room. The two then change roles, the blindfolded partner becoming the guide and vice-versa. A variation on this is for the guide to stand to one side and call out instructions to the blindfolded partner enabling him to safely negotiate the classroom floor over which a variety of objects have been scattered. Experiences such as these can lead naturally to group plays based on the lives of Helen Keller, or Louis Braille.

7. *Music.* Music is a particularly effective stimulus for creating character and the time and effort involved is well spent in cataloguing the discs in the drama department and the teacher's own record library under the character headings and emotional states, if any, suggested by the music:

> *Losing a grip on reality:*
> *Fontana Mix*, Cage.
> *Visage*, Berio.
> *Clowns:*
> "Galop" from *The Comedians*, Kabalevsky.

"The Entree" from the ballet *Les Patineurs*, Meyerbeer. *See also* Appendix II for more examples.

8. *Narration over Music.* The effectiveness of music as a stimulus to character can be enhanced at times by adding a narration, either given spontaneously by the teacher, or prepared beforehand on tape. To create the roles of men lost in the polar wastes the following extract could be recorded over a section of Vaughan Williams' "Seventh Symphony:"

"I can only write at lunch and then only occasionally. The cold is intense, — 40 degrees at midday. My companions are unendingly cheerful, but we are all on the verge of serious frostbites, and though we constantly talk of fetching through I don't think any one of us believes it in his heart.

We are cold on the march now, and at all times except meals. Yesterday we had to lay up for a blizzard and today we move dreadfully slowly. We are at No. 14 pony camp, only two pony marches from One Ton Depot. We leave here our theodolite, a camera, and Oates' sleeping bags. Diaries, etc., and geological specimens carried at Wilson's special request, will be found with us or on our sledge.

Sunday, March 18—Today, lunch, we are 21 miles from the depot. Ill fortune presses, but better may come. We have had more wind and drift from ahead yesterday; had to stop marching; wind NW, force 4, temp. — 35 degrees. No human being could face it, and we are worn out nearly.

My right foot has gone, nearly all the toes—two days ago I was proud possessor of best feet. These are the steps of my downfall. Like an ass I mixed a small spoonful of curry powder with my melted pemmican—it gave me violent indigestion. I lay awake and in pain all night; woke and felt done on the march; foot went and I didn't know it. A very small measure of neglect and have a foot which is not pleasant to contemplate. Bowers takes first place in condition, but there is not much to choose after all. The others are still confident of getting through—or pretend to be—I don't know! We have the last half fill of oil in our primus and a very small quantity of spirit—this alone between us and thirst. The wind is fair for the moment, and that is perhaps a fact to help. The mileage would have seemed ridiculously small on our outward journey.

Monday, March 19.—Lunch. We camped with difficulty last night, and were dreadfully cold till after our supper of cold pemmican and biscuit and a half a pannikin of cocoa cooked over the spirit. Then, contrary to expectation, we got warm and all slept well. Today we started in the usual dragging manner. Sledge dreadfully heavy. We are 15½ miles from the depot and ought to get there in three days. What progress! We have two days' food but barely a day's fuel. All our feet are getting bad—Wilson's best, my right foot worst, left all right. There is no chance to nurse one's feet till we can get hot food into us. Amputation is the least I can hope for now, but will the trouble spread? That is the serious question. The weather doesn't give us a chance—the wind from N to NW and — 40 degrees temp. today.

Wednesday, March 21.—Got within 11 miles of depot Monday

night; had to lay up all yesterday in severe blizzard. Today forlorn hope, Wilson and Bowers going to depot for fuel.

Thursday, March 22 and 23.—Blizzard bad as ever—Wilson and Bowers unable to start—tomorrow last chance—no fuel and only one or two of food left—must be near the end. Have decided it shall be natural—we shall march for the depot with or without our effects and die in our tracks.

Thursday, March 29.—Since the 21st we have had a continuous gale from WSW and SW. We had fuel to make two cups of tea apiece and bare food for two days on the 20th. Every day we have been ready to start for our depot 11 miles away, but outside the door of the tent it remains a scene of whirling drift. I do not think we can hope for any better things now. We shall stick it out to the end, but we are getting weaker, of course, and the end cannot be far."

Robert Falcon Scott, *Scott's Last Expedition*, John Murray Ltd.

Emotional states can be heightened by recording a poem over a suitable piece of music. Grief, for example, is an emotion often required of children in their drama lessons, whether it be as a wife lamenting the death of her husband slain in battle, or a peasant farmer, in a drought-stricken area of India, whose child has died from malnutrition. Careful foundations must be laid. To ask children to exhibit feelings of grief in a vacuum will only produce embarrassed giggles, as happened to me when I tried, with insufficient preparation, to "direct" a funeral cortège. Poems dealing with the subject of grief, such as the following, could be read over a recording of Bloch's *Schelomo*, or Ravel's *Pavane pour une Infante défunte*.

REMEMBRANCE

Cold in the earth—and the deep snow piled above thee,
Far, far removed, cold in the dreary grave!
Have I forgot, my only Love, to love thee,
Severed at last by Time's all-severing wave?

Now, when alone, do my thoughts no longer hover
Over the mountains, on that northern shore,
Resting their wings where heath and fern-leaves cover
Thy noble heart for ever, ever more?

Cold in the earth—and fifteen wild Decembers
From those brown hills, have melted into spring:
Faithful, indeed, is the spirit that remembers
After such years of change and suffering!

Sweet love of youth, forgive, if I forget thee,
While the world's tide is bearing me along;
Other desires and other hopes beset me,
Hopes which obscure, but cannot do thee wrong!

No later light has lightened up my heaven,
No second morn has ever shone for me;
All my life's bliss from thy dear life was given,
All my life's bliss is in the grave with thee.

But when the days of golden dreams had perished,
And even Despair was powerless to destroy,
Then did I learn how existence could be cherished,
Strengthened, and fed, without the aid of joy.

Then did I check the tears of useless passion—
Weaned my young soul from yearning after thine;
Sternly denied its burning wish to hasten
Down to that tomb already more than mine.

And, even yet, I dare not let it languish,
Dare not indulge in memory's rapturous pain;
Once drinking deep of that divinest anguish,
How could I seek the empty world again?

                                        Emily Brontë

In the *Penguin Book of English Verse*, edited by John Hayward, are
Shakespeare's *Song* from Cymbeline and Bishop King's *Exequy on his
Wife*, which could also be looked at.

Feelings of grief can also be stimulated by asking children to
recapture the emotion they felt when a favourite pet died; but the
teacher must be sensitive here. A friend of mine was working on an
improvisation dealing with a pit disaster, when one of the girls in the
class suddenly burst into tears. He discovered later that only a fort-
night previously, her own father had died in a type of accident similar
to the one they were improvising in the class room. Fortunately, such
terrible coincidences are rare, but the teacher must, if possible, guard
against them. There are many who feel that the drama teacher, by
using emotionally-charged words and music, is flirting dangerously
with the emotions of young children and mixed-media stimuli of the
type mentioned above is best left out of the drama syllabus. But drama
has always dealt with the strong human emotions of grief and love,
suffering and joy, and to be over-cautious is to rule out much that
is dramatically worthwhile and relevant to the needs of the children.

9. *Music and Movement.* Many different types of character can be stimulated by using *Laban's Eight Basic Effort Actions* (see Chapter IV, *Modern Educational Dance*, Rudolf Laban, Macdonald & Evans Ltd.), especially if each effort is accompanied by a suitable piece of music:

Character:	A robot
Music	*Intermezzo*, Mimaroglu
Movement	The Thrust or Punch
Character:	A person in a dream sequence
Music	*The Birth of the Blues*
Movement	The Float
Character:	A giant
Music	*'Promenade''* from *Pictures at an Exhibition*, Mussorgsky-Ravel
Movement	The Press
Character:	An Elizabethan Dandy
Music	Third movement, Prokofiev's *Classical Symphony*
Movement	The Flick
Character:	An Irish washerwoman
Music	Theme, Corelli's *Violin Sonata No. 12*
Movement	Wringing
Character:	A mischievous gnome
Music	First movement, Shostakovich's *First Symphony*
Movement	The Dab
Character:	A medieval knight armed with a two-handed sword
Music	*Zorba's Dance*, Theodorakis
Movement	The Slash
Character:	A Princess
Music	Slow movement, Mozart's *Clarinet Concerto*
Movement	The Glide

These are stimuli for the outward characteristics of a role. Once the movements have been mastered, then the children must work towards putting flesh on the bare bones of movement with their own imaginative responses. Again, it will repay the drama teacher to listen to as much music as possible, with a view to cataloguing each piece or movement, plus the character suggested, under one or other of the eight Basic Effort Actions.

Listed below are four characters often met with in educational drama with suggestions for the type of stimuli that can be used in creating these roles.

An Astronaut
 Things to do: Watch the movements of a bouncing balloon. Try
to move in a similar way.
 Music to listen to: Fantasy in Orbit, Tom Dissevelt.
 Literary research: Read Peter Ryan, *The Invasion of the Moon 1969,*
the story of Apollo 11 (a Penguin Special).
 Improvisation: Astronauts lost in space.

A Red Indian
 Things to do: Look at the photographs of Red Indians in *Touch
The Earth* (compiled T. C. McLuhan, Sphere Books Ltd.),
and the pictures in *Indians of the Americas* (Matthew W. Stirling,
the National Geographic Society).
 Learn some of the Red Indian sign language shown in *Indian
Talk*, "Iron Eyes" Cody, New English Library. *The Golden
Book of Indian Crafts and Lore*, Ben Hunt, Golden Press, New
York, shows how to make Red Indian clothing and equipment.
Learn the basic Indian dance steps shown in this book.
 Music to listen to: Learn some of the Red Indian songs in *The
Indians' Book*, recorded and edited by Natalie Curtis, Dover
Publications, New York.
 Literary stimulus:
"Brothers! I have listened to many talks from our Great Father.
When he first came over the wide waters, he was but a little man
... very little. His legs were cramped by sitting long in his big boat,
and he begged for a little land to light his fire on. ... But when
the white man had warmed himself before the Indians' fire and
filled himself with their hominy, he became very large. With a step
he bestrode the mountains, and his feet covered the plains and the
valleys. His hand grasped the eastern and the western sea, and his
head rested on the moon. Then he became our Great Father. He
loved his red children, and he said, 'Get a little further, lest I tread
on thee. ...'
 Brothers I have listened to a great many talks from our great
father. But they always began and ended in this—'Get a little
further; you are too near me.' " Katharine C. Turner, *Red Men
Calling on the Great White Father*, copyright 1951, University of Oklahoma Press.

  Improvisation: The American government breaks a treaty and
the Red Indians go on the warpath.

An American Negro
 Things to do: Listen to the voice of Martin Luther King on

The Great March to Freedom, Tamla Motown, TML 11076, and *Dr. Martin Luther King Junior In the Struggle for Freedom and Human Dignity*. Hallmark CHM 631.

Learn some of the freedom songs:
"If you miss me at the back of the Bus."
"Keep your eyes on the Prize."
"I ain't scared of your Jail."
"We shall Overcome."

These can be found on the record, *We Shall Overcome*, Pete Seeger, CBS, BPG 62209.

Music to listen to: Listen to recordings of the Blues, especially those of Huddie Leadbetter (Leadbelly) and Mississippi John Hurt.

Literary research: The Long Freedom Road, Janet Harris, Constable Young Books Ltd.

The Past That Would Not Die, Walter Lord, Hamish Hamilton.

Literary stimulus:

"We are an oppressed, economically depressed colonial people. We were brought here, from Africa and other parts of the world of palm and sun, under duress, and have passed all our days here under duress. The people who run this country will never let us succeed to power. Everything in history that was of any value was taken by force. We must organise our thoughts, get behind the revolutionary vanguard, make the correct alliances this time. We must fall on our enemies, the enemies of all righteousness, with a ruthless relentless will to win! History sweeps on, we must not let it escape our influence this time!!!!

I am an extremist. I call for extreme measures to solve extreme problems. Where face and freedom are concerned I do not use or prescribe half measures. To me life without control over the determining factors is not worth the effort of drawing breath. Without self-determination I am extremely displeased.

International capitalism cannot be destroyed without the extremes of struggle. The entire colonial world is watching the blacks inside the U.S., wondering and waiting for us to come to our senses. Their problems and struggles with the American monster are much more difficult than they would be if we actively aided them. We are on the inside. We are the only ones (besides the very small white minority left) who can get at the monster's heart without subjecting the world to nuclear fire. We have a momentous historical role to act out if we will. The whole world for all time in the future will love us and remember us as the righteous people who made it possible for the world to live on. If we fail through fear and lack of aggressive imagination, then the slaves of the future will curse us, as we sometimes curse those of yesterday. I don't want to die and leave a few sad songs and a hump in the ground as my only monument. I want to leave a world that is liberated from trash, pollution, racism, poverty, nation-states, nation-state wars and armies, from pomp, bigotry, parochialism, a thousand different brands of untruth, and licentious usurious economics." (*Soledad Brother*, George Jackson.)

Improvisation: Aspects of the American Civil Rights Movement among the Negroes in the early 1960s.

A Tramp

Things to do: Stuff paper into your shoes to make walking uncomfortable. Change clothes with your friends. Wear your jackets inside out. Rough up your hair and generally make yourselves look as untidy as you can. Lie on the floor and cover yourself with a newspaper.

Sound effects: Listen to HMV Sound Effects: Wind. 7 FX 10.

Literary research: Read *Bury Me In My Boots*, Sally Trench.

Improvisation: The experiences of a boy or a girl who has run away from home and is living with dossers and tramps.

To help with characterisation, the drama teacher should try to build up a "resources centre" where many different types of stimuli will be available.

B. *Play construction*

Play reading among the young has gone out of fashion, but a study of worthwhile one-act plays can prove a useful stimulus in helping children in the creation of their own group plays. There are similarities here with creative writing, where, for example, children are encouraged to study a selection of detective stories before attempting the genre themselves. Embryo playwrights study the work of their peers, and, children improvising in groups are, in effect, "playwrights," therefore a study and discussion of one-act plays is essential if group drama is to be taken seriously. Suitable plays, many of them in school editions, are listed below.

Collections:

Five Plays, from *Write a Play*, Blond Educational.

Eight One-Act Plays, Nelson.

Conflicting Generations, selected and edited by Michael Marland, Longman.

English One-Act Plays of Today, selected and introduced by Donald Fitzjohn, Oxford University Press.

Switch On—Switch Off and Other Plays, Janet McNeill, Faber & Faber.

The Long Christmas Dinner and Other Plays in One Act, Thornton Wilder, Penguin Books.

Theatre Today, edited by David Thompson, Longman.

Single Plays

Zoo Story, Edward Albee, in Penguin (Absurd Drama).

The Monkey's Paw, W. W. Jacobs.

The Emperor Jones, Eugene O'Neill.

The Last Word, James Broughton.

The Typists, Murray Schisgal.

C. *The set*. Time should be set aside to allow children to "play around" with the furniture available—chairs, tables, rostrums, etc.— to discover the effects that can be achieved with only the minimum of equipment. With older children, the teacher should take the opportunity of discussing the different types of staging that have evolved through the ages and allow the children, preferably when they are secure within the conventions of theatre-in-the-round, to experiment with the various other theatrical forms—arena, open—and the variants on these: "L" staging, amphitheatre, space staging, split staging, horseshoe seating, and horseshoe or caliper staging as outlined in Chapter Four of *The School Play*, Richard Courtney, Cassell & Co. Also in this context, the work of Jerzy Grotowski (see pp. 157–64, *Towards a Poor Theatre*, Methuen & Co.) and Stephen Joseph's *Planning For New Forms of Theatre*, published by Messrs Strand Electric, merit attention.

D. *Music and sound effects*. Every drama department should have a comprehensive record library (*see* Appendix 2 for a list of suitable records). Time should be spent explaining to the children the use of the record player and tape recorder, the care of records, and how to record from disc to tape. A rota system can be organised within each group, allowing every child in turn to be responsible for the selection and playing of suitable music and sound effects, to add atmosphere to the plays concerned. Children should also be encouraged to create their own sound effects (see pp. 78–81, H. Woodman, *The Drama Tape Guide*, Focal Press).

E. *Planting*. Planting is another aspect of educational drama which is especially important particularly when acting without the aid of representational sets. It is the device whereby the setting for the scene, or play, is indicated by an actor or actors concerned. For example, a child explaining how much he hates sentry duty in the mist and the rain and how he would give anything to be posted back to the bright sunshine of Rome rather than have to skirmish with the Picts and Scots, would indicate to the audience that he was a Roman soldier stationed on Hadrian's Wall. Similarly, a girl telling another: "I don't know how you can live in this pig sty. Look at the walls, they're dripping with damp! And those grey sheets on the bed!" might be visiting a junky friend who has "dropped-out" from society. Planting is also used to provide the audience with details of past events, potted biographies of a character or characters, appearing later in the play; in fact, any information required by the audience for a full understanding of the action.

F. *Style.* A discussion on dramatic styles, melodrama, tragedy, comedy, tragi-comedy, low comedy, farce, slapstick, realism, and surrealism is also an important consideration, as is discussion of the type of play which needs a consistent style of acting and when and how to mix varying styles smoothly into a single performance.

Once all these elements of educational drama have been fully discussed, exercises can be given further to reinforce them; members of the audience can be primed to look out for a particular aspect in the group plays under consideration, and be prepared to discuss it.

"Today, you have been looking closely at characterisation. Let's consider Jennifer. Do you think she was an effective queen? If so, give your reasons. If not, why not? And what about Jack? Did he make a convincing ship's captain? What were the qualities of seamanship, if any, that came across? Is that how you think a person might behave who has seen his best friend being carried off by a monster?"

Apropos of a discussion on sets:

"Did group A's arrangement of chairs and rostrums remind you of the inside of a bank? If not, why not? And group C, were you convinced that by upending sets of chairs they created a jungle effect, or did they just get in the way of the action?"

And on planting:

> "Did group D plant adequately enough? A person was shot at the beginning of their play. Did they establish his character sufficiently well for us to understand why he was murdered?"

And play construction:

> "Did group B achieve a satisfactory ending, or did the long-drawn-out climax detract from the plays denouement?"

Criticisms must always be constructive, never destructive. The teacher should never allow a child to criticise without qualification, the critic concerned must always be prepared to explain what he or she would have done in the circumstances. The ability to criticise, and the forming of artistic standards, are an important part of the drama lesson. Helpful information thus acquired, can be reinforced by exercises given to the children concerned and improvements should always be noted.

Maintaining Records

Dramatic progression is particularly important in group work and the teacher would be well-advised to keep a record of the work undertaken. Such a record is also important for ensuring that each child is given a fair chance of exploring his or her potential. It is so easy to allow the more gifted children to take the main roles week after week and overlook the fact that the inhibited, or less gifted, are left with the walk-on parts. Ideally, the extroverts should be prepared to step down at times and allow the less gifted children to take the leading roles. The psychological damage done to a sensitive child playing subservient roles for the whole period of his or her dramatic life in school must inevitably outweigh all the benefits that drama can bring. The keeping of records is, therefore, very important. This need only be a rough and ready guide, enabling the teacher to push a quiet girl into an important part when he feels that the time is ripe—how often that decision turns out to be the right one. One of the joys of teaching drama is to see a child one has always considered to be a mouse suddenly blossom forth and become a lion.

Alongside individual reports should go a record of the work done each week by the various groups. Of course, the membership of groups will occasionally alter, as old friendships die and new ones are formed, but, as experience has shown, membership remains fairly constant throughout the year. Group records are necessary in order to prevent repetitiveness in presentation, to enable the teacher to challenge a weak group, and encourage sensitivity among the extroverts.

For example, let us take an imaginary group, A. This group is composed of five rather shy girls. The first week found them creating a play set in a hat shop; half the girls were shop assistants, the other half customers trying on hats. There was very little movement, a minimum of inaudible conversation and the play fizzled out with one of the customers stealing a hat, but the assistants making no attempt to do anything about it. Next week, the teacher, armed with his record book, knows that something must be done to help these girls break down their inhibitions. Perhaps they might attempt a play in which an old woman is accused of having dealings with the devil. Brought before a hastily constituted court, she is found guilty and sentenced to be burned at the stake. The play ends with the accusers dancing gleefully around the bonfire.

Group B consists of eight extrovert boys. Their play concerns a bank robbery. This involves a great deal of fighting and the dialogue, such as it is, cannot be heard for the noise they are making as the gangsters fight it out with the manager, the tellers, the customers, and eventually the police. Sensitivity is the requirement here. Again, armed with his record, the teacher plans their next group improvisation. They obviously prefer fighting to acting, and to prohibit them from fighting would serve no useful purpose and only breed resentment (the last thing a drama teacher wants). Therefore, their next play must, inevitably, include a fight, but if this can be delayed by appealing to the boys' imagination there will be a quiet period at the beginning of the play allowing time for dialogue development. The teacher splits the boys up into two groups. The members of the larger group are rich merchants travelling through bandit-infested country. They stop for the night in a lonely valley, posting guards to keep watch in case of an attack by bandits. The members of the smaller group become the bandits living in the hills. As soon as the merchants have settled for the night, the bandits creep up to their encampment without making a sound. Stress is laid on the fact that if the bandits do make a noise the guards will hear them and alert the rest, and the bandits, though heavily armed, are few in number. They must creep up to each guard and kill him in turn before they can turn their attention to the rich pickings available in the merchants' waggons. By means of this scenario, the boys of group B will begin to learn something of that sensitivity without which there can be no dramatic progression.

Sometimes it is possible to involve the whole audience as spectators, within a group presentation, *e.g.* at a boxing match, or a night club. This could serve as a transitional stage between group work and class work, especially if the teacher does not feel confident in undertaking class work from the outset.

There is little possibility of extending group work beyond the limits of the lesson, especially with younger children. Group plays are basically one-off plays, characters remain undeveloped, the format is always that of the one-act play. There is little chance for research, unless each group is working on the same topic, and then the presentation, because of its very repetitiveness, proves tiresome for the audience. Perhaps the ideal solution lies in a mixture of group work and class work of the type that took place in the scenario on *The Goblin of Oyeyama.*

CHAPTER 3

"ALL HUMAN LIFE IS HERE"
Drama from Scratch

Creating a play from scratch with a class of children based upon their ideas, experiences and imagination is probably the most neglected area of educational play-making, perhaps because of the demands that it makes upon the teacher. And yet, of all the methods of teaching drama in schools, this is the one that I find the most satisfying. "All human life is here," past, present—and future; all human striving, and failure is grist to the dramatic mill. The scope for the imagination is boundless, the opportunities for characterisation are unlimited. From astronauts lost in deep space to an oil rig keeling over in the North Sea, from the primitive hunt of Cromagnard cave dwellers to the sophisticated modern warfare of a battle in South East Asia, from the fury of a typhoon to a train derailment, from an encounter with a ghost to a team of doctors fighting to save the life of an important political figure—the dramatic possibilities are endless.

There can, of course, be no preparation for this type of drama, but a broad general knowledge stands the teacher in good stead when dealing with the variety of topics met with from class to class. To be able to talk about coal-mining from first-hand experience would be extremely useful to children creating a play dealing with a mining disaster. Similarly, for the teacher to have read something of the conditions that prevailed in Hiroshima after the dropping of the first atomic bomb would be of assistance in helping children to realise the effects of a nuclear holocaust upon a party of survivors.

How Drama from Scratch Works

The following pages are based on a series of drama-from-scratch lessons taken with a class of twenty-five mixed-ability first-year boys in a Yorkshire Comprehensive school, most of whom had never done drama before.

The simplest way of beginning a series of drama from scratch lessons is to ask the children:

"What would you like to do a play about?"

Five hands shoot up immediately.

First Child: Monsters ...
Second Child: Cowboys and Indians....
Third Child: Space travel....
Fourth Child: A bank robbery....
Fifth Child: Smugglers.

I have never known this method fail with children; something seen on television, a popular news story of the day, or one or more of the all-time favourites mentioned above, ideas are always forthcoming.

The teacher should accept any suggestion, however ludicrous or wrongly intentioned. Often, some of the best drama-from-scratch lessons develop from facetious remarks made in this way. A flippant remark often masks a genuine desire to explore some field of human experience that would prove embarrassing to the child concerned if made more explicit. Once, when a class of school-leavers was asked what they would like to do a play about, one boy, with a bored expression on his face, said "kipping." Instead of rejecting his preference for sleep rather than drama, we discussed "kipping"—What type of people "kip" as opposed to those who sleep. "Kipping," it was decided, was a word used by manual labourers, and, after further discussion, an interesting improvisation developed. Set in a boarding house, it concerned two gangs of construction workers: one gang "kipped" during the night and worked during the day, while the other group worked during the night and "kipped" during the day, each group using the same beds. The drama teacher cannot afford to alienate children, if he rejects a questionable contribution there is a possibility that this may deter others in the class with more valuable suggestions to offer.

Once the suggestions have been received the teacher runs through the list:

Q. We have five suggestions: monsters, cowboys and Indians, space travel, a bank robbery, and smugglers. I will go through the list again and this time I would like you to vote for the subject that appeals to you most. Remember, you only have one vote.

The smuggling topic won by a narrow majority. Should two subjects tie in popularity, let the class vote again to decide upon the outcome.

To clarify the situation, the teacher asks the children for information about the life and work of smugglers; and gradually a story begins to emerge concerning a group of nineteenth-century south-coast fishermen who used to slip across the Channel to buy French wine which was then shipped back to a secret hideout under cover of darkness in order to avoid paying customs duty. The wine was later sold at a handsome profit.

As with dramatising a scenario, the aim is always to begin at an exciting point in the story. The children decide to set the first scene in France, showing a meeting between the smugglers and a group of French merchants with casks of wine for sale.

SCENE ONE

Q. Where does the scene take place?
R. On a French quayside.
Q. What happens?
R. The smugglers buy wine from the merchants.
Q. Is it a straightforward sale, or do the smugglers have to bargain with the merchants?
R. The smugglers bargain.
Q. Why?
R. Because they feel that the merchants are charging them too much. The smugglers try to bring down the price.
Q. Do they succeed?
R. No, there is an argument.
Q. What happens then?
R. A fight breaks out. One of the smugglers pulls a knife and stabs one of the Frenchmen.
Q. Why does the smuggler carry a knife?
R. He's a fisherman, he needs it for his work.
Q. Would the smuggler use his knife as soon as the argument breaks out?
R. No.
Q. Why?
R. Well, people don't get mad straight away—you get angrier and angrier.
Q. At what point in the argument might the stabbing take place?
R. If the Frenchman insulted him.
Q. What insult might lead our smuggler to stab, and possibly kill?
R. If he called him a thieving rogue.

To reinforce this:

> **Q.** But it wouldn't happen immediately?
> **R.** No.
> **Q.** Only after they had spent some time arguing?
> **R.** Yes.

The drama teacher, by virtue of his training, is constantly placed in a dilemma: should he use theatrical conventions in helping children to shape a scene, or ignore them completely, leaving children to work out the results for themselves. A case in point arises over the stabbing. If left to themselves, young boys will begin to fight as soon as an argument breaks out, no dialogue, no dramatic build-up, just a confused mêlée on the floor. Of course, a fight need not be a confused mêlée on the floor, it can be worked out systematically, but at the time, these first-year boys lacked the necessary discipline for the arrangement of a fight sequence. In spite of what may be said to the contrary, children enjoy discipline: they prefer to act within a controlled framework, gradually building up to a fight rather than hurling themselves into it from the outset. Therefore, it is preferable to sustain the argument between the Frenchmen and the smuggler for as long as possible rather than let the stabbing occur at the very beginning.

The smuggler's boat was to be on the stage, the steps making an effective gangplank. A boy was chosen to stab the Frenchman.

> **Q.** (To the boy concerned) What happens after you've knifed the Frenchman?
> **R.** I run back to the boat.
> **T.** Why?
> **R.** I'd be scared of what might happen, what they might do to me.

The class decided that some of the other smugglers would have made their way back to the boat, with or without their casks of wine (depending upon the outcome of the bargaining) before the knifing takes place.

The initial discussion on a drama from scratch scenario is always a lengthy and, at times, confusing process. Ideas are constantly being put forward for acceptance or rejection—and not necessarily in the order in which they will occur in the play—and it is the drama teacher's responsibility to retain and organise this material into a coherent scenario whilst at the same time keeping one jump ahead of the children to forestall future difficulties, attend to discipline, and be constantly on the lookout for any signs of boredom on the part of the children. If the children do become restive because the discussion does not seem to be getting anywhere, it is a good idea to break off and try an improvisation. Afterwards, the children are then in a much better position to see what does and does not work. One can then resume the discussion, which will have greater validity because of the run-through.

> Q. What would the other smugglers who were still buying the wine do when they realised that one of their friends had knifed a Frenchman?
> R. They'd get back to the boat as soon as possible.
> Q. Why?
> R. Because the other merchants might call for help and there could be trouble.
> Q. What about the smugglers back on board? What would they be doing?
> R. They'd be getting the boat ready to sail.
> Q. How would they do that?
> R. They'd let out the sails ... get ready to cast off ... when the last smuggler was back on board someone would take up the gangplank.
> Q. Do any of the merchants try to follow the smugglers on board?
> R. Yes.
> Q. How many?
> R. All of them.
> Q. What about their wounded friend?
> R. Oh, yes, one of them would stay behind to look after him.
> Q. What happens when they rush the boat?
> R. (From the smugglers) We push them overboard.
> Q. So the boat leaves the harbour and the merchants are left with a wounded, possibly a dying man, on their hands?
> R. Yes.

A great deal of information had been elicited through a lengthy discussion.

> Q. I would like you now to split up into five groups, five in a group, three of you will be smugglers, the other two Frenchmen. (When this has been done) Merchants, will you decide upon an asking price for your wine; smugglers, will you decide how much you are prepared

to pay for it. A heated discussion will break out in each group over the price charged. The smugglers will decide amongst themselves whether to pay the price or return to England empty-handed. If you do refuse to pay, smugglers, the merchants must then decide whether to bring down their price or seek customers elsewhere. Now, we have the smuggler who kills the Frenchman, haven't we? Quickly decide which Frenchman you are going to stab. (To the other four groups.) Two of you are going to make your way back to the boat before the smuggler knifes the Frenchman. Which two groups will that be? (Two groups volunteer.) Choose a skipper and decide amongst yourselves who is going to unfurl the sails, who is going to cast off and who is going to haul up the gangplank after the last smuggler has returned on board. Frenchmen, decide who is going to lead you in the attempt to board the smuggler's boat.

Now to set the scene: if the smugglers will go on to the stage. That is your boat. Wine merchants, if you could be waiting here on the hall floor. Now, when I have finished speaking, the smugglers go down the gang-plank to meet the merchants.

The teacher almost always has to say something like '. . . when I have finished speaking. . .' otherwise the children, who are usually so keyed up at this point, will start the scene as soon as the teacher pauses for breath, without being fully aware of what they have to do.

Q. Both sides haggle over the price of wine. You decide to either buy or not, to drop the price asked or not. Two groups of smugglers return to the boat. The two groups involved in the knifing group begin to argue heatedly, the Frenchman insults the smuggler and you (to the smuggler concerned) pull out your knife and stab him. Horrified now by what you have done, you run back on board the boat and the other smugglers on the quay, when they realise what has happened, join you. The merchants close around their wounded companion. On board, preparations are well in hand for a speedy departure and, as the last smuggler climbs aboard, the gangplank is raised. The merchants race to the boat and try to climb aboard but the smugglers line the sides and push you away. The boat leaves the quayside and the merchants return to their wounded colleague.

The children run through the scene.

SCENE TWO

> **Q.** Well, and what happens next? Is that the end of the story—the smugglers arrive back in England, the merchant either dies or recovers? Or, does something happen because of the knifing?
> **R.** Something happens because of the knifing.
> **Q.** What happens? (A pause.)
> **Q.** Well, what would you do if your best friend was knifed and the person responsible got away?
> **R.** I'd go to the police.

If there is a problem over motive always relate to the children's own experience.

> **Q.** Do you think the merchants would go to the police?
> **R.** Yes.
> **Q.** But what could the police do? The smugglers are away on the high seas.
> **R.** They could get a boat and chase after them.
> **Q.** Could they?
> **R.** No, they wouldn't have a boat. They'd have to get someone else who had.
> **R.** The French customs.
> **Q.** Would they be able to overtake the smugglers?
> **R.** Yes, they'd have a faster boat than the smugglers. They'd have to catch their own smugglers.
> **Q.** Where do we begin Scene Two then?
> **R.** With the French customs overtaking the smugglers' boat.

As there was a great deal of discussion in the last scene, it is best to give something practical to do here, as soon as possible.

> **Q.** Would there be more customs officials than smugglers?
> **R.** No, about the same number.
> **Q.** I would like half the class to be smugglers and the other half to play French customs officials. Those who would like to be customs officials go and stand over there (to the right) and those who would like to be smugglers, go and stand over there (to the left).

The class divides roughly into two halves.

Q. Now, customs officials, would you "build" me your customs launch. Use chairs to mark out the shape, and rostrums, tables, and chairs, for the deck and other parts of the ship that you think you will need for this scene. Choose a Chief Customs Officer to lead you, and decide who does what on board.

Such instructions have to be given fairly quickly, the smugglers, too, are awaiting their instructions. The customs officers go away to "build" their launch. The teacher turns to the smugglers:

Q. Would you "build" your boat in the same manner and elect someone to play the part of the skipper. Decide who is going to be at the wheel, etc., and place your boat alongside the customs launch.

The teacher keeps an eye on what is happening, trying to visualise probable events in order to make valid suggestions regarding location.

Q. (To the smugglers) Are you going to put some cabins below deck.
R. Yes, that's a good idea. Come on!

The boats are soon ready; the class meet together for a further discussion.

Q. Now, tell me what happens from the moment the smugglers sight the French customs launch to the end of the scene.
R. Well, the smugglers would try to give the customs launch the slip.
Q. Smugglers, what reason have you for supposing that the customs launch is after you?
R. Because they're heading straight for us.
R. Can you get your boat to go any faster, smugglers?
R. We could put up more sail.
Q. Would those responsible for the sails see to that. What is happening aboard your launch, customs officials?
R. We're gaining on them.
Q. Why is that?
R. We have a faster boat.
Q. Customs officials, do you overtake them?
R. Yes.

There is some pleasant banter here from the smugglers, but also the realisation that, unless the customs boat did overtake them, there would be no confrontation, and no satisfactory ending to the scene.

Q. What happens when you get close to the fishing boat?

R. We ask them to heave-to.

Q. Do you heave-to, smugglers?

R. We'd have to, wouldn't we?

Q. Why?

R. Because they'd have guns.

Q. Why wouldn't you carry guns?

R. We're fishermen, fishermen don't carry guns.

Q. What happens then?

R. The customs officers tell the smugglers that they want the smuggler who did the stabbing.

Q. Shall we give him a name rather than keep calling him "the smuggler who did the stabbing." What shall we call him?

R. Sam.

Q. (To the boy concerned.) Right, you're Sam.

Q. How is the Frenchman by the way? Has he recovered?

R. No, he died.

Q. So it's murder?

R. Yes.

Q. Are you smugglers going to give Sam up?

R. No.

Q. What are you going to do with him? You know they'll search your boat.

R. We'll hide him and tell the customs that he fell overboard.

Q. Wouldn't it save a lot of trouble if you gave him up?

R. No, you don't sprag on your mates.

Q. Where would you hide him?

R. Somewhere where the customs officers wouldn't think of looking for him... in one of the casks.

Q. But they are full of wine, aren't they?

R. We brought some spare ones with us.

Q. When do you hide in the cask, Sam?

R. As soon as I hear the customs officer telling the skipper that they're after me.

Q. What happens next?

R. The customs officers board the fishing boat.

Q. Why? I thought you were going to tell them that Sam fell overboard.

R. We want to have a look for ourselves.
Q. How many customs officials board the fishing boat?
R. All of us.
Q. Would you all go?
R. Yes.

Already they are envisaging the free-for-all that will undoubtedly take place if the teacher allows an unstructured confrontation between the smugglers and the customs officials in the small area set aside as the fishing boat. An effective scene could be ruined. Further questions are necessary.

Q. (To the customs officials) What is the danger of holding a potential enemy too closely at gunpoint?
R. They might jump you and start a fight.
Q. If a number of you were holding your enemies at gunpoint and they did jump you, why would it be dangerous to open fire on them?
R. Because you might hit some of your own men instead.
Q. And that's just the problem you are faced with, isn't it, customs officials, if you all board the fishing boat: the danger of the smugglers gaining the advantage and of hitting some of your own people if you open fire at them?
Q. Is there a way of controlling the smugglers, customs officials, so that they do not gain the initiative?
R. If some of the customs officials were left behind on the launch to cover those searching the fishing boat.
Q. Customs officials, would you allow the smugglers to carry on with their jobs while you are searching their boat?
R. No, we'd line them up against the side.
Q. Why?
R. So there'd be less chance of trouble.
Q. And what about the smugglers who might be lurking below decks?
R. Some of us would have to go below and get them, and line them up with the others.
Q. Why must you be very careful where you line up the smugglers?
R. What do you mean?
Q. Let me explain on the blackboard (*see* **Fig.** 3).

If you have the smugglers lined up on the far side of the boat from the customs launch, for example, with the

customs officers searching here and their friends covering them from here, what might happen?

R. The customs officials searching the boat are between the
smugglers and their friends covering them from the
launch.

Q. And what does that mean?

R. It means that the smugglers could grab hold of them
and use them as shields.

Q. Exactly.

The drama teacher must always think ahead in order to try to
forestall possible breakdowns in dramatic tension. Chaos would have
resulted if the smugglers began to use the customs officials as "shields."
Such detailed plotting of a confrontation is only necessary where the

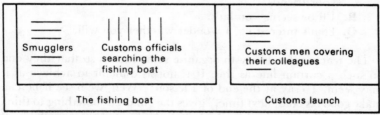

Fig. 3. Unworkable confrontation.

unplanned actions of a few might fragment a situation at a time when
the children need the safety of a disciplined structure within which
to work. The teacher was dealing with boys, most of whom had done
no drama before, and it is generally unwise to allow the unexpected
until children have had some experience of the disciplines involved
in working together as a class. Once they have gained experience,
there is nothing more rewarding for the drama teacher than to see
a scene effectively transformed by a child, or a group of children,
doing the unexpected. But, in spite of what has been said, there must
be no attempt to stifle creativity. If the children had insisted on the
smugglers defeating the customs officials, they were perfectly at liberty
to suggest this and try it out for themselves.

Q. (To the customs officials.) Do you find Sam?

R. Yes.

Q. How do you manage to find him if he is hidden away
in a cask?

R. He sneezes and gives the game away.

Q. What happens next?

R. We arrest him and take him to the launch.

Q. Do you try to rescue him, smugglers?

R. No, they've got guns. We might be killed. (It is reassuring to have confirmation that the discussion on this point has not been wasted and has been taken imaginatively to heart.)

Q. Are you only after Sam?

R. Yes.

Q. Why not the rest of the crew?

R. They've done nothing wrong.

Q. They are smugglers.

R. Yes, but you're only a smuggler if you bring things into a country, not out. They've paid for the wine.

Q. As you are being handed over the side into the French launch, Sam, is there anything that you might say to your friends?

R. I'll be seeing you lads.

Q. That's interesting, I wonder whether you will.

The teacher should try to organise some lessons so that they end on such a curtain line as this. It is not as difficult to achieve as it may seem. To say at the end of a lesson: "Well, we'll see if he can make good his boast next time," gives the children something to think about, and look forward to. And, with the limited time available, it is an advantage to have them enthusiastic at the start of the next lesson rather than have to spend valuable time re-awakening their interest in the story. The scene is now run-through as planned.

SCENE THREE

Q. At the end of Scene Two (pointing to Sam) you said, "I'll be seeing you, lads." Well, what happened to you in France? Were you executed for the murder?

R. No, I escaped from prison.

There has tended to be more discussion than drama so far and a change of lesson plan is indicated. Here is an opportunity for the children to engage in a very popular form of group work. They are set a problem and asked to solve it dramatically.

Q. Go into four groups. (The teacher sets the scene.) Imagine a French prison, possibly a stone fortress. High walls, armed guards—most probably the prisoners are chained to the floor in small cells which are locked and barred. In your groups, choose one person to be Sam;

the rest of you will be prison guards, officials, other prisoners, etc. Now show me how Sam escaped.

SCENE FOUR

Q. (To Sam) So you escaped from prison. What did you do after that?

R. I made my way back to England.

Q. What would you do as soon as you got back?

R. I'd look up my mates.

Q. Where might you find them?

R. Drinking in a pub.

Q. Describe the pub to me.

R. Wooden tables, chairs....

The boy who began to answer is put in charge of the rest of the class; under his supervision they are to create the interior of the tavern out of the tables, chairs, and rostrums available.

Q. Don't forget the bar. Can we have a landlord. (They quickly create a tavern setting.)
Now, smugglers, what are you talking about as you sit drinking?

R. We're talking about the money we've made on the last job.

Q. Sam joins you. He has escaped from a French prison. Are you pleased to see him?

R. We're surprised.

Q. What does he talk about?

R. How he escaped. (Another boy is chosen to play Sam)

Q. You can tell them of the escape that took place in your group. Is there anything Sam might want from you?

R. He'd want his share of the money.

Q. Have you got it for him?

R. No.

Q. Why is that?

R. We've spent it ... and anyway, he didn't bring any wine back with him.

Q. So, when he asks for his share, you tell him there's nothing for him?

R. Yes. Anyway he shouldn't have killed the Frenchman. We don't want him any more.

Q. You've changed your mind towards him now that he's back?

R. Yes.

Q. What does he do when you tell him?

R. He gets angry.

Q. Is that all?

R. Yes. We'd bray him up if he tried anything on us.

Q. Well, there's no money for you, Sam. What might you do?

R. I'd go to the customs and shop them.

R. You haven't any proof.

SAM. I've got plenty of proof. What about the store of wine in the cave, there's plenty of proof there.

Q. Would you tell your friends that you were going to the customs?

R. Not likely. I'd just go.

The children run through the scene in the tavern ending with Sam leaving to inform the customs.

SCENE FIVE

Q. What is the outcome?

R. The English customs come and arrest the smugglers.

Half the class elect to be English customs officials and a Chief Customs Officer is chosen; the rest continue as smugglers.

Q. Now, customs officers, you have been told that a crowd of smugglers is gathered in ... let's give the tavern a name. ...

R. The Red Boar.

Q. ... gathered in the Red Boar. How would you deploy your men? Would you send them all in through the one door?

R. No, some of the smugglers might escape out at the back.

Q. What would you do then?

R. We'd surround the pub, leave some men outside to catch those who escaped, and the rest would split up and go in by different ways.

Q. How many exits are there?

R. Three. (The children delineate the tavern area with chairs leaving three openings as exits.)

Q. Now, remember, you're not ghosts, you're smugglers. You can't walk through walls. You can only escape via the exits marked by the gaps in the chairs.

Q. What happens when the customs men burst into the tavern?

R. The officer tells the smugglers that he has come to arrest them. There's a fight.

Q. Who wins?

R. The customs officers.

Q. What does the landlord do?

R. He's on the side of the customs.

Q. What happens then?

R. The smugglers are led away.

Q. The smugglers, then, will continue drinking in the tavern. (To the customs officials) Find a place for your customs post, and, remember, it's not a race, take your time. Decide on a signal to begin the raid; a shouted word of command might alert the smugglers. After you have arrested them bring them back to their seats.

It is always preferable to have a base to come back to after a declimax. Sam goes to the customs post to inform on his friends. He tells the customs officials that smugglers are drinking in the Red Boar. The customs officials descend upon the ring of chairs that, for the time being, delineate the walls of the tavern. The boy playing the Chief Customs Officer stations some of his men around the chairs to catch escaping smugglers; he gives the signal and leads the rest into the tavern to arrest the smugglers. There is a fight, those trying to escape are picked up outside, while the rest are rounded up and taken back to their seats.

It is important at this point to reverse roles, the customs officers becoming smugglers and vice-versa, and then let them run through the scene again, so that all the boys have a chance of being on the winning side—it is important for prestige.

SCENE SIX

Q. What happens next?

R. Sam is rewarded by the customs and the smugglers are hanged.

At this point, a boy with a strong sense of justice interrupted to ask about Sam. He pointed out that, although Sam killed a Frenchman and spragged on his mates, he had received a reward.

Q. (To the class) Well, what do you think happened to him?

There are various suggestions: he was killed by a relative of one of the smugglers; a friend or relative of the murdered Frenchman traced him back to England and killed him out of revenge; after his friends were hanged, his conscience troubled him so much that he killed himself.

The children went into groups and made up their own endings to the story. Further discussions took place and the play was eventually shaped and polished to the children's satisfaction. A final run-through of the whole play completed the project.

Scenario:
The Smugglers

CHARACTERS   The smugglers
                              French wine merchants
                              Sam

SCENE ONE   A French quayside
1. The merchants wait on the quayside. The smugglers tie up their boat and join them. They haggle over the price of the wine. Some of the smugglers carry their casks back to the fishing boat.
2. A heated argument breaks out between one of the smugglers (Sam) and a Frenchman. The Frenchman calls Sam a thieving rogue. Sam pulls out a knife and stabs the Frenchman. Sam and the rest of the smugglers race back to the boat pursued by the Frenchmen. One Frenchman stays behind to look after his wounded colleague.
3. The smugglers, once on board, quickly prepare the boat for sea: some unfurl the sails, while others cast off the mooring ropes. As the last smuggler climbs aboard, one of the crew hauls the gangplank in after him.
4. The Frenchmen try to climb on board but are repelled by the smugglers.
5. The boat heads for the open sea. Some of the Frenchmen run to the customs post and inform the officials there of what has taken place.

CHARACTERS   The English skipper
                            The smugglers
                            Chief Customs Officer
                            Customs officials
                            A French merchant

SCENE TWO In the Channel
1. A French customs launch sets off in pursuit of the smugglers. The gap between the two vessels narrows.

Customs officers	*Smugglers*
1. Some of the customs officers are running the launch, a group of them are engaged in loading a cannon. the rest line the sides.	1. The smugglers are doing all they can to elude the customs launch, but the Frenchmen are gaining on them.
2. The Chief Customs Officer orders the English skipper to drop anchor.	2. Realising the hopelessness of the situation, the skipper orders the anchor to be dropped.

The customs launch moves alongside.

2. The Chief Customs Officer orders the smugglers to hand Sam over. The merchant has since died and the charge is now one of murder. Below decks, Sam hides in an empty cask. The English skipper tells the Chief Customs Officer that Sam fell overboard. The Officer does not believe him and tells the skipper that they are going to search his boat.
3. The Chief Customs Officer positions some of his men along the side of the launch armed with muskets to fire on the smugglers if there is any sign of resistance. He then orders those on deck to line up with their hands above their heads.
4. The Chief Customs Officer leads some of his men on board the fishing boat. While some of them are lifting the hatch covers and searching under the ropes and bundles of tarpaulin littering the deck, a handful of picked men go below. Sam sneezes. He is hauled out of the cask and brought up on deck where he is recognised by one of the merchants brought along to make an identification.
5. Sam is dragged aboard the customs launch. "I'll be seeing you, lads!" he boasts.

CHARACTERS Sam
Prison guards
Officials
Other prisoners

SCENE THREE In and around a French prison
1. In groups, show how Sam escapes from prison and makes his way back to England.

CHARACTERS The smugglers
            Sam
            The landlord of the Red Boar

SCENE FOUR Inside the Red Boar tavern.

1. The smugglers are drinking and celebrating their success.
2. Sam enters. The smugglers are surprised to see him. He tells them how he escaped from a French prison and made his way back to England.
3. He asks for his share in the profits. They tell him that they have spent it, and, anyway, he did not bring any wine back with him. He is too hot-tempered, they are dispensing with his services. Sam becomes very angry, but there is nothing that he can do—at the moment.
4. He leaves the Red Boar and makes his way to the English customs post.
5. The smugglers continue with their celebrations.

CHARACTERS The smugglers
            The landlord
            Sam
            Chief Customs Officer
            English customs officials

SCENE FOUR The Red Boar tavern; a customs post

Tavern	*Customs post*
1. The smugglers continue with their drinking and celebrating.	1. Sam goes to the customs post and tells the Chief Customs Officer that there are smugglers drinking in the Red Boar. He offers proof.
	2. The Chief Customs Officer rounds up his men. He leads them to the Red Boar. They surround the tavern. Some of them are chosen to stay outside, those selected to go inside are divided into three groups. Each group enters the tavern by a different door.

3. The customs officers rush into the Red Boar. The Chief Customs Officer tells the smugglers that he has come to arrest them. A fight

breaks out. The customs officers arrest the smugglers; those managing to escape are picked up by the customs officers stationed outside. The smugglers are taken to the customs post.

4. Sam is rewarded; the smugglers are hanged.

5. The play ends with children presenting group plays showing what happened to Sam.

The play is over. By no stretch of the imagination could it be called great child drama but these children, with little previous experience, had produced a worthwhile play. They were now ready to go on and tackle a more demanding scenario. Therein lies dramatic progression. What had they learnt from the experience?

1. They had solved a number of problems. "Drama is problem-solving," Mrs Dorothy Heathcote.*

2. They had learnt something about dramatic shape.

3. They had learnt something of the life of a nineteenth-century smuggler, albeit sketchily. Some had been motivated to read about the history of smuggling and several had discovered copies of Masefield's *Jim Davies* in the library which they were reading avidly.

4. They had learnt that drama is a worthwhile, enjoyable activity.

5. They had used their imagination both in the narrative and in the practical staging.

6. They had had several interesting discussions; excellent training for future debate.

7. They had learnt more about human motivation. Drama provides a useful introduction to psychology.

Of course, this is only one way of tackling drama from scratch. Many drama teachers may feel that there has been too much discussion and not enough drama, but one must always guard against vagueness in structuring dramatic situations. It is indefensible for a drama teacher to allow a scene to flounder because children are uncertain of the action and the parts they are required to play.

Mrs. Heathcote has warned: "Beware of catering for wants rather than needs" and this applies particularly to material chosen by the children themselves. A run of smuggling plays, or those dealing with cowboys and Indians tend to produce a similarity of format and, because something has worked once, there is a tendency to repeat it ad infinitum. "All human life is here" and variety is the spice of life in the drama lesson as in reality. A record should be kept of all drama from scratch plays to avoid repetition. If similar themes do keep recurring, the voting procedure can be held in abeyance for a

* Two articles by Mrs. Heathcote are especially valuable—"Drama and Education: Subject or System", in *Drama and Theatre in Education*, edited Nigel Dodd and Winifred Hickson, Heinemann; "Drama as Challenge", in *The Uses of Drama*, edited John Hodgson, Eyre Methuen.

while and suggestions, that in normal circumstances would be rejected, can be tried out, depending upon the teacher's enthusiasm and ability to whet the children's dramatic appetites.

The success of any drama lesson can be measured by the way in which children make the characters their own. In the previous example "Sam", mentioning the smuggled spirits in the cave, is an example of this. He was thinking ahead, imaginatively building up a picture of smuggling activities and his part in them. A similar example of this occurred with a "problem child" I once had. Despite constant attempts to motivate him in subjects and characterisations in which I knew he was interested, and giving him as much creative freedom as I dare, this boy always ended up by taking advantage, disrupting as many other members of the class as he could in the process. He saw drama as "mucking about" and no amount of discussion would convince him otherwise. Until, that is, one day I spied him with a friend, lurking behind a rostrum box. At best he was probably carving his initials, at worst lighting a cigarette. The scenario at the time concerned the effects of the blitz upon the people living in London. To the accompaniment of sound effects of sirens, and an aerial bombardment, Red Cross men attended to the wounded, and wardens were helping those who could walk down the air raid shelters. I moved over to the box with considerable trepidation. Charlie was lying on the floor with his friend bending over him. Charlie was obviously dying and his friend was trying to catch his last words. "Look after my plants, when I'm gone," he was gasping, "keep them well-watered." I tiptoed away, Charlie had at last found a part that fitted his ebullient character. On another occasion, I was fortunate to be teaching in a school which had a small wood adjacent to the playing field. One of the topics suggested by the children was on the theme of William Golding's *Lord of the Flies*, and, the weather being sunny I took the class out among the trees to try to give them something of the feeling of life on a tropical island. The girls prepared a "fire" while the boys went out hunting for wild animals. At the end of a tree-lined path I saw another boy, who had caused me much concern in the past, seemingly lashing out at a bush with a large stick. Fearing that an act of wilful vandalism was taking place I hastened to the spot only to find the bush untouched and to be told that a wild pig was lurking inside and he was in the process of killing it for supper.

Choosing the right medium of expression is as much a problem for the drama teacher as it is for the writer. Once, dealing with the population explosion, I herded a class of children into an extremely small area and watched their initial good humour swiftly disintegrate into frayed tempers as they became more and more harassed by the close proximity of their friends. As a play it could not be judged a great success. Fortunately, I had the same class for the next lesson which happened to be creative writing. I set them an essay on the population explosion and received some of the best pieces of writing I have ever had on the perils of overcrowding.

Often, especially with older children, the discussion proves more important than the drama.

The drama teacher must be sensitive to the varying abilities of the children and know those who can safely be left to their own devices and those who must be watched. He should never send a group of children known to be troublesome to another classroom to practice, even if it means that the rest of the class will be better behaved in consequence. They will only disturb other teachers. Never send inexperienced groups to different parts of the hall or class room until they clearly understand what is expected of them. It is the witnessing of slip-shod, only partially-understood actions, that causes some people to give educational drama a bad name. Never allow children to become out of control, always know that by means of a signal— a raised hand, a bang on a drum, or a spoken command you can stop them at any time. There is no class worse than a badly-disciplined drama class; the scope for mischief is so much greater, especially if the work takes place in the school hall.

Allow children to relax into their parts, for example, in the smuggler's play, let the smugglers in the Red Boar settle down in the scene, let them buy each other drinks, tell stories, do not introduce the escaped prisoner Sam until you feel that the children are ready to move on. Educational drama is not theatre, there is no audience to be considered, allow the children time to become absorbed. But equally, do not give them too long to settle into a scene. If the celebrations go on too long in the Red Boar, some of the children will become "drunk," and, if there has been no discussion on the creation of a drunken character, the children concerned will probably create the worst kind of cliché drunk causing the scene to degenerate into a crude parody of what it might have been. Once children go "over the top" it is very difficult to bring them back without having to resort to a threatening attitude which should be alien to the tolerably permissive atmosphere in the drama class room.

CHAPTER 4

THE SET-UP SITUATION
"Jungle Ordeal"

Educational drama is a tool to be used at the discretion of the teacher as and when the opportunity presents itself. The more stimulating the lesson, the greater will be the children's involvement. Once children have been sufficiently stimulated by the presentation of a story, an idea, or a set of facts, the dramatic processes involved become self-generating. Present children with an exciting starting-point, provide them with the relevant information, and they can be safely left to their own devices. *Jungle Ordeal* is an example of one way in which drama can be used to add a new dimension to a geography lesson.

Jungle Ordeal

The year is 1950. An airliner on a routine flight across South America, from Rio de Janeiro in Brazil to Quito in Ecuador, develops engine trouble 150 miles from its destination and the pilot has to make a crash landing in the jungle.

Preliminary work on sound effects

Make a tape recording of an aeroplane taking off, in flight, developing engine trouble, and crashing. This can be done by recording the sound of a vacuum cleaner. Switch the vacuum cleaner on for take-off, keep it running for the flight, switch it on and off for the engine trouble, and make a gargling noise with your mouth close to the microphone for the crash. Or, alternatively, use Sound Effects record HMV 7 FX 13, *Aeroplanes—Air Liner*. Side One: 1. Passing Overhead, 2. Engine Noise or Roar, 3. Nose Dive, Crash and Fire; Side Two: 1. Warming Up and Taking Off, 2. Landing and Taxi-ing, 3. Flying Full Boost.

SCENE ONE Rio de Janeiro airport

CHARACTERS Crew of the plane—pilot, co-pilot, radio opera-
tor, navigator, stewards, air hostesses
Passengers
Airport announcer

The children should decide which particular character they would
like to play and then with chairs, tables, rostrums, create the interior
of the plane in the centre of the class room or hall. The aircrew start
up the engines ready for take-off and the stewards and air hostesses
go to the galley and prepare food and drinks for the flight.

The children should decide who they are and why they are travelling on this particular flight. The passengers include a businessman,
a wife going out to join her husband, a party of nuns returning to
a convent, members of a football team.

Put out circles of chairs at one end of the room and sit down.
You are in the airport lounge waiting for your flight. You
talk among yourselves about who you are and why you are
going to Quito.

1. When the crew of the plane are ready the announcer gives details
of the flight: "Would passengers for flight number..." (Details to
be improvised)
2. The passengers make their way to the plane. The air hostesses wait
by the doors and see the passengers to their seats.

Stimulus for improvisation: air crash

In order to simulate conditions during a plane crash it is important
that the children have some understanding of the sequence of events
from the development of engine trouble to the passengers abandoning
the wreck. The teacher, or members of the class, read aloud the following extracts:

"The aircraft's first impact with the ground occurred three
hundred and thirty-five feet short of the threshold of the runway.
The passengers felt it in various degrees depending on their seat
position. Some felt it as no more than the extra-heavy bump of a
bad landing. Others felt it much more violently. One man, sitting
over the undercarriage could 'feel and hear the (landing) gear rip-
ping off the aircraft and the crunching of it scraping on its belly.'
The aircraft continued sliding on its fuselage for about half-a-mile,
eventually swinging off to the right of the runway. One engine

broke away as it swung and hurtled a hundred and forty feet on its own.

"Despite the violence of the impact, none of the crew or passengers were apparently injured by it. All were still left with a chance to escape. But speed was vital. The difference between death and survival was compressed into that first minute or two. Everything depended on passengers' quickness of reaction and how well the emergency routines and the safety equipment worked.

"A leg of the broken landing gear had pushed a large hole into the right-hand rear side of the fuselage, rupturing fuel lines situated a few inches inside. Fire broke out almost instantly, caused either by a spark from the scraping of metal on the runway or from severed generator leads. Flames burst through the fuselage where the gear had penetrated and were licking menacingly at the floor below the passenger seats. The cabin began to fill with choking clouds of smoke. The lights flickered briefly then went out, adding darkness to the confusion.

"In those first bewildering moments as the aircraft skidded along, one of the stewardesses shouted to the passengers to keep their seats until it stopped. Most did so, possibly in obedience to her instructions. But it is more likely that they were simply too shocked and helpless to move, unsure of which way survival lay.

"Some of those in the forward part of the cabin seemed unaware of the blaze aft, until someone shouted 'My God, we're on fire. Let's get out of here.' Some passengers were already scrambling to find the handle of the nearest emergency exit, or groping forward along the aisle towards the front door. A stewardess was struggling with the handle, hampered by the press of people behind her, and it was not until the second officer came back to help that they got it open.

"By then the queue had been waiting for ten or fifteen seconds. 'It seemed like an age,' said one survivor later. Another, who escaped less than a minute after the crash, estimated that he would have succumbed to the smoke and heat in a few more seconds. Those out first remembered little jostling and few voices raised, possibly because everyone was trying to save every gasp of breath they could. Those who died were suffocated. This was shown by the high carboxyhemoglobin concentration in the victims.

"Preliminary indications showed that the interior furnishings accelerated the spread of the fire, contributing to the heavy black smoke, and hence to the fatalities. One man, who did not get out until the flames were running the length of the cabin ceiling, recalled that 'it was impossible to get near any of the window exits, due to the crowding of the people . . . practically everyone was hysterical with a great deal of screaming and shouting.'

"The man seated by the starboard wing exit, who had taken trouble to work out a hatch-opening routine, was one of the first out. He got the hatch open quickly, while the aircraft was still moving, but was blown flat on his back as soon as he got the panel out. He struggled up again, went head first through the hatch onto the wing and escaped with minor burns and bruises.

"Once out, survivors went on reacting almost unthinkingly. Some ran away as far as they could. Some hovered in a daze by the aircraft, although dimly aware of the considerable risk of explosion (a few were sprawled on the ground, unable to move because of broken or twisted ankles or semi-asphyxiation by the smoke). One passenger recalled with bewilderment how he had run away, taken off his jacket, folded it with extreme neatness and care, and placed it on a clean patch of grass. Only then had he returned to help. One of the F.A.A. inspectors bravely crawled back up the safety chute to try to rescue a passenger. Seeing that it was sheer suicide others pulled him back.

"Within a few minutes at most, watchers outside thought it impossible that anyone should still be living in the inferno. The airport crash trucks arrived within three-and-a-half minutes but since the fire was largely internal, the hoses were not fully effective. One survivor claimed that the first truck had run out of foam before the others arrived.

"At least three people remained alive aboard the aircraft. It is possibly the most astonishing example of survival in the air accident records. One of this fortunate trio was a stewardess, Annette Folz. In her testimony to the Civil Aeronautics Board enquiry she described how, after the impact, she managed to open the aft pressure door. This leads to another 'access door' and a central stairway which is lowered hydraulically under normal circumstances to allow passengers to board and alight at the rear of the plane. Initially Miss Folz could not open the access door because her hands were too badly burnt (when her hair caught fire she had had to put it out with her hands). She found two men crouched on the stairs. The stairway was jammed almost against the ground outside, and there appeared to be no escape that way. So Miss Folz turned back to the cabin, intending to try to help evacuation at another exit. By then most of the cabin was on fire and she could see that it would have been 'sure suicide' to try that way. 'I remembered what we were told in training school, "If there's a solid block of fire in front of you, don't go through it".'

"The two men were at the very end of the stairs laying down. I curled up right behind them into a little ball to get away from most of the smoke and fire and I started breathing through my jacket. I couldn't see any possible means of escape for us. I thought for sure that I was going to die. I then began to pray and review my life. It was getting hotter and hotter on the stairwell. The two men weren't talking so I asked one, 'Sir, do you think we're going to get out of here?' His answer was "Yes." I couldn't believe it so I asked, 'Alive?'. He then said "Yes," again. It was wonderful to see that he was optimistic.

"By then the fire was getting closer and the aft pressure door itself was alight.... Then they noticed a two-inch crack in the fuselage through which their vital supply of fresh air was coming. Miss Folz put her hand through it and waved. The firemen saw it, directed foam on the tail, and passed another hose inside for one of the men to use. The firemen got them out at last, after they had survived between twenty-five and thirty minutes on the burning plane." John Godson, *Unsafe at any Height*, Anthony Blond.

Then the following instructions for crew and passengers may be read to the class:

"Emergency landing on land:
1. Fasten your seat belt tightly.
2. Pull your chair to a fully upright position.
3. Bend forward with one arm across your knees.
4. Place your pillow on your lap.
5. Put your head on the pillow, with your other arm over your head.
6. Push and brace your arms forward.
7. Wait for the moment of impact. You will be warned just before it comes." Bruce Cassidy, *Survival Handbook*, Tower Publications.

A discussion then follows, directed at the various groups.

Crew members: Why does the plane develop engine trouble? How do you try to keep the plane airborne? What happens when you realise that the plane is losing height and there is nothing you can do about it? When do you tell the passengers you are going to attempt a crash-landing? You spot a clearing in the jungle below. What is the procedure for a crash-landing?
Air hostesses: What can you do to calm the passengers? What is the drill for a crash-landing? Where are the emergency exits?
All: What happens to the human body during a plane crash? What happens to the plane when it crashes? Does it burst into flames?

Decide what is going to happen to you during the crash. Are you going to be killed, are you seriously injured, or do you escape with minor cuts and bruises?

SCENE TWO: Inside the aircraft

1. (Sound effects—a plane taking off) The air hostesses help the passengers fasten their seat belts. The plane takes off. The passengers unfasten their seat belts and everything goes smoothly at first. The air hostesses go round asking the passengers what they would like to eat and drink. The passengers talk amongst themselves and the pilot joins them and talks about the flight.
2. Sound effects. The plane develops engine trouble and it crashes. Do you try to get out of the plane as fast as you can if you are uninjured, or do you stay behind and try to help those in need?

The plane has crashed in a remote part of the jungle ... in the territory of the Aucas. ...

Stimulus for improvisation: The Aucas

The *Aucas* (pronounced ow-cah) are a race of primitive Indians who live deep in the heart of the Ecuadorian jungle between the Napo and Villano rivers, one hundred and fifty miles south-east of Quito, the capital city.

They live in villages consisting of a few large huts, each sheltering from twenty to fifty Indians. These huts consist of a sloping roof of palm leaves constructed over a ridge pole which is supported by a number of posts twenty feet in height. Sometimes the structure is finished off by adding three-foot high walls of split bamboo, but usually the sides are left open exposing the occupants to wind and rain. The gable ends are rounded, giving the building an elliptical shape when viewed from the air. A small opening at each end serves as a doorway. Inside the huts each family has its own living area around a stone fireplace with a wooden mantle shelf. The smoke from the many fires quickly coats the ceiling with tar which helps to preserve it and also acts as an insect repellent. The Aucas sleep on hammocks plaited from palm leaf fibre. The leaves are torn off and the stalk is boiled and spread out in the sun to dry. It is then rolled by the women between the palms of their hands, making strong twine of varying thickness, from slender thread used in the making of clothes, to the thicker varieties used in the manufacture of fishnets, which are plaited on wooden hoops, and hammocks.

It takes roughly one year to obtain the twine to make one hammock. If there are no walls to the hut the hammocks are hung high in the roof so that the occupants will not be drenched by the rain as it splashes up from the floor. Their simple utensils lie scattered about the hut: a few clay pots, plaited baskets, dishes made out of gourds cut in half, and a bundle of rubbing sticks for lighting the seed wool from the balsa tree which acts as tinder when making the fire. A rack of smoked meat hangs over the fire, while up in the sloping beams of the roof, always ready to hand, are the weapons of the hunt, the weapons of war—the nine-foot-long spears of *chonta* wood and the blowpipes with their lethal darts which an Auca can fire with deadly accuracy up to a range of fifty yards. A fishnet and a few stone hatchets complete the worldly possessions of these primitive people.

The *chonta* spear is sharpened at each end and one end is barbed. It is decorated with brilliantly coloured toucan feathers. Each male Auca has nine or ten spears in his possession, and during the hunt they are used to kill the larger creatures: wild pigs, tapirs, alligators and anacondas; the blowpipe is reserved for smaller animals and birds: woolly spider monkeys, howler monkeys, macaws, squirrels, and toucans.

The long blowpipe is fashioned out of palmwood and has a wide mouthpiece shaped like a matchbox. When not in use, the darts are always carried in a waterproof case coated with a pitch-like substance. The ends of the darts are dipped in *curare*, a poison which is produced from the bark of certain tropical evergreen trees. The bark is shredded and placed in a funnel made from a broad leaf. Water is poured over the bark and the funnel is placed upon a framework of sticks so that the liquid can drip into a container placed underneath. When all the brown-coloured liquid has dripped into the container, it is gently heated over a slow fire. Periodically, the skin that forms on the surface is skimmed off with a dart and scraped onto a piece of pottery where it thickens as it cools. This is curare. The head of each dart is dipped into the poison and placed on a rack near the fire to dry. A groove is made just below the poisoned tip with a sharp piranha tooth to stop monkeys from pulling the darts out of their bodies. If they try to do so the stem breaks off leaving the poisoned tip firmly embedded in the flesh. An Auca will wait for hours, imitating the call of wild birds, eventually enticing them within range of his lethal darts. He always carries a wad of kapok in a gourd attached to his darts' case. The kapok is wrapped around the end of the dart so that it fits snugly into the bore of his blowpipe.

From an early age the Auca boy is trained in the use of weapons.

Starting with the smaller spears used for killing fish, he will stand for hours by the side of a fast-flowing stream trying to hit small objects thrown into the water by his friends, until he is expert enough to handle the large *chonta* spears used by the men. Life-size human shapes carved out of balsa wood are used for target practice, the boys moving further and further away as their aim becomes more and more accurate.

The men spend a great deal of their time hunting; travelling far from their homes and going for many hours without food following the trail of a herd of wild pigs or stalking a savage puma. They return from the hunt covered in wood ticks which are removed by their families and killed by crushing them between their teeth.

The women and boys join the men on their fishing expeditions. The boys are sent on ahead to search out a likely stretch of water where the fish are most numerous. When a school of fish is located the men either use their special spears, leaving the women to catch the fry in their scoop nets, or they trail the crushed roots of the barabasco plant through the water. These plants give off a poison-ous substance which dissolves in the water and stuns the fish enabling them to be lifted out by hand or caught by the women in their nets.

Some of the women accompany the men on their numerous raids into neighbouring territory. Acting as porters, they leave the men free to use their spears should they walk into an ambush. During a battle the women pass the spears to their menfolk. The Aucas usually spring a surprise attack at night and they always ensure that they are numerically stronger than their enemies.

A favourite spot for an Auca ambush is at the bend in a river where they wait for unsuspecting travellers. As the river curves, strong currents drive the travellers and their boats towards the wait-ing Aucas, who, at a given signal, hurl their spears at the voyagers, just at the moment when, unprotected, they are attempting to pole away from the shore.

To protect their own property the Aucas dig camouflaged pits lined with *chonta* spears on the trails leading to their villages.

The Aucas are constantly making raids upon their friendly neighbours, the *Quichuas* (pronounced keech-wa), robbing them of their axes, machetes, knives, scissors, and shovels. They also steal their glass beads to take home to their womenfolk. These imple-ments are highly-prized by the Aucas, especially the machetes, which are much more effective for hacking a way through the dense jungle than their own simple axes fashioned from pieces of stone. They have been known to kill each other for the possession of a machete and one axe was once responsible for the death of seven

Aucas. After a raid they always burn down their houses and move
on for fear of reprisals.

Manioc, or cassava root, is the Aucas main food, the equivalent
of our bread and potatoes. When boiled, it has a similar taste and
texture to the parsnip. They will eat a small portion of meat or
fish followed by a large quantity of manioc. They also eat boiled
yucca, plantains, ground nuts, *chonta* fruit, maize, bananas, sweet
potatoes, yams, smoked meats and boiled or smoked fish. Large
white grubs which are found in palm trees are eaten either raw
or cooked in the ashes of the fire. They find the piranha a very
tasty dish, but the armoured catfish is the most succulent of all.
They smoke large quantities of meat as they have no salt to preserve
it. They drink *chicha*, which is made by the women. Quantities
of manioc are boiled, chewed and put to one side for a couple of
days to allow the starch in the manioc to change to sugar through
the action of the digestive enzymes in the spittle. It is then mixed
with water and consumed. It is a lumpy, milky liquid and is very
nourishing. Unlike the Quichuas, they do not let the chicha fer-
ment. As an alternative to chicha, they also make a drink from plan-
tain by squeezing the fruit to a pulp and mixing it with water. Plan-
tain leaves are used as tablecloths, and talking is forbidden at meal
times. Because of the lack of sugar in their diet they suffer very
little from toothache.

The women spend their time cooking, preparing chicha, and
growing plantains and manioc in the clearings that have been
hacked out of the jungle by the men. Manioc takes five months
to grow, and a crop of plaintains is ready at the end of a year. Being
a semi-nomadic people, they are continually on the move and the
men are constantly having to clear new areas of the jungle. When
not out hunting, the men spend their time making and sharpening
their weapons.

They possess very few clothes. The women wear skirts made of
bark cloth and enjoy displaying the jewellery captured from the
Quichuas, and necklaces which they make themselves from monkey
teeth strung on pieces of twine. They sometimes paint their faces
using the dye from achiote berries. The men are completely naked,
wearing only plugs of balsa wood attached to the lobes of their ears.
During their dances they don magnificent woven headbands of red
and yellow toucan feathers. Both the men and the women wear
their hair long, the women slightly longer than the men with a
fringe across their foreheads. The women cut their hair with clam
shells.

Girls marry between the ages of twelve and fifteen. There is no
marriage ceremony, the man simply asks the girl's parents if she

can be his wife, and, providing that he is not the girl's cousin and the parents approve of him, they are considered married. The young couple spend a month with his in-laws and he has to supply his father-in-law with a share of the game that he kills while out hunting, then he is free to set up his own fireplace in the big hut. If an Auca chooses a wife from another tribe he is forbidden from taking a further bride from among his own people.

The almost continuous warfare waged by the Aucas against neighbouring tribes and amongst themselves has taken its tragic toll. Many of the children have no fathers and the women greatly outnumber the men. Consequently, the men take more than one wife and also become responsible for the upbringing of their dead comrades' children. Each wife serves her own family first at meal-times, then the orphans and widows that are under her husband's protection. When boys are badly behaved their parents beat them with jungle vines, or nettles.

The dead are buried in a sitting position under the floor of the big house. Food is left to help them in their long journey in the after-life and the relatives are content if, on waking the following morning, they find that it has gone, even though it has probably been taken by rats.

Aucas are a very sociable people and think nothing of waking up at three o'clock in the morning to tell their friends or relatives that it is raining. This conversation soon wakes the whole hut and the most trivial remarks are cheerfully relayed from house to house as if it was mid-afternoon rather than the middle of the night.

Food, hunting, and the killing of their enemies, are the main topics of conversation among the men. An Auca will explain, with much excitement, and in great detail, how he avenged his father's murder.

There are no dogs but they make pets of young boars, monkeys, and parrots, and take delight in describing the flights of birds in a style reminiscent of a television sports commentator reporting a horse race or a motoring event:

> "Two birds of paradise, male and female, have just flown into the lower branches of that kapok tree. The female has come out now, and..."

The other Aucas eagerly follow the birds' movements as they are described.

They possess their own tales and legends. One, similar to the biblical story of Noah's Ark, tells how fire flashed down from heaven and destroyed all the human race except the Aucas who hid themselves under the leaves of the sweet potato and were saved. When the earth cooled, they crawled from under their flimsy shelters and re-peopled the earth. Another story concerns a small turtle who, one day, as he was out walking in the forest met a fierce jaguar. The jaguar bullied and threatened the little turtle who replied by telling him what fine teeth he had. The jaguar opened his mouth to show them off to advantage whereupon the little turtle jumped inside the jaguar's mouth, seized him by the throat, and killed him.

They have no chief to rule over them, and no councils. Everyone is left to make his own decisions. Each man is his own chief.

Vocabulary

Apaika	Moon
Apu	River
Awum irimi?	What is your name?
Ayuma	Wood bee = Aeroplane
Ba-ah!	Take that!
Bah	No
Baru	There
Biti winki pungi amupa	I want to approach you
Biti miti punimupa	I like you; I want to be your friend
Ganimui	We are friends
Huininamai	Don't run away
Nimu	Stars
Owuka	The sun maker, God.
Puinani	Welcome
Tomamoni	All of us
Wi mponimopa	I don't remember

From the sixteenth century onwards, the Aucas have savagely defended their territory against foreign invasion, earning for themselves the Quichua title, Auca, or Savage. This word is unknown to the Aucas, they always refer to themselves as the *Cuuri*. They are also known as *Los Infiels*—the Heathens.

Through the years, their grim determination to defend their territory has earned them grudging respect, and any foreigner who ignored their warning line of nine-foot *chonta* spears across a jungle trail, passed on at his peril. They had no need to write "Trespassers will be assassinated!"—it was an unwritten law. Travellers soon learned to heed the warning of the deadly *chonta* spears.

There came a time, though, between 1875 and 1925, when mens' greed overcame their fear. This was the age of the great South American rubber boom when men from all over the world travelled to the jungles of the Oriente to tap the wild rubber trees and sell the precious liquid in a wild scramble to get rich quick. Carrying guns and licensed to kill, the tappers, joined by gold prospectors, held the view that primitive people, like outlaws, had no rights— they should expect no justice or mercy—and consequently, they received none. When a party of Aucas appeared to defend their land against these foreign invaders they were butchered to a man to avoid reprisals. Others were coaxed from their homes by offers of gifts and friendship. When the Aucas appeared, leaving their weapons behind in their houses, the rubber tappers and gold prospectors overpowered them, sold them into slavery on the surrounding haciendas, and burned their houses to the ground. Realising that they were fighting an unequal battle, the Aucas hid themselves away in the great forest.

Eventually, with the development of rubber plantations in the Dutch East Indies and Malaya, interest in South American rubber declined and the rubber tappers went home.

Deep in the almost impenetrable jungle, the Aucas licked their wounds. In their minds the foreigners had become synonymous with death, and they hated them with an overwhelming hatred. From now on, every stranger was an enemy, and every stranger must die....

Improvisations

An Auca raid

Divide yourselves up into two groups: a group of Quichuas and a group of Aucas.

It is evening and the Quichuas lie down in their hammocks to sleep. A party of Aucas creep silently through the jungle towards the Quichua settlement, stealthily moving through the huts taking machetes, knives and axes, from beside the sleeping Quichuas. One of the Aucus disturbs a Quichua girl. She wakes and seeing the Auca in her hut lets out a scream. The Aucus, realising that they have been discovered, make off into the jungle. Hearing the girl's screams, two Quichua brothers, armed with rifles, rush out of their hut firing wildly at the Aucus as they flee into the jungle.

Now change over. The Quichuas becoming Aucas and vice-versa.

Spirits

When an Auca dies it is believed that the spirit leaves the body and returns to the jungle to be close to the familiar scenes of its manhood, but it must never enter the big house of its relatives.

> Imagine that you are such a spirit floating invisibly through the jungle. As you pass your friends you can whisper to each other as the Auca spirits are supposed to do.

Evil spirits

There is one evil spirit that haunts the jungle trails. He is a skeleton but his heart can still be seen beating through the bones.

> Find a partner. One of you becomes an Auca, the other the evil spirit. It is said that whenever the evil spirit encounters a person on his own it savagely attacks and murders him. Then the ground begins to quake and the Indians listen and know. This is their way of explaining earthquakes. A lonely Auca walks down a jungle path, suddenly, the spirit of the evil one appears. . . .
> Change roles: the evil spirit becomes the Auca and vice-versa.

The Medicine man

When an Auca becomes ill his sickness is believed to have been brought on by a medicine man in another tribe. If a patient is suffering from a snake bite they believe that an unknown enemy medicine man talked with the snake and persuaded it to bite the victim. The patient has to bring in his own medicine man to attempt a cure.

> Find a partner. One of you becomes the patient and the other the medicine man. The patient lies on the floor. The medicine man consumes large quantities of a powerful drink known as *Aya Huasca*. He then begins to breathe upon his patient, starting at the head and working down to the feet. The patient feels strength coming back into his body. Slowly he begins to sit up as the power of the medicine man's breath drives away the evil that is attempting to destroy him.

An Auca dance

Make a long line across the floor, boy and girl alternatively and put your hands on each other's shoulders. When
the music begins, jump one step forward making sure that
your feet all come down on the floor at the same time. Before
you begin the dance, decide which way you are going. You
can either jump backwards or forwards alternatively, or,
you can move forward for a few jumps and then jump backwards to the spot that you originally started from.

Once the facts about the Aucas have been assimilated the class is
split into two groups: the members of one group taking the part of
the Aucas, while the other group are the survivors of the plane crash.
What happens then? Do the Aucas massacre the survivors? Or do
they feel sorry for them and help them to return to civilisation? Are
the survivors rescued by a search party? Or do they escape from the
Aucas only to die of starvation in the jungle?

Bibliography

Blomberg, R., *The Naked Aucas*, George Allen & Unwin.
Elliot, Elisabeth, *Shadow of the Almighty*, Hodder & Stoughton.
—— *The Savage my Kinsman*, Hodder & Stoughton.
—— *Through Gates of Splendour*, Hodder & Stoughton.
Hitt, R., *Jungle Pilot*, Hodder & Stoughton.
Wallace, *The Dayuma Story*, Hodder & Stoughton.

Although dealing with the music of another South American tribe,
the Jivaro, "Legend of the Jivaro" by Yma Sumac, Capitol T 770
is a useful record for accompanying any movement sequences in *Jungle
Ordeal*.

CHAPTER 5

"SMALL BOYS FOR SMALL FLUES"

Drama as the Focal Point for Integrated Studies

In an age of ever-narrowing specialisation, particularly in the field of advanced academic study, teachers, especially primary school teachers, are increasingly structuring their lessons on the basis of integrated studies. Geography combines with religious education in a study of local churches; music joins with physical education to create a dance drama on the theme of witches; and English goes hand in hand with history in giving children a wider understanding of the medieval mystery plays.

If an integrated approach is adopted, the preliminary question is always to decide which particular subject should initiate such a scheme. In secondary schools, most heads of department like to think of their subject as the one most suited to be the focal point for integrated work. The head of the geography department might argue that an integrated course should begin with a study of the local environment, gradually moving outwards to embrace a world view, while the head of the English department might feel that such a scheme should begin with a personal affection such as discontent, suffering, pleasure, beauty, etc. In the light of such vested interests, it might appear presumptuous of the drama teacher to declare his subject as the ideal focal point for integrated work, especially as it is still a matter of some debate whether drama is a subject at all in the accepted sense of the word. Yet the drama teacher, by the very nature of his subject, is in a unique position to be, if not the instigator, at least the catalyst in such a scheme. Children learn most eagerly the things they like doing best, and educational drama enjoys immense popularity. The idea of doing a play, for example, on the life of Captain Cook has much more appeal than a narrative exposition by the teacher followed by a written exercise. However gifted the teacher's narrative skill, or the vividness of a film or filmstrip, there can never be the same feeling of involvement on the part of the children if the end product is a written exercise rather than a dramatisation. This is in no way to denigrate the importance of written work

80

in schools, but only to comment upon children's reactions to two differing forms of expression.

If the means of expression then is drama there is much more incentive on the part of the children to learn. As we have seen educational drama provides the ideal motivation for learning, and nowhere more so than at the centre of an integrated studies project, represented here diagrammatically (*see* Fig. 4).

A topic is chosen, an aspect of which is then, through discussion with the children, transformed into an unpolished improvisation, an

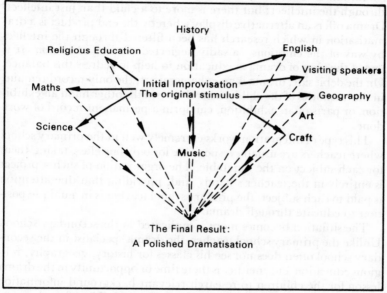

Fig. 4. Drama as the centre of an integrated studies project.

unsatisfactory end in itself because of its superficiality as there is much knowledge yet to be acquired. The children at this point will only possess a limited amount of knowledge about the topic in question. But the need soon arises for some form of research to be undertaken, whether it be to find out the cost of a loaf of bread in France in 1787 in an integrated studies project on the French Revolution; or the design of James Watt's steam engine; or, why, in 1064, Harold landed on the coast of Normandy to be detained and handed over to William the Conqueror when dealing with the events leading up to the Battle of Hastings.

Information required for a dramatisation leads to research, which is undertaken not to be hidden away behind the covers of an exercise book to be seen only by the teacher, but to form an integral part of the play. Without research, the play would remain a superficial and unsatisfactory improvisation. The boy playing the part of James Watt has a real incentive to find out all he can about the early steam engine if his part is to have credibility. The children playing French peasants in 1787 need to know the cost of a loaf of bread as a peg on which to hang their grievances. Harold and his followers need a motivation for sailing off to Normandy.

The end product of an integrated studies project is usually an exhibition of some kind, a display of research that has been filtered through the intellect; but there is more to a child than just intellect. Drama offers an alternative display whereby the end product is a dramatisation in which research has been filtered through the intellect by way of the emotions—a sadly neglected area in education. It is one of the aims of drama in education to help to redress this balance. On the debit side, drama is an ephemeral art, the only record remains in the memories of the children involved; on the other hand an exhibition, or parts of an exhibition, can form a permanent record of work done.

This type of integration works extremely well in the primary school where teachers are usually responsible for only one class, taking them for each subject on the timetable. The organisation of such a project is entirely in the teacher's hands, and, providing that due attention is paid to each subject, the primary school teacher is in a unique position to educate through drama.

The situation becomes more complicated in the secondary school. Unlike the primary school teacher, the drama specialist in the secondary school often does not see his classes for history, geography, religious education, etc., neither is there time or opportunity in the drama lesson for the children to research relevant background information for the particular topic the teacher has in mind. Therefore, he must seek the co-operation of other members of staff. The children in 2Q, for example, are keen to do a play about pirates. The drama teacher goes to the head of the history department and asks if it is possible for some background information on pirates to be given to this class.

"Sorry," replies the head of history consulting his syllabus, "but 2Q are down to do the Romans."

"But," remonstrates the drama teacher, "they are much more interested in pirates than they are in the Romans."

"I can't help that," says the head of the history department. "I have a syllabus to get through, a syllabus I spent hours working on, and I don't intend to jump about from one unrelated section to another to suit the children's particular whims and fancies. It's just not on."

Perhaps a partial solution to this problem can be found if a drama teacher seeking integrated facilities obtains copies of syllabuses from the main subject departments, enabling him to pick out those topics which particularly lend themselves to dramatisation, providing that he has the time available in which to prepare the work and the co-operation of the staff in allowing the children to undertake the research in the parent subject concerned.

On the other hand a drama teacher may be brought in to assist in a team-teaching project, on the surface an ideal set-up for integrating subjects through drama; but the situation even here often proves to be far short of ideal. At one school in which I taught, all the first-year children were engaged upon a study of the local environment and I was brought in as a drama teacher to help in a project on roads. One group of children was drawing a map of the major road networks; another group was researching tolls and tollgates, and a further group was studying road construction with particular reference to a motorway project nearing completion in the area. I was given a group of children and it was suggested that we might like to produce a polished improvisation on the theme of highwaymen, a subject of particular local interest as Dick Turpin had been arrested at an inn close by the school. Work began on the play. Five weeks went by and I felt that the time had come for the children to show their work to the rest of the first year. I went to see the head of the geography department who was masterminding the project and told him that the play was ready.

"A play about Dick Turpin?" he said with a puzzled frown.

"Yes, you asked me to create a play about highwaymen with my group."

"Oh yes, so I did," he said, "But we've finished with roads, we're on to windmills now. Look, why don't you do a play about Don Quixote."

This illustrates the different time-scales involved in, say, completing a map on the one hand, and bringing an improvisation to a level where it is worth showing to an audience on the other. A map might take two or three lessons at most and can be completed, if necessary, for homework. It takes much longer to reach a satisfactory standard in drama and the work usually has to be completed in lesson time, especially if the drama teacher is busy rehearsing the end of term play after four o'clock.

Integration through drama at secondary level is complicated by all these factors. But many drama teachers look forward to a time when a drama-based curriculum at secondary level could be a reality. To achieve this, modified syllabuses, thematically linked, would have to be amicably worked out between the heads of departments

concerned. Richard Courtney in *Play, Drama and Thought* has presented a theoretical justification for education by means of drama;
it is now up to interested drama teachers to prove that such a method
can work out in practice.

Integrated Drama in Practice

So far reference has only been made to partial integration, drama
linked with one particular subject. *Small Boys For Small Flues* is the
record of a fully-integrated studies scheme based on the lives of nineteenth-century climbing boys, undertaken with a mixed class in their
final year at primary school. These children had never taken educational drama before, and this topic was chosen because of its particular appeal to the young. The opening scenes deal mainly with
the climbing boys themselves, thus enabling the children to identify
fairly easily with the characters, settling safely into their parts before
more demanding roles were expected of them. Children love to climb
trees and crawl through drain pipes; there was a foundation here upon
which to build, as they will already have experienced through play
some aspects of a climbing boy's lot. They enjoy learning about how
children lived at other times and in other places. This is also the age
at which a social conscience begins to develop and the scenario, dealing as it does with the inhumanity of sending little children to clean
narrow soot-clogged chimneys, was designed to give their feelings adequate scope for expression. There were no costume difficulties, at least
not for the children playing climbing boys; in reality they wore cast-
off clothing begged from home, while in the classroom the actors were
encouraged to exchange articles of clothing with their friends, wear
their jackets inside out, ruffle up their hair and generally make themselves as dishevelled as possible—a rare treat in school! As most of
the drama work had to be taken in the class room, the scenario was
structured to give the maximum dramatic conflict within physically
limiting confines. Finally, there is always the danger of distorting historical truth to serve the demands of the drama and the needs of the
children taking part. *Small Boys for Small Flues* overcame this problem
with a basically fictitious scenario stressing freedom within a set of
social conditions rather than restrictions imposed by a series of well-
documented historical events.

The stages involved from play to presentation can be written out
as an equation:

Interest   +stimula-
              tion   +narration+improvisation+
research +discussion +dramatisation

= the most worthwhile educational experience we are so far capable of giving children in the humanities.

Interest

The project began with the teacher discussing various social aspects of the year 1828 (*see* Talking Points 1828, Chapter Six), the year in which the scenario takes place. Interest was aroused by comparing and contrasting life then with life today. Basic facts about climbing boys (*see* Chapter Six) were then given to the children.

Stimulation

Having whetted the children's interest in climbing boys, the next stage was for the children to become climbing boys themselves. They ruffled their hair, turned their jackets and cardigans inside out, took their shoes and socks off, changed articles of clothing with their friends, boys rolled up their trouser legs. A house-point was given to the untidiest child.

The physical conditions of the climbing boys were described in detail and the children were asked to imagine themselves with hacking coughs, knock-knees, humped backs, their feet and legs resembling the letter S. They were then asked to walk about the room imagining that they were climbing boys returning to their cellar homes after a hard day's work in the chimneys. There is a tendency here for some children, either through embarrassment on the girls' side, or a feeling on the part of the boys that drama is "for sissys," to giggle nervously or behave in an extremely silly and uncontrolled manner. Therefore, the more stimuli one can use to help children overcome these difficulties, the better. To heighten atmosphere and aid characterisation the teacher played the second movement of Dvořák's "New World" Symphony over which was read the following poem:

> Sweep! Sweep! Sweep!
> A small boy for a small chimney!
> Sweep! Sweep! Sweep!

> Yes, open your doors, you fine ladies,
> Pay sixpence to our master sweep;
> We'll get not a farthing between us,
> Just a sack full of soot for our sleep.

Yes, open your doors, you fine ladies,
Don't look at the sores on our knees;
Let's get at the soot in the chimney.
We're as tough as the bark on the trees.

Yes, open your doors, you fine ladies,
Stay close should we utter a cry;
You don't want your chimney a coffin,
But in soot we so easily die.

Yes, open your doors, you fine ladies,
We're apprenticed and know our trade;
We learnt it the hard way, they kicked us
For all the mistakes that we made.

Yes, open your doors, you fine ladies
Joe's one of a short-living crew
Beset with the chimney sweep's cancer
From a-staying too long in the flue.

Narration

Having experienced something of what it felt like to be climbing boys, the children returned to their places and listened to a synopsis of the story.

Jack Sourgull is sold by his parents to Charlie Crouch, a climbing master. Jack's apprenticeship began as soon as his parents were off Crouch's premises. He was bundled unceremoniously into the fireplace and forced to climb the chimney. His cries for help were heard by a rich businessman's wife, Mrs. Winchester-Grey, whose coach had broken down outside the doorway of Crouch's cellar. Finding Jack in the process of being forced up the chimney, Mrs. Winchester-Grey orders Crouch to bring him down. Crouch refuses. Feeling sorry for the boys, she invites them to an open-air dinner of sausages and ale; and after listening to some of their stories of ill-treatment and the conditions under which they had to work, she begins a campaign to have the practice of using climbing boys abolished.

A fire then breaks out in her own chimney and a kitchen girl is sent for the nearest sweep, who happens to be Crouch. Crouch is still in the process of teaching Jack his "trade," and as he is the only boy on the premises at the time, he is cajoled and threatened into climbing the chimney and putting out the fire. He dies in the process.

Scenario:
Small Boys for Small Flues

CHARACTERS Climbing boys
Charlie Crouch, a master chimney sweep
Ned, a journeyman sweep
William Sourgull, a poor clerk
Emily Sourgull, his wife
Jack Sourgull, their son
Mrs. Winchester-Grey, a businessman's wife

SCENE ONE Crouch's cellar

The home of the climbing boys. Sacks of soot are spread over the floor for the boys to sleep on. There is a fireplace on one wall. It is an evening in the year 1828. (Make a square of chairs for the walls of the cellar. Use chairs and boxes to make the fireplace. Chairs for the chimney can stretch across the classroom floor.)

1. One by one, the climbing boys return to the cellar, tired after a hard day sweeping chimneys. They flop on to the bags of soot. Some sleep. Others talk about their work.

2. Charlie Crouch enters with Ned, his assistant. Ned carries a sack on his back. He opens it, and tosses hunks of bread and cheese to the boys.

3. They push and shove, trying to get as much of the bread and cheese as they can.

4. While they are eating, Crouch asks them about the day's work. He praises those who have worked hard, and ill-treats those who have been lazy.

5. There is a knock on the door. Crouch opens it and lets in Mr. and Mrs. Sourgull, and their son Jack. At first, Crouch thinks that Sourgull is a customer. Sourgull tells Crouch that he wants to apprentice Jack to a climbing master. He has seven children and cannot afford to look after them all. Jack, being the eldest, must leave home in order that more money can be spent on the rest of the family. Would Crouch be interested in buying him? Mrs. Sourgull sobs in the background. Crouch asks how old Jack is. Sourgull says that he is eight years old. Crouch complains that Jack is too big; he only buys small boys. "A small boy for a small flue," that is his motto. Crouch asks Sourgull how much he thinks Jack is worth. Sourgull asks £3. Crouch says he will give ten shillings for him. They haggle. Sourgull asks less, Crouch offers more. They eventually fix a price. Crouch hands over

the money, and Jack becomes his possession. Mr. and Mrs. Sourgull leave.

6. Crouch says that Jack must begin his apprenticeship at once. He tells Jack to take off his shoes and socks. Jack is much too frightened to refuse. Crouch tells him to climb the chimney. Jack shakes his head. Crouch drags him to the fireplace and pushes him up the chimney. He asks Ned for a pin. Crouch takes the pin and orders one of the boys to get into the fireplace underneath Jack. He is to drive Jack up the chimney pricking his bare feet with the pin if he hesitates. Jack and the climbing boy disappear up the chimney. Jack yells out as he is pricked with the pin.

7. Mrs. Winchester-Grey pushes her way into the cellar. She tells Crouch that she was on her way home by coach, but one of her horses has gone lame. Does he know where she can find a blacksmith?

She hears Jack's screams coming from the chimney and asks Crouch what is happening. He says that he is training an apprentice climbing boy. She tells him that the boy must be in great pain to be screaming like that. Crouch says that it is none of her business. She asks the boys what is happening. They tell her about the other boy and the pin. She is shocked. She never realised before how the boys are taught their trade; she is usually in bed when her own chimneys are swept. She tells Crouch to bring the boy down at once. Crouch refuses. He asks her to leave. They argue. Crouch tells her that he will do what he likes on his own property. He has a job to do and now would she kindly leave him to get on with it. She realises that there is nothing she can do; Crouch is determined not to bring the boy down. At the door she turns: "You haven't heard the last of this," she says as she leaves the cellar.

"Stop boys climbing chimneys and your houses will soon burn down," shouts Crouch.

8. Jack is brought down from the chimney. He is bruised, sore, and terribly frightened. "I'll have you broken in in no time," leers Crouch.

9. Crouch tells the boys to get to sleep. They lie down on the sacks of soot. Jack sobs quietly to himself.

10. Crouch and Ned leave. Crouch locks the cellar door behind him.

(The children go into groups of not more than eight and make up a play about something that might have happened to them had they been climbing boys.)

CHARACTERS Mrs. Winchester-Grey
            Waitresses
            Ned
            Climbing boys
            A gatecrasher

SCENE TWO In the open air. Mrs. Winchester-Grey has invited
Crouch's boys to a feast. It is 6.45 p.m.

Put lines of desks down the classroom with chairs around them.
Put out as many chairs as there are climbing boys.

This scene is based on a description of James White's annual feast
for chimney sweepers as described by Charles Lamb in his essay
"Praise of Chimney Sweepers" from *Essays of Elia*.

1. Waitresses stand by the tables with pans of sizzling sausages.
2. Another sweep's boy tries to sit at one of the tables. They chase
him away shouting and yelling good-naturedly.
3. The climbing boys rush over to the tables. They greet Mrs.
Winchester-Grey and scramble and jostle to get a seat.
4. The waitresses go round handing out the sausages and mugs of ale.
The boys eat hungrily, calling all the while for more. Mrs.
Winchester-Grey walks up and down the lines of tables asking the
boys if they are enjoying themselves.
5. When the meal is over they all sing:

TIPPITIWITCHET
This morning early
My malady was such
I in my tea took brandy,
And took a drop too much.
Tol lol lol (hiccup)
Tol lol lol de rol de lay.

But stop! I must not wag hard—
My head aches, if you please,
One pinch of Irish Blackguard
I'll take to give me ease.
Tol lol lol (sneezes)
Tol lol lol de rol de lay.

Now I'm quite drowsy growing,
For this very morn
I rose when cock was crowing,
Excuse me if I yawn.
Tol lol lol (yawns)
Tol lol lol de rol de lay.

I'm not in cue for frolic,
Can't my spirits keep,
Love, most melancholic,
'Tis that which makes me weep.

Tol lol lol (weeps)
Tol lol lol de rol de lay.

I'm not in mood for crying,
Care's a silly calf,
If to get fat you're trying
Then my way's to laugh.
Tol lol lol (laughs)
Tol lol lol de rol de lay.

Fig. 5. Music for Tippitiwitchet.

6. Ned stands up and proposes a toast to "The King" (George IV). They all stand up and shout "The King!" They drink a toast, shake hands, and hug each other. Ned proposes another toast, "To the sweeping brush, may it do the job for us." Standing up, they all drink a toast to the sweeping brush. "To the soot!"..."To Mrs. Winchester-Grey!"... (Discuss what other toasts climbing boys could make. If any child has an idea, he should stand up and propose his toast.) The other boys stand up and repeat what has been proposed.
7. Ned thanks Mrs. Winchester-Grey for her hospitality.
8. Mrs. Winchester-Grey tells the boys that she is going to do all she can to prevent them from climbing chimneys. The boys clap and cheer. To help her to do this she wants them to tell her about the things that have happened to them. She starts them talking by asking leading questions such as: "Have you ever been trapped in a chimney?" "Have any of you been beaten by your employer?" etc. Mrs. Winchester-Grey takes notes as the boys tell their stories.
9. Ned tells Mrs. Winchester-Grey that they must go back to their cellar now as they have to be up at 5 a.m. the next morning to sweep chimneys.

10. They each say goodnight to Mrs. Winchester-Grey. She gives each boy a shilling. The boys return to the cellar.

CHARACTERS Other climbing boys
Tim, a climbing boy
Ned
Crouch

SCENE THREE Crouch's cellar the next morning. It is 4.45 a.m.
1. The boys are sleeping soundly.
2. Crouch comes in. He yells at them to wake up. Tim, who is sleeping by the door, jumps up. He drops his shilling which he has been clutching in his hand. It rolls into a corner.
3. Crouch picks it up and asks Tim where he got it from. The noise wakes the other boys.
4. Tim says that the money was given to him. Crouch does not believe him and accuses Tim of keeping back money that rightfully belongs to him. Tim tells Crouch of the feast given by Mrs. Winchester-Grey and how she gave each of the climbing boys a shilling. They argue. Crouch puts the shilling into his pocket.
5. Crouch turns to the other boys. One of them has his shilling in his hand. Crouch snatches it away. He forces the others to give up their shillings. One boy refuses. Crouch beats him. The rest meekly hand over their shillings.
6. When all the money has been collected, the boys tell Crouch that Ned too has a shilling. He asks Ned to give it to him. Ned is furious, but hands it over.
7. Crouch tells them to go out to work. They complain that they have had no breakfast. "You had a good meal last night, didn't you? Let that do for your breakfast as well."
8. The boys leave. Crouch sits down at a table, and counts the money. He chuckles to himself. A climbing boy creeps back, takes one of the shillings from the table and makes off before Crouch realises what has happened.

———————————

Mrs. Winchester-Grey places an advertisement in The Times newspaper asking for all those who are interested in stopping the practice of using boys to sweep chimneys to attend a meeting.

———————————

CHARACTERS   Mrs. Winchester-Grey

Some of the climbing boys who had stories to tell in Scene Two

Large group of people who oppose the use of climbing boys

Smaller group determined to keep boys climbing chimneys—this group includes some chimney sweeps

SCENE FOUR   A large room

Chairs have been set out for a meeting. There is a table and chair for Mrs. Winchester-Grey.

1. Mrs. Winchester-Grey enters the room with some of the climbing boys. She wants them to tell their stories again just as they did at the open-air feast. They are to speak up and not be frightened.

2. People begin to arrive. Mrs. Winchester-Grey talks to some of them. They take their seats.

3. Mrs. Winchester-Grey begins the meeting. She tells the audience that they have come together to discuss what can be done to stop boys climbing chimneys. She gives her reasons why the boys should be prohibited from climbing chimneys.

What are they?

4. She asks each of the boys in turn to tell his story. (People in the audience who do not want to see an end to climbing boys interrupt. Mrs. Winchester-Grey tells them to wait, they will have their chance to speak later.)

5. She gets one of the climbing boys to stand up on a chair. She points out his knock-knees, the callouses on his elbows, bruises on his back and other signs of ill-treatment. She then asks the audience if they have anything to say.

6. Those for and against argue their case (for the reasons for keeping climbing boys, *see* the section on Sweeping Machines, Chapter 6).

7. When everyone has spoken, Mrs. Winchester-Grey takes a vote. She asks those who favour the use of climbing boys to raise their hands, and counts them. She then asks those who oppose the use of climbing boys to raise their hands, and counts them also.

8. She tells the audience that the majority want to stop boys climbing chimneys. She asks the members of the audience if anyone has any suggestions about what can be done.

(What ideas do you have, audience?)

"It is not against the law," says one of the audience. "It

is for children under eight years of age," pipes up another, "but the authorities turn a blind eye to it." "Therefore," adds a third, "we must find a way of sweeping chimneys that does not involve climbing boys."

9. Mrs. Winchester-Grey says that a bricklayer and chimney sweep, Mr. Joseph Glass, has produced an excellent machine for sweeping chimneys. She will do what she can to popularise it.
10. The meeting comes to an end.

Machines were loaned out to master sweeps, but they were loath to use them. It meant that they would have to do most of the work themselves. They preferred to stay at home and leave the work to their boys. They sabotaged the idea of the machines, therefore, from the start.

Before acting out the following improvisation, the children should be given the material in the section on Sweeping Machines in Chapter 6.

CHARACTERS   Housekeeper
       Female servants
       Chimney sweep
       Climbing boy

SCENE FIVE The sitting room of a large private house.
1. The housekeeper is talking to the servants. She tells them that a chimney sweep is coming to demonstrate a machine for sweeping chimneys that will do the work that used to be done by climbing boys.
2. The chimney sweep arrives with his boy. He explains to the housekeeper how the machine works. He says that it is an unsatisfactory way of sweeping chimneys. Climbing boys are much more efficient.
3. The sweep begins to use the machine. He is very careless. Soot falls down the chimney. It showers over the chairs, tables and carpets. (As you cannot use real soot, create the effects of a heavy fall by coughing, brushing it off your clothes, and most important, by the housekeeper's comments to the sweep about the mess he is making.)
4. The housekeeper is furious. She says that the carpets will take hours to clean. What will the mistress of the house say? The sweep says he did warn her beforehand that it was an unsatisfactory method of sweeping chimneys.
5. The housekeeper tells him to pack up his machine and go. She

never wants to see it again. The chimneys will in future be swept by climbing boys. They don't make any mess.

6. The sweep packs up the machine. "See," he tells the climbing boy, "I told you. They'll never replace boys like you with a machine."

7. They go off leaving the housekeeper and the servants to clean up the mess.

CHARACTERS Cook
Kitchen-maids
Cook-maids
Scullery-maids
Kitchen-girl

SCENE SIX Mrs. Winchester-Grey's kitchen; it is 6.30 p.m. on August 12th, 1828

The chimney can be made out of a large roll of corrugated paper standing on its end, with a hole cut in the front for the fireplace.

1. The cook and her staff are preparing a meal. Mrs. Winchester-Grey is giving a dinner for members of her Society For Superseding Climbing Boys.

2. A kitchen maid accidently knocks a pan of boiling fat on to the fire. Flames shoot up the chimney, setting fire to the soot. Burning soot showers down the chimney and settles on the food set out around the kitchen.

3. The cook and her staff step back in fear. A scullery-maid screams. The cook tells the kitchen-girl to run to the nearest chimney sweep and get a climbing boy to come and put out the fire.

4. In the meantime she closes the doors and windows to cut down the draught. She sprinkles some salt on the fire, then pours some water on to make steam.

CHARACTERS Crouch
Jack Sourgull
Kitchen girl

SCENE SEVEN Crouch's cellar

1. Crouch is sitting on a sack of soot.

2. Jack Sourgull drops down the chimney. (He has been on a practice climb.)

3. Crouch tells him to climb back up the chimney again.

4. Jack says that his knees and elbows are red raw.

5. Crouch tells him not to worry. A few more climbs and his skin will be as tough as an elephant's hide.

6. The kitchen-girl rushes in and tells Crouch of the fire in Mrs. Winchester-Grey's chimney. Will he come and see what he can do to put it out?

7. Crouch tells Jack to come with him. They go off with the kitchen-girl.

CHARACTERS Cook
          Kitchen and scullery maids
          Kitchen-girl
          Crouch
          Jack Sourgull
          Passers-by
          Neighbours
          A climbing boy
          Mrs. Winchester-Grey

SCENE EIGHT Mrs. Winchester-Grey's kitchen

1. More and more burning soot showers down the chimney. The cook and her staff are doing what they can to protect the food. Neighbours and passers-by rush in to give help. They all crowd into the kitchen. They are followed by a group of layabouts attracted by the noise and commotion.

2. The kitchen-girl returns with Crouch and Jack.

3. Crouch takes one look at the room and orders Jack up the chimney to put out the fire.

4. Jack tells Crouch that he lacks experience. His knees and elbows are too sore for any more climbing today.

5. Crouch offers him a shilling as a bribe. Jack refuses. The gate-crashers offer suggestions.

6. Crouch threatens him. Jack agrees to do what he can. Crouch tells him to pull his shirt over his head. He asks the cook for some water. He soaks Jack's shirt. He gives Jack a brush which has also been soaked in water and tells him to push the burning soot up the chimney in front of him. "Keep going and the fire won't harm you. If you don't, you'll get burnt."

7. Jack disappears up the chimney. The layabouts take this opportunity of grabbing anything of value and creeping off into the street.

8. One of the scullery-maids complains about Crouch's treatment of Jack. "Rather a toasted boy, than a burnt dinner," replies Crouch.

9. Crouch explains that this is the only way to put out a chimney fire, unless they want to wait until it burns itself out, with the possibility of burning the house down as well.

10. Jack climbs down again. He tells Crouch that the chimney is too hot. He cannot move the soot.

11. Crouch beats him, and orders him up the chimney, pushing him back into the fireplace.

12. Again, the scullery-maid and several of the other girls accuse Crouch of ill-treatment. Jack's screams can be heard for some time, and then there is silence. Twenty minutes later....

13. Crouch sends the kitchen-girl back to the cellar to see if any of the climbing boys have returned from work. If she finds one, she is to bring him back to Mrs. Winchester-Grey's with a rope. The kitchen-girl goes out.

14. They wait for Jack to come down. One of the scullery-maids thinks that he is dead. "Sleeping, more like," says Crouch. "They're a lazy lot."

15. The kitchen-girl comes back with another climbing boy. Crouch tells him to go up the chimney and find out wnat has happened to Jack. The boy reaches Jack and ties the rope round his legs.

16. The others wait. Mrs. Winchester-Grey comes into the kitchen. She has been out and has only just heard about the fire. The other climbing boy comes back down the chimney and tells them that he has managed to reach Jack and has tied the rope around his legs. He hands Crouch the rope and they both pull as hard as they can. Others help but they cannot free Jack. He is stuck. "Let him stay there then," says Crouch, preparing to leave.

17. Mrs. Winchester-Grey is furious. "You're not going to leave him up there, are you?" Crouch walks to the door. Mrs. Winchester-Grey stops him. They argue. "It's your chimney, you get him out," says Crouch as he and the other climbing boy leave.

18. Mrs. Winchester-Grey sends the kitchen girl for a builder to come and rescue Jack.

CHARACTERS Mrs. Winchester-Grey
Members of her family and staff
Passers-by
Builder
Jack (his body)

SCENE NINE Mrs. Winchester-Grey's kitchen

1. Mrs. Winchester-Grey and members of her family and staff are anxiously waiting by the fireplace. One or two of them are looking to see if they can see Jack up the chimney. They try calling him but there is no reply.

2. The builder arrives. He begins to hammer away at the bricks above the fireplace. (He could cut a hole at the back of the corrugated paper.) He tells them that he has found Jack. Helped by the others,

he lifts Jack's body out through the hole he has made in the wall on to one of the tables in the kitchen. Jack is dead. The builder says that the chimney was very hot. He shows them Jack's elbows and knees which are burned to the bone. He tells them that Jack was trapped in a narrow passage just before a bend in the chimney. "He must have suffocated in the heat and the smoke."

3. Mrs. Winchester-Grey says that Crouch shall pay for this. She will take him to court for manslaughter.

CHARACTERS Judge
               Members of the jury
               Crouch
               Clerk
               Counsel for the prosecution
               Counsel for the defence
               Witnesses for the prosecution:
                   Mrs. Winchester-Grey
                   Her family and staff
                   Climbing boy who tried to rescue Jack
                   Police officer
                   Surgeon
               Witnesses for the defence

SCENE TEN The courtroom (*see* Fig. 6 for layout)
Witnesses for the prosecution should discuss evidence with Counsel for the prosecution so that all the evidence tallies. The class should discuss who would be a witness for the defence—the climbing boys? Ned, or a friend of Crouch's, a satisfied customer? They should make up their own list.

1. Members of the court take their places. (The order of the trial follows closely that of William Corder for the murder of Maria Marten in 1828.)

2. The judge takes his seat on the bench.

3. Crouch is brought into court.

4. The Clerk reads over the names of the members of the jury.

5. The jury are sworn in by the Clerk. Each one steps into the jury box and takes the oath: "I swear by Almighty God that I will well and truly try and true deliverance make between our Sovereign Lord the King and the prisoner at the bar whom I shall have in charge and a true verdict give according to the evidence."

6. The Clerk reads the indictment. "Charles Crouch, you are charged on indictment that you, on the"... (suggest that the Clerk makes up his own indictment).

7. He asks Crouch whether he pleads guilty or not guilty.
How do you plead, Crouch?

8. The counsel for the prosecution stands up and tells the judge and jury the reasons why Crouch is on trial.

9. The clerk calls the witnesses for the prosecution one at a time. They each go into the witness box and are questioned first by the counsel for the prosecution and then cross-examined by the counsel for the defence. The counsel for the prosecution may re-examine if he likes.

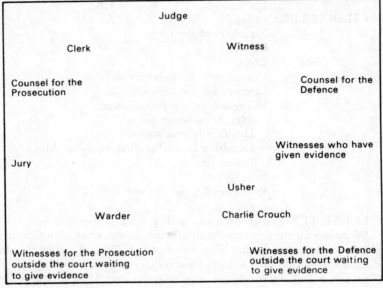

Fig. 6. Courtroom.

10. The case for the prosecution comes to an end.

11. Crouch goes into the witness box and is questioned by the counsel for the prosecution.

12. The clerk calls the witnesses for the defence. They each go into the witness box and say pleasant things about Crouch. They are each questioned by the counsel for the prosecution.

13. The counsel for the defence makes his speech.

14. The counsel for the prosecution makes his speech.

15. The judge sums up the evidence that has been heard.

16. The clerk asks the jury to consider their verdict.

      Discuss amongst yourselves, jury, whether you think that Crouch is guilty of manslaughter or not.

17. The clerk stands up and asks:
"Members of the jury, are you agreed upon your verdict?"
"We are," says the foreman of the jury.
"How say you then—do you find the prisoner, Charles Crouch,
guilty, or not guilty of the manslaughter of Jack Sourgull?"
18. If not guilty, Crouch is allowed to go free.
19. If guilty, the judge asks Crouch if he has anything to say.

Have you, Crouch?

The judge then pronounces sentence: ten years' transportation to Van
Dieman's Land, present-day Tasmania.

How does the story end? If Crouch is found not guilty, does Mrs.
Winchester-Grey find another way to stop him? Can members of her
Society help? If Crouch is transported, what happens to his climbing
boys? Are they taken to a workhouse to be apprenticed to other chimney sweeps? Do they become thieves and cat burglars? Or do the
members of Mrs. Winchester-Grey's Society look after them? The
children should make up the final scene(s) of the play themselves.

Each scene was then taken in turn and parts were re-distributed
at the beginning of each scene. By the end of the first run-through
each child had taken at least one of the leading roles. The initial acting
was still very much at the play stage, but by the third or fourth week,
the self-conscious giggles and over-reactions had given way to total
absorption as the children became increasingly involved in the story.

Research and Discussion

The first run-through was a good illustration of utilitarian drama.
The children knew very little about climbing boys apart from the
teacher's brief introductory talk, but had discovered something more
about themselves and the world around them. They had discovered
something of what it means to be dispossessed and at the mercy of
a rogue such as Charlie Crouch. The girls playing the part of Mrs.
Winchester-Grey had discovered some of the difficulties in chairing
a stormy meeting. Counsels for the defence and prosecution had
learned something of the power of language in twisting people's words
to suit their own particular line of argument. Children who had
always been extremely shy of speaking in front of the rest of the class
now stood up in court and gave their evidence, assured and confident.

The advance in personal growth fully justified the time that had so far been spent on the scenario.

But this was to be an illustration of educational drama as the focal point for integrated studies. A historian, for example, would find little in the play so far to commend it. The dialogue abounded in anachronisms. Mrs. Winchester-Grey used the telephone to call her friends, the servants prepared dinner on an electric cooker, and the boy who gate-crashed the climbing boys' feast made his getaway on a No. 9 bus! Imagination and emotion were there in abundance, but there was just no sense of feeling for the period in question. The educational dimension had now to be added. Drama at this level requires the teacher to have a plentiful supply of source material available: books, pictures, Jackdaw folders, filmstrips, films, etc. The material in Chapter 6 composed the "kit" that was used as a basis for the children's research into the lives and social conditions of the climbing boys.

By giving each child the opportunity of playing most of the leading parts, the teacher now had a fairly good idea of which child to cast in a particular role. Each character or group of characters was then given a specific piece of research to do, relevant to the role or roles they would be playing. The children were now keen to find out all they could about the characters they had been called upon to play, realising that their success in these parts depended to a certain extent upon the expertise they could bring to bear on their characterisations. The feedback of information in this specific research transformed a superficial improvisation into a worthwhile dramatisation. The doubling up of some of the minor parts ensured adequate research for all concerned.

1. Ned, Jack and all those playing the parts of climbing boys studied the sections on The Climbing Boys and Chimney Sweepers' Slang in Chapter 6. They were encouraged to use as much of this jargon as they could in order to give their language an air of authenticity.
2. Charlie Crouch studied the sections on The Climbing Boys, Master Sweeps, Sweeping Machines and Chimney Sweepers' Slang.
3. Mr. and Mrs. Sourgull studied the section Boys for Sale.
4. Mrs. Winchester-Grey studied the section on Sweeping Machines, also background information on life among the upper middle classes in the reign of George IV in such books as *Illustrated English Social History*, Vol. IV, G. M. Trevelyan, Longman; *A History of Everyday Things in England*, Vol. III, 1733–1851, Marjorie and C. H. B. Quennell, Batsford; *Life in Regency England*, R. J. White, Batsford.
5. The cook and kitchen staff studied Chapter X in *What the Butler Saw*, E. S. Turner, Michael Joseph.
6. The judge, members of the jury, the clerk of the court, counsels

for the prosecution and defence and the police officer studied trial procedure found in such books as *The Courts of Justice*, Wilfrid J. Jenkins, Wheaton, and *The Criminal Law*, F. T. Giles, Penguin Books.
7. The surgeon who carried out the post mortem on Jack studied the Post Mortem on a Climbing Boy in Chapter 6.
8. Each member of the cast read Talking Points, 1828; the information contained there was used to enliven the dialogue as and when necessary.

Apart from the specific research, general research was also carried out and lessons in all subjects were chosen for their possible links with the theme of the play and the year 1828. This provided additional material.

1. *Religious education.* A study of the life of Jonas Hanway, English philanthropist and champion of the rights of climbing boys (see John Hutchins, *Jonas Hanway 1712–1786*, S.P.C.K.).

2. *English.*
   Oliver Twist, Charles Dickens
   The Water Babies, Charles Kingsley
   The Early Visitor, Ian Serailler
   "*Sooeep*," Walter de la Mare
   "*The Chimney Sweeper*," William Blake
Also poems dealing with outcasts, rejects and misfits, in *Conflict*, edited Rhodri Jones, Heinemann Educational Books Ltd.
   A debate might be held on the motion "The climbing boy is a better chimney sweeper than the machine."
   Creative Writing might involve the compilation of a pamphlet outlining, by means of imaginary case histories, the inhumanity of the climbing boy system.

3. *History.* Each child prepares a five-minute lecture on one of the following topics.

      1. George IV
      2. From coal fires to central heating
      3. Lord Shaftesbury
      4. Male fashions in 1828
      5. Female fashions in 1828
      6. Transportation
      7. Van Dieman's Land
      8. The modern chimney sweep
      9. The barouch
     10. The murder of Maria Marten

11. The apprenticeship system
12. Grimaldi
13. The Royal Gardens, Vauxhall
14. The Quadrille
15. Bartholomew Fair
16. The debtor's prison
17. Public executions
18. Travel by stage coach
19. The Resurrectionists
20. Smuggling
21. The steam carriage
22. "Phiz"
23. Henry Grey Bennet
24. The Annual Register
25. Charles Lamb
26. The Duke of Wellington as Prime Minister
27. David Porter
28. Joseph Glass
29. Sir Robert Peel
30. Charles Kingsley

When completed these can be written up and bound together into a booklet on the year 1828.

4. *Geography*. How your city, town or village has developed since 1828.

5. *Science*. Find out all you can about the state of medicine in 1828.

6. Music. Listen to a recording of Britten's *Let's Make an Opera*. Learn the song "*Tippitiwitchet*," p. 89–90.

7. *Art*. Draw and paint some backcloths for use in the play.

8. *Craft*. Make sectional models out of cardboard of the various types of twisting flues the climbing boys had to climb.

9. *Arithmetic*. Measure the maximum width of each member in the class and make a chart showing the size of chimney they would each be able to climb. As a contrast, also show the smallest flue a climbing boy was capable of sweeping.

10. *Technical drawing*. Design and draw your own chimney-sweeping machine.

11. *Physical education*. A dance drama based on *The Water Babies*.

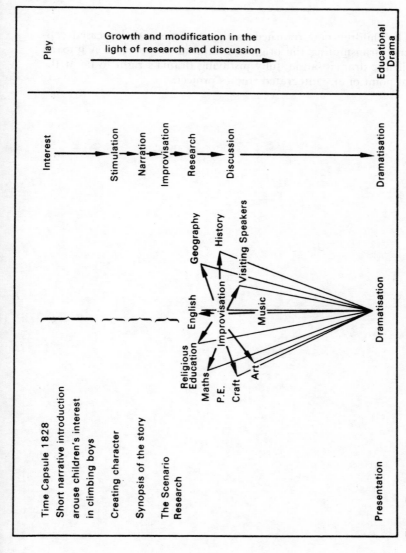

Fig. 7. Drama as the focal point of an integrated studies project on climbing boys.

Visiting speaker. Look in the Yellow Pages of the Telephone Directory and see if there are any sweeps still working in your area. Try to get one to come to school and talk about his work. Failing that, is it possible to contact a retired sweep?

The children now returned to the scenario with increased confidence transmuting the original utilitarian improvisation into an authentic dramatisation, fully justifying drama's right to be at the focal point of any integrated studies project.

CHAPTER 6

"SMALL BOYS FOR SMALL FLUES"
Source Material

The Climbing Boys

Why climbing boys?

Small boys were used to sweep chimneys from the end of the sixteenth century right up to 1875. Prior to the Elizabethan era, chimneys had always been fairly wide, enabling them to be swept with a brush attached to the end of a long pole, or by a sack of straw dropped down on the end of a length of rope. Some even had iron ladders on the inside so that a person could climb right to the top. Another method of cleaning was to set light to the soot and let it burn itself out.

However, from the seventeenth century onwards, the shape and size of chimneys began to change. For the sake of warmth, fireplaces began to appear in most rooms, and additional flues had to be built to carry away the increased volume of smoke. The more flues, the narrower they became. Also, old buildings, instead of being pulled down to make room for the new as they are today, were renovated and further rooms added, each with its own fireplace. The new flues were connected to the existing ones, creating a maze of narrow passages winding and twisting their way up behind the walls to the sky above, like giant lianas in a tropical rain forest. Because of their shape, they could not be swept by any of the conventional means in use at the time. Their very narrowness ruled out any possibility of setting light to the soot; the fire risk was too great.

The only humane way of cleaning such chimneys would have been for the builders to install register doors in all the rooms with a fireplace thus enabling the soot to be raked out when the chimney needed sweeping. But the owners of these houses would not allow their elegant rooms to be spoiled by unsightly-looking doors; the only alternative lay in the use of climbing boys.

Boys for sale

At first the boys were imported from Italy, but this proved expensive, especially when the streets and workhouses of England were full of pauper children ideally suited to the task.

An Act of Parliament had been passed in 1788 making it illegal for children under eight years of age to be used as chimney sweeps, but it was widely ignored. To save public money, workhouse officials gladly apprenticed the small undernourished children under their care to chimney sweeps more interested in the apprenticeship fee offered than in the welfare of the children concerned. And as the flues became narrower and narrower (some only seven inches square), this trade in undersized children that no one else wanted increased at an alarming rate. "Small boys for small flues," advertised the sweeps of the time.

Some parents unable to support their large families actually sold their children to chimney sweeps for sums ranging from £1 to five guineas. Providing he was fit, the smaller the boy, the higher the price. One small child fetched a record eight pounds five shillings. Parents sold to the highest bidder, and consoled themselves with the thought that they were apprenticing their offspring to a worthwhile trade. Most children never saw their parents again.

Some children were stolen from home by unscrupulous rogues and sold to climbing masters in faraway towns, others were hoodwinked. One boy was given a shilling by a master sweep who told him that by accepting the gift he automatically became his apprentice. Mothers told their children, "Don't wander or the sweep will get you."

Apprenticeship usually began at the age of seven, although six-year-olds were preferred, and it was not uncommon for a boy to begin climbing at the age of four. Thomas Allen was three-and-a-half when he was apprenticed by his parents in a tavern in the year 1795. Part of the agreement called for the parents or guardian to swear on oath, if need be, that their child was eight years old at the time he was articled.

"Be it ever so humble"

Conditions varied from master to master. There were those who genuinely cared for their boys and provided them with food, decent clothes and a proper bed for the night; but a damp, dirty cellar served as home for the majority, and bed was a pile of straw, or a few sacks of soot covered over with a cleaning cloth. One fifteen-year-old apprentice shared a verminous room ten feet square with four pigs. When questioned about the pigs, the master said he did not keep them outside as they might die of the cold.

The first climb

Once apprenticed, a boy was sent on his first climb. Some were bribed with the offer of a plum pudding, or a halfpenny, but the majority were beaten black and blue if they failed to co-operate. An experienced boy was always sent up with the new lad to show him where to place his hands and feet and to catch him should he fall. Callous masters would send the experienced boy up armed with a pin to jab into the young apprentice's bare feet if he paused for breath. Sometimes a pile of straw burning in the hearth was used as an incentive. What terrors the boys must have experienced in those pitch-black, suffocating flues, as the rough brickwork scraped and tore their soft skin to shreds! They returned to the hearth, their knees, elbows, and thighs streaming with blood.

Before the new boy could become a chimney sweep, his skin had to be toughened up. This was done by rubbing salt into the open wounds in front of a hot fire. The pain must have been excruciating. Threats of a beating, or the offer of a halfpenny ensured that they kept up the massage. Even humane masters made the boys climb a little each day during "the sores." Constant practice was necessary to toughen up the skin. Soot found its way into the cuts causing infection, and the festering sores which resulted took weeks to heal, eventually forming scars the size of a shilling piece. After many months, thick calluses appeared, forming a protective covering against the rough brickwork in the chimney. A few masters wrapped the knees and elbows of their apprentices in cloth to protect them until they had learned to climb, but this was considered a new-fangled method and even kind masters would have nothing to do with the "padding" as it was called.

Apprenticeship

It took ten to twenty practice climbs for an apprentice to master his trade. The apprenticeship lasted for seven years.

Some boys wore clothes made for them by their master's wives from old rags, others begged them from the householders whose chimneys they swept. Most went barefoot. For additional warmth during the winter they wrapped themselves in the cloth used to catch the soot that fell down the chimney, or draped the soot sack around their necks like a shawl. To protect their eyes and mouth when climbing they wore a peaked cap made of calico, and tucked in at the back of the neck to keep as much soot as possible out of their clothing.

The boys began work at three or four o'clock in the morning and finished around midday. A boy either "cried the streets," or worked only for those householders who had a regular contract with his master.

Crying the streets meant walking up and down the rows of houses touting for business by crying "Sweep for the Soot O! Sweep! Sweep! Sweep! Soot Ho! Swee ... up!" Wealthy sweeps complained that boys who cried the streets took away their business and lowered standards in the trade.

Sometimes one of the boys would be taken by his master to sweep the chimneys of one of the big houses usually situated at a distance from the master's home. They travelled by horse and cart if the sweep was wealthy enough to own one, and the boy would take advantage of the opportunity to have an extra sleep in the back of the cart. Often, the servants, annoyed at having to get up early, would keep master and apprentice waiting on the doorstep for ages before letting them in. Winter was the worst time. Bare feet froze to the pavement and there was little comfort once inside. The fires had all been put out the night before in anticipation of their coming so the rooms were damp and cold.

A wide chimney was easy to climb. The boy ducked into the hearth, reached up for a handhold, hauled up his legs until he found two projecting bricks on which to place his feet and scraped away as much soot as he could with the metal scraper provided. Then he would reach up and begin the process all over again. Most of the soot was brought down by the action of the boy's body as he climbed up to the top. He also carried a brush but this was only used if there were turns or flaws in the chimney.

The narrow chimneys were the difficult ones to climb. Here, the boys had to make themselves as thin as possible. They reached up with one arm above their heads, the other tucked down by their sides. By pressing on the elbow of their upraised arm hard against the side of the chimney they managed to obtain enough grip to enable them to drag their feet up, bending their knees as they did so. When they had drawn up their knees as far as they would go, they supported themselves on their haunches by wedging their knees and heels against the sides of the flue. This enabled them to reach up again with their outstretched arm, gaining a fresh support with their elbow, and begin all over again. Reaching up with their arm, supporting themselves with their elbow, and then bringing up their knees, using their scraper as best they could. This method was known as "slanting." If the boy's outstretched arm slipped down, he could find himself wedged in the chimney until help arrived. They breathed in large quantities of soot in the process, and, if the fire had only just been put out, they choked on sulphurous fumes. Sweat poured off them as they struggled for the tiny pin-point of light high above. They proved, for the benefit of the owner of the house, that they had reached the top, by sticking their head or their brush out of the chimney pot and calling out, "All up!" They slid down in the same way that they had climbed up.

George Elson was given as much as sixpence for sweeping a chimney, but if a boy had a cruel master, all the money was taken from him leaving him with nothing but a coating of soot for his pains. If a boy complained that a chimney was too narrow, a cruel master would order him to take his clothes off, beat him, and send him back to try once again. Some boys could climb a chimney as fast as a person could climb the stairs. When a boy had finished sweeping, the lady of the house would often ask for a small quantity of soot. Because the boys' teeth gleamed white in their dirty faces it was erroneously believed that soot made the finest tooth paste available.

The boys were free in the afternoons and they gambled away any money they had earned playing games of chuck and toss in the gutter.

They not only swept chimneys, they had to core (smooth) the rough surfaces of newly constructed ones, clearing away the piles of rubble carelessly left behind by the builders. This was dangerous work, and many boys were struck by large chunks of falling masonry dislodged from above. They rescued trapped cats, and removed bird's nests. George Elson once had to clear a chimney of a swarm of bees that had temporarily taken up lodgings there. Because they worked when most other people were asleep, some boys were tempted to pocket any valuables left lying about but the masters had their reputations to consider and strongly discouraged theft. The boys were more likely to be in the pay of burglars, providing them with layouts of the large houses they visited, indicating where the valuables were to be found.

One boy estimated that, in eleven years of climbing, he had worked his way up through 130 miles of soot.

They relied upon their masters to provide them with food, usually one meal a day—at supper time, or they had to find their own. However, the servants in the big houses would often feed them scraps left over from meals taken the day before. After sweeping the chimneys, the boys would rub off as much soot as they could before going down to the servant's hall, where, if they were lucky, a breakfast of hot venison and cold roast beef washed down with tea, coffee or ale, awaited them, although many had to make do with bread and jam. But it was not in the sweep's interest to starve his boys; they needed to be thin and wiry, but the work also required a great deal of energy which could only come from a sparse, but adequate, diet.

The best masters tried to ensure that their boys washed regularly. In summer they would take their apprentices down to the river every Sunday morning, but during the winter the boys often went dirty. One climbing boy was drowned while bathing in the Serpentine which discouraged the others. An old wives' tale laid down that washing softened the skin, a misguided belief that did much to discourage cleanliness. One boy slept black for fifteen months, his only contact with water was going out in the rain.

The hazards

Chimney sweeping was extremely dangerous work. A boy climbing down a chimney could lose his hold and slide all the way to the bottom scraping his flesh to the bone. As the chimneys became narrower, the dangers of becoming jammed intensified. One boy boasted that he could run up and down a flue fourteen inches square; but a rucked-up shirt, or a turned down waistband in a flue only seven inches square could pinion a boy like a strait-jacket. A projecting lump of mortar in a chimney that had not been properly cored could have the same effect. George Elson often climbed without trousers to prevent himself from becoming wedged on the way down by an accumulation of soot in the pockets. When a boy became stuck in a chimney, his terror must have known no bounds, screaming as best as his soot-filled lungs would allow, hoping upon hope that someone would hear him and bring help in time, before he suffocated. Down below, oblivious to his plight, his master would fret and fume at the delay. To free a trapped boy, another apprentice was sent up the chimney with instructions to tie a rope around the trapped boy's legs in an attempt to haul him down. Sometimes a pile of dry straw was burned in the hearth in the hope that the heat scorching the boy's feet would cause him to wriggle and thus free himself. Wet straw proved ineffective, it produced smoke sending the boy to sleep.

Some of the larger houses presented such a maze of twisting chimneys that it was possible for a boy to lose his way, and overcome by fumes, slide down on to a lighted fire, or fall into a morass of soot in a horizontal flue and suffocate before help could arrive. One boy was lost for six hours in the flues in Goldsmith's Hall. Another climbed up into a chimney pot to clean it, but it broke away and crashed down to the courtyard below with the boy still inside it. Fortunately he was unharmed and emerged "like a chicken out of an egg."

The most dangerous and unpleasant chimneys to climb were the cold wet ones, these proved extremely slippery, while the rotting plaster gave off a most foul smell.

But of all the hazards encountered by the climbing boys, the worst was a chimney fire. Soot built up in the chimneys and if not swept regularly there was always the danger that a flame from a roaring fire could set it alight. And if one of the beams ran through the chimney wall, there was the danger of this catching fire and setting light to the whole house. Because of the danger to property that could be caused by a chimney fire, boys were bribed with offers of sixpence or even a shilling to climb up and extinguish the burning soot. Sometimes water was poured down first to cool the chimney sufficiently to enable the boy to climb in safety, but usually there was no time for this, chimney-sweeping being a highly competitive business, if one master suffered pangs of conscience about using one of his boys, there were always others who would have no such compunction.

The boy chosen would first soak his shirt in water to prevent any burning soot that might fall on it from setting it alight. The front of the shirt would be pinned over his face as additional protection. And then holding a wet cloth in his hand he would climb the chimney as swiftly as possible, pushing the burning soot ahead of him. When one boy became exhausted, another was sent up to take his place. The main danger lay in the horizontal flues where a boy could inadvertently push some of the burning soot behind him and then find himself trapped between two fires.

A minor problem concerned the attitude of other children. Parents would frighten naughty children with tales of the bogeyman coming to get them, and when they saw a climbing boy they would warn their offspring: "Here's the bogeyman come to put you in his black bag. You'll take him, won't you?" Children grew up disliking sweeps and would often insult climbing boys they met in the street, and when the opportunity arose, tip over their sacks of soot.

The effects of climbing

Soot made eyes and faces smart. Most climbing boys suffered from weak sight which was aggravated by rubbing their eyes with their dirty hands. Their limbs remained stunted from the unnatural positions in which they had to work while their bones were soft and still growing. The constant pressure against the chimney wall could dislodge a kneecap, leaving a leg stunted and deformed. The boys were knock-kneed from continually squatting on their haunches, their legs and feet shaped like the letter S. Their ankle joints swelled, their backs became deformed through carrying wet soot cloths and heavy bags of soot over long distances. Their flesh was torn on the jagged mortar in the chimneys that had not been properly cored.

They fell into blazing fires and burned themselves severely. They suffered from asthma and consumption from sleeping on sacks in damp cold cellars and by going out into the chill morning air inadequately clothed. They were undernourished from eating the wrong diet. They suffered from lung complaints from breathing in soot and sulphurous fumes. Many had the chimney sweep's cancer, the "sooty warts" as it was called. Cramp was a constant companion brought on by holding themselves in one position over long periods at a stretch.

But this was their life, they knew no other. To run away meant risking starvation. In fact, if they complained, many masters would threaten to send them back to their parents knowing full well that they could not afford to look after them.

Apprenticed for redundancy

Jonas Hanway once met a blind twelve-year-old ex-chimney sweep who had worked since he was five years old. He was three feet seven inches tall and unable to move on his twisted legs without the aid of crutches. He had served his seven years' apprenticeship and was now redundant. Where could such a boy find work? This was the problem with chimney sweeping: whereas most apprenticeships trained a boy for life, a chimney sweep outgrew his usefulness. What then? Those still fit enough joined the army or the navy, became gypsies, or even took up acting. Some stayed on to become journeyman sweeps, assistants to their masters. They were paid two shillings a week and given board and lodgings, but had to provide their own clothes and other necessities. Two shillings a week was barely enough to keep them in shoe leather. Promotion had its problems. To supplement their miserable wages, they stole from the boys under their charge, or cheated them out of their money by games of chuck and toss. They were often more cruel to the boys than their masters. Journeymen were continually moving from one master to another in the hope of a better life.

And what of the rest? To those unfit for work a life of crime seemed the only alternative. The agility they had acquired in climbing chimneys often stood them in good stead as cat burglars. One of the cleverest thieves of the last century was an ex-climbing boy who had run away from his master. In fact some masters actually hired out their ex-apprentices to thieves and robbers. And after that? Most of them grew old before their time and died in workhouses, or ended their days on the road as tramps and vagrants.

But in spite of the dangers, the fears and uncertainties, these boys still kept their sense of humour. One of their most popular stories concerned a climbing boy who had been given permission by a farmer to sleep in his barn for the night on a pile of straw. During the night, the boy awoke to the sound of two men entering the barn. They carried a sack and a lantern, and at once made for a pile of corn near where the climbing boy lay pretending to be asleep. While one of the men held the lantern aloft, the other began shovelling corn into the sack. The dim light given off by the lantern hampered his work. "Confound it," grumbled the man with the light, "I wish we had someone to hold up the lantern." At which the sweep jumped up and shouted, "I will." Whereupon the thieves, seeing the black face of the climbing boy, uttered cries of, "It's the devil!" and fled in terror from the barn leaving lantern, sack and shovel behind them.

Master Sweeps

There were 400 masters and 1000 climbing boys in England in 1817. It cost comparatively little to set up in business as a master sweep once the apprenticeship-money had been paid, and, of course, in the case of workhouse boys, the sweeps were paid for taking them off the ratepayers' hands. A sweep would need some rope, a few bags for the soot, a ladder, brushes and scrapers, and possibly the hire of a barrow when business was booming. Any hovel would do as a home for the apprentices and a place to store the soot. An unscrupulous sweep did not even have to provide them with clothes as he could send them out begging for cast-offs from his customers. It was a profitable business for such a small outlay. A boy could sweep four chimneys in a day which would bring in an average of nine pence per chimney. Therefore, a sweep with six boys, the number allowable by law, could make a yearly profit of £270, no mean sum in those days. Added to this was the money he received for the sale of soot to farmers who used it on the land as a fertiliser. Each bushel cost the farmer seven pence, and each chimney swept would yield half a bushel to a bushel of soot. Small wonder that the number of master sweeps rose so rapidly throughout the first half of the nineteenth century.

Master sweeps were of two kinds: those who had begun life as climbing boys and worked their way up to become their own masters, and those who had taken up the work in adult life for want of anything better. Many craftsmen, for example, whose work had been taken over by machinery in the rapidly developing industrial revolution, took to the trade. Those who had been climbing boys themselves became the cruellest masters. They had suffered, therefore they saw to it that their boys did too. It was always the unscrupulous ones who took the frailest and youngest children, those especially in need of care and consideration.

The busiest season was in the winter months from November to May. Some masters took on more boys than they needed, and hired them out during the winter months at six pence a day. During the slack summer months, these boys were left to their own devices to live as best they could. Some would be sent out begging for cast-off clothes which their masters would sell in the second-hand clothes shops or to the rag and bone men. Boys who came home empty-handed were cruelly beaten.

Sweeping chimneys was looked down on as a dirty, smelly trade, and many masters, socially ostracised, frittered away their profits on heavy drinking.

But there were considerate masters, too. George Elson, for example, was given free board, had his clothes provided, on top of which he received a wage of £2 per year.

Some sweeps had brightly-painted signs on the walls of their houses to advertise their trade. A picture would show a master and his boy hurrying to a house with bright yellow flames coming out of the chimney. Underneath would be details of the services available. They also had business cards printed, like the one below dating from 1867:

> "William Burges, chimney sweeper, No. 36 Bolton Street, Chorley, flatters himself in having boys of the best size for such branches of business suitable for a Tunnel or Chimney, and that it is now in his power to render his assistance in a more extensive manner than he usually has done. He also carries his boys from room to room occasionally to prevent them staining or marking any room floor with their feet."

Sweeps had their own special festival which took place each year on the first of May. Companies of sweeps would parade the streets dressed in paper finery, jumping up and down, rattling shovels and brushes together in order to attract attention. The larger companies would have a fiddler and a "Jack in Green." This character was always played by one of the sweeps who would be enclosed in a wicker or wooden frame shaped like a sugar loaf, and decorated with green leaves or bunches of flowers, completely hiding the man inside. A Lord and Lady of the May would follow the fiddler in a stately procession. For three days they made street collections and on the third night there would be a feast held in one of the popular public houses. The masters took most of the profits from these collections, but any money left over was used to buy clothes for the boys.

Sweeping Machines

The practice of sending boys to sweep chimneys could have been abolished in 1803. In that year George Smart invented the Scandiscope, a machine for cleaning chimneys:

"His cleaning machine consists of an expanding brush somewhat like an umbrella which is raised by a series of hollow rods or tubes which fix into ferrules; a cord runs through these tubes, and by a contrivance may be drawn tight, and fastened by means of a pulley and screws. A cloth is placed before the chimney, and the machine worked through an opening in it. This cloth is fastened up by means of a bar and slider, by which it may be made fast to chimney-pieces of very different sizes."

Gentleman's Magazine, 1803.

The newly-formed Society For The Superseding Of Climbing Boys, promoted the idea. Some sweeps, too poor to buy a machine themselves, were presented with free ones in a blaze of publicity. Smart's machine was found to be successful in ninety-five cases out of a hundred, sharp angles in the chimneys accounting for the lack of success with the other five per cent. But these could have been swept, too, if the house-owners had permitted the building of soot doors giving access to the soot that could not be removed by the machine. But the owners refused to have the appearances of their fine rooms altered just to suit the demands of an upstart Society. If a chimney was not fit for a Scandiscope, argued the Society, then it was not fit for a climbing boy either.

Smart's invention met with an unfavourable reception. Unscrupulous masters rejected it out of hand. A climbing boy could be sent out on his own; a machine needed the master and the journeyman present to operate it. Most sweeps were lazy and preferred to spend their time in the public houses. Generous housewives fed the boys and gave them their cast-off clothing which the masters sold to the local rag and bone men. No one fed or clothed a machine. Machines cost money: the market price in 1817 was £2·3 shillings. Boys could be picked up for much less than that, and if sent out to beg for their food, cost nothing to maintain. Machines wore out and had to be replaced, boys had to climb even when they were ill. With a machine, anyone could set up as a sweep, and the masters argued that the additional sweeps thus created would rapidly bring down prices and in the long run, lead to mass unemployment amongst the boys who would be forced back to the workhouses adding an extra burden on the already overcharged ratepayers.

Masters, if persuaded to try the machines, made as much mess with them as possible, causing the housewives to beg for a climbing boy next time. Some masters placed slates on top of the chimneys and, when the brush reached the obstruction, would complain that the machines were ineffective. They argued that the machines did not clean out the recesses in the same way that a boy did, thus increasing the risk of fire. Some masters bribed the servants in the big houses to gain their employment, and the servants feared that these perks would end if machines were used. By 1817 only sixty machines were in operation.

In 1827, Joseph Glass improved upon Smart's model and swept 823 chimneys during the year 1827, only meeting with difficulties in thirteen of these; difficulties which a little alteration to the chimneys concerned, at small expense, could easily have overcome. He even managed to sweep chimneys which boys could not climb. The following is a description of Glass's machine as given by the Society for the Superseding of Climbing Boys.

"The brush, of which [Fig. 8(a)] is a section, is made of a round stock a, commonly alder, and pierced with small holes, into which bunches, formed of strips of the best whale-bone are inserted, and made fast by glue. These strips b are 8 to 8½ inches in length; which renders the brush, including the stock, about 20 inches in diameter. It therefore completely fills, and consequently effectively cleanses, the largest flues, which are never more than 14 inches square, and seldom more than 14 inches by 9. To make it pass more readily up the chimney, a small wheel f is fixed to the top of the stock a. At the end of the stock c is a very strong brass ferrule with a wormed socket, which receives the screw of the first joint d.

[Fig. 8(b)] is a representation, in their actual size, of the ferrules. The three first portions labelled [in Fig. 8(a)], a d d, 2½ feet in length, are made of good cane; the rest, e of ground ash, and of the same length; the number used depending, of course, upon the height of the chimney: these gradually become stronger towards the bottom, and are affixed to each other, as the brush is forced higher up the chimney, by means of the brass screws and sockets, ... before described.

The superiority of this machine consists in its extreme pliability, lightness, strength, and aptitude to turn by a little force applied at the bottom. It has been effectually used in crooked chimneys, where Smart's machine has not been able to pass. A machine has been made at Bath, somewhat on the same principle; the joints or portions, made of several slight canes twisted together, are, however, fastened by a small iron screw, which has been found too weak.

The whole machine is clumsy, and is so very pliable, that the force exerted below cannot drive it up the chimney. J. Glass, who is a bricklayer, a manufacturer of his machines, and a cleanser of chimneys by them, has given great satisfaction to those who have employed him. He sweeps the chimneys of the excise, the King's New Palace, Lloyd's Coffee-house, part of those of Somerset House, and of several insurance offices, banking houses, etc.

[Fig. 8(c)] is a cloth to fix over the fire-place, to prevent the falling soot from flying about the room. The joints of the machine are worked through the little sleeve in the middle.

[Fig. 8(d)] is an apparatus called the ball and brush. An iron ball is attached to one end of a long rope, in the middle of which is fastened a brush very similar to the one in the cane machine. The ball is let down the chimney by a man at the top of the house, and received by another at the bottom: they work it up and down, till the chimney is thoroughly cleansed. This apparatus is only used in very crooked flues which have no part quite horizontal. It is now nearly superseded by the introduction of the cane machine.

[Fig. 8(e)] is the end of a house, showing the sections of flues in the different stories, as they are occasionally formed. A is a flue with a horizontal part, which rarely occurs, but which can only be adapted to a machine by the insertion of a small iron door at G, or by the removal of two bricks at that corner, when it is swept; either of which may be done at a trifling expense. The machine then works from G to the top, from G to the opposite corner of the horizontal part, and from the fireplace to the same. These are the flues which are very dangerous to the boys, and which are never well swept by them, unless there is an opening at G; for when a boy has swept all the upper part, there must be a great collection of soot at G; through which, when he descends, he is obliged to work his way by main force, at the imminent hazard of being suffocated. The quantity of soot that he can force along a horizontal part, 30, 40, and even 60 feet long, and which is so small as not to admit of his turning himself round, must be very little indeed, in comparison to the quantity obtained from the perpendicular part.

B, C, and D are flues of the common form, as they exist in ninety-five cases out of a hundred.

E and F are crooked flues, which have hitherto been cleansed by the ball and brush, but which may now be done by the cane machine which is represented in g [Fig. 8(e)]. It is very desirable, however, that such flues should never be built.

The cane machine is recommended on account of its extreme pliability, and as being more durable; and though at first the most

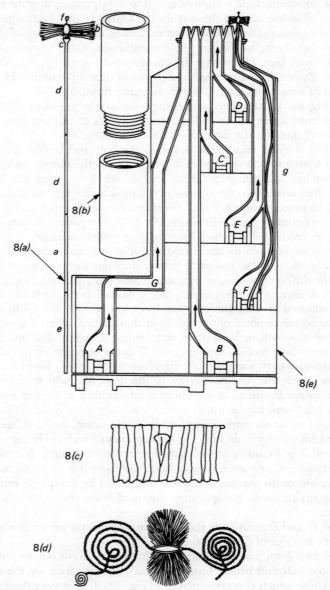

Fig. 8. Joseph Glass' Sweeping Machine.

expensive, it will eventually be found to be the cheapest."
                    Mechanics' Magazine, Saturday April 12th, 1828.

> "Some wooden tubes, a brush, and rope,
>   Are all you need employ;
>   Pray order, maids, the Scandiscope,
>   and not the climbing boy."

Went the publicity jingle. But the same arguments were advanced
as had been used about Smart's machine, and the practice of using
climbing boys continued.

Report of a Post-Mortem on a Climbing Boy Who Died Trying to put out a Chimney Fire (*The Times*, August 14th, 1847)

"The medical man who examined the body after death stated
that he found several slight burns and bruises on various parts of
the body. There were several severe ones on the back, caused
apparently by blows. These, however, had not been the cause of
death. The post mortem alone afforded no certain evidence of what
was the immediate cause of death; but coupled with the evidence,
satisfied the medical man that his death had been caused by convulsions produced by suffocation. The convulsions which had pre-
ceded death would diminish the appearances of suffocation in the
lungs."

Legislation

1788. An Act of Parliament was passed forbidding boys under eight
years of age from sweeping chimneys. No sweep was to employ more
than six boys at a time. Each apprentice had to wear a brass plate
in his cap on which was inscribed his name and the address of his
master. No boy was to be ill-treated or rented out to work for other
sweeps. The master had to provide the boys with food and lodgings
and two sets of clothes; one set for climbing, the other to be worn
on Sundays. On Sundays they were to have a bath and be sent off
to Sunday School. The Act was widely ignored.

1803. The Society For Superseding The Necessity Of Climbing Boys
was formed to promote the use of the Scandiscope, a sweeping brush
aimed at replacing climbing boys.

1808. Slavery was abolished.

1817. Parliament set up a Select Committee to look into the problem. The members came to the conclusion that most chimneys could be effectively swept by using a Scandiscope.

1834. An Act of Parliament was passed forbidding boys under ten years of age from climbing chimneys, but parents and workhouse officials continued to falsify their children's ages. No master was allowed to employ more than four apprentices, plus two other boys undergoing a two-monthly trial period. At the end of this probationary period, the boys were examined by two Justices of the Peace who would refuse to sign indentures if the boys did not wish to continue in the trade.

Boys were not to extinguish chimney fires, they were not to be ill-treated, and crying the streets was forbidden. Anyone found guilty of constructing a chimney smaller than fourteen inches by nine inches (the minimum size capable of taking the Scandiscope) could be fined a maximum of £100. Again the Act was widely ignored, Parliament did not have the facilities at hand for its enforcement.

1840. An Act of Parliament was passed forbidding boys under twenty-one years of age from being apprenticed to climb chimneys or extinguish chimney fires. No boy under sixteen years of age was allowed to assist the sweep in his work. Again, this Act was widely ignored and it was left to informers to notify the authorities of a breach in the regulations. Sweeps would use boys to carry their brushes and then, once inside a house, down would come the blinds shutting out the scene from prying eyes and up the chimney would go the boy. Fines varied from £5 to £10, but magistrates were slow to convict men breaking the law by sweeping the magistrates' own chimneys. If brought before the magistrates, boys under threat of punishment from their masters, would deny all knowledge of climbing.

1847. John Gordon, a chimney sweep, was sentenced to ten years' transportation to Van Dieman's Land for causing the death of a climbing boy by sending him to extinguish a fire in a factory chimney.

1863. Charles Kingsley published *The Water Babies*, a book that had a great influence on changing public opinion regarding the use of climbing boys, but during the 1860s the number of climbing boys increased.

1864. An Act of Parliament was passed forbidding sweeps to employ any child under ten years of age except on their own premises, or to allow any child under sixteen years of age to be with a sweep while he was cleaning chimneys. The Act of 1840 had laid down a maximum fine of £10 and a minimum fine of £5, but the present act stressed only that the maximum fine should be £10, no minimum fine was laid down. Therefore, any sweep brought before a magistrate was only fined a token sum which encouraged him to go on breaking the law.

1875. Lord Salisbury's *Chimney Sweeper's Bill* finally put an end to the employment of climbing boys after nearly one hundred years of legislation. Master sweeps were henceforth required to register with the police each year on payment of an annual fee of five shillings. Anyone found breaking the Acts of 1840 or 1864 could have their licence taken away and be barred from sweeping. For the first time, the police were given powers to enforce the Act.

The inhuman employment of climbing boys was at an end.

Talking Points, 1828

These have been taken from *The Times* newspaper of 1828, and the *Annual Register*.

Accidents

"Mr. Aulder, a coal merchant, residing in Goswell-Street Rd, was killed, close to the Green Man public house Finchley Bottoms, by the Barnet Coach running against his gig."

"On the evening of Thursday last, as the coach of Mr Mort, of this town, was proceeding down Bridge-Street, to the Bridge Inn, the horses gave a sudden turn down to their stables, which are situated in that neighbourhood, in consequence of which the wheels ran upon the causeway, and unfortunately crushed a poor woman against the wall of Mr. Mort's house, in such a manner as to produce instant death. The deceased was the wife of an industrious man of the name of Jonathan Ashcroft, who is empoyed at the gas works in this town: she was very near-sighted and deaf, and it is conjectured had those afflictions not attended her, the unhappy event might not have happened. The coach had been to Wigan by a private party, and Captain Brook of the 67th. Regiment, now lying in this town, held the reins; but we are given to understand that no blame attaches to him, and that the occurrence was purely accidental. The deceased was in the 56th. year of her age."

Believe It or not

"Another extraordinary pair of eyes—The following story of an English child with an inscription on the eyes appears in the Manchester Guardian.—The French child with 'Empereur Napoleon' on his eyes, that now attracts so much attention in the metropolis, is perhaps surpassed by another boy, 11 years of age, who was lately in this town, having the name of his father, 'John Wood' perfectly legible on the iris of his right eye, and the date of his birth, '1817' on that of his left. A gentleman in High-Street who examined the boy, vouched for us the truth of his statement. The letters are of a faint, or light blue colour. Those on the right eye, particularly the word 'Wood' are distinguished without much difficulty, but not so the date on his left. It should, however, be observed that there is great difficulty in getting the child to keep from blinking, and that rolling motion of the eye so unfavourable to minute observation."

Chimneys sweepers' dinner

"On thursday (May 1st.) the third anniversary dinner of the Society of Master Chimney Sweepers of the metropolis took place at White Conduit-House. The society was formed by a few masters in the trade, for the purpose of putting an end to a practice which has been for many years prevalent—that of allowing their apprentices to perambulate the streets on May days to the annoyance of the public; in lieu of which they are now treated with a substantial dinner at some of the large taverns in the outskirts of the town, where they have an opportunity of enjoying themselves, without the risk of accidents, to which they were formerly subjected. The apprentices went in procession through some of the principal streets, headed by a band of music; and on its arrival before the Mansion-house, the Lord Mayor, on witnessing the healthy and cleanly appearance of the boys, expressed much pleasure, and as a token of his approbation, subscribed a handsome sum of money towards defraying the expenses of the day. The sight of the apprentices partaking of a good substantial dinner of roast beef and plum pudding, in the extensive grounds belonging to the tavern, was extremely gratifying to a large concourse of persons, who assembled on the occasion.

Subsequently to the apprentices having dined, the masters themselves sat down to an excellent dinner.

After *Non nobis, Domine*, was sung by some professional vocalists, and the usual loyal and patriotic toasts had gone round, the Chairman (Mr. Duck) gave an account of the prosperous advancement of the Society. He then alluded to certain reports that the individuals belonging to it were inimical to the introduction of the machine for cleaning chimneys; the reverse, however, was the case; for they made a point of using the machine when it could be brought into operation with effect. He further stated, that it was the opinion of Colonel Stephenson, as well as of Messrs Smirke and Nash, the architects, that owing to the construction of the chimnies in most of the buildings in the metropolis, it was impossible to clean them with the apparatus.

Mr. Watson said that he was present, a few evenings since, at a lecture delivered by Dr. Birkbeck, on the utility of the machine to supersede the necessity of the climbing-boy. The doctor, he admitted, argued candidly and fairly on the subject, and produced an improvement on Glass's machine, which was unquestionably the best invention of the kind; yet, with all its perfections, he (Mr. Watson) was convinced that it would never answer the expectations of those who entertained such a favourable opinion of its efficacy in cleansing chimnies. In the course of the lecture, the doctor said that the machine must succeed in all cases where it is used, if the prejudice of the master chimney-sweepers did not interfere with the trial. It was true that the machine so eloquently eulogised by the doctor would answer in cleansing perpendicular chimnies, but where there were impediments from various causes, no machine, however pliable would overcome them.

Several master chimney sweepers addressed the chair in the course of the afternoon, and excited much amusement by the display of their eloquence. One of them commenced 'I'm blowed, but if we had Dr. Bucbuck, or whatever you may call him, here at our dinner, I think we should soon make a conwert of him to our opinions. Gemmen, I say it is unpossible that ere chimney (pointing to the chimney in the room) can be swept unless one of us goes up it; and I'll give you a proof of it now.' The speaker began to doff his long coat, and would have run up the chimney in earnest, had he not been prevented by some of his brother tradesmen, who caught hold of him by the legs just as his body was about disappearing from the company. When he alighted on the floor, he said that he did not mind a fig getting a sooty shirt, so that he succeeded in showing the strangers present, how little danger was to be apprehended in doing the work as it should be done, and that was by encouraging climbing boys. He had ascended upwards of 5,000 chimneys in his life, of all sorts and sizes, and never yet met with an accident.

This speech was followed by another equally effective on the subject and the glass having by this time circulated freely, everyone was then for speechifying, until at length the chairman ordered the band to strike up; the voices of the speakers were drowned in the thunders of the big drum. The doors of the room were flung open, which was the signal for the commencement of the ball, and in rushed, with the impetuosity of a torrent, about 150 women, all eager to commence tripping it on the light fantastic toe. To dance then they did begin in earnest, but the room became so dreadfully hot from the numbers in it, that many were obliged to quit, and those who did, on getting into the fresh air, felt as if they had escaped out of an atmosphere equally as oppressive as that of the black hole at Calcutta is represented to have been.

With the exception of the above little casualty, everything went on extremely smooth, and the ball was kept up with great spirit until a late hour."

Education

"A Clergyman, late of Cambridge University, LL.D., living in a mansion 6 miles from London, respectfully informs Noblemen and Gentlemen, that long experience in teaching has not only convinced him that it is principally the teacher's fault if pupils do not improve, but that boys may be made at an early age good Latin and Greek scholars, without flagellation; in proof of which, he begs to add, that pupils who began their education under his care read, at the age of 11, Virgil and Xenophon, make sense verses, and write Greek as well as Latin exercises and at the age of 12 read Homer, speak French, draw maps without copies, study algebra and Euclid, write themes, etc. Terms, including single bed, tea twice a day, and every school expense, 60 guineas if under 14, and if above, 80. Pupils dine with the principal. Three vacancies."

"Lower Tooting Establishment for Young Ladies, on the following terms: from 5 to 7 years, £16 per annum; from 7 to 10, £8 ditto, from 10 to 12, £20 ditto: are boarded and carefully instructed in the English and French language, writing, arithmetic, music, and all kinds of plain and ornamental needlework: every attention is paid to the health and rapid improvement of the pupils. Situation truly respectable, only 7 miles from London."

Entertainments

"Equestrian Balloon Ascent, in honour of His Majesty's Birthday.—Mr. Charles Green, the veteran aeronaut, patronised by his Gracious Majesty, at whose Coronation he made his first ascent, begs leave to announce to the Nobility, Gentry, his Friends, and the Public generally, that he purposes making his Hundredth Ascent, from the White Conduit Gardens, Pentonville, on Wednesday, August 13th. 1828, at 5 o'clock in the afternoon, on which occasion, should the evening prove calm, he will, without his car, ascend on horseback. The docile and highly trained animal, on which Mr. Green will ascend, has on 3 former occasions borne him safely through the aerial regions. In the event of rain, there will be found sufficient shelter for upwards of 1,000 persons. Tickets of admission 2s. A band of music will be stationed in the gardens. N.B. Should the evening prove unfavourable for the equestrian ascent, Mr. Green will, to prevent any disappointment, ascend in his car in the usual manner. Mr. Green regrets not being able to ascend on the 12th. instant, in consequence of the gardens being particularly engaged that day."

Mr. Charles Green ascended in his balloon, having a pony along with him. The following is his account of the excursion:

"At half past six o'clock on Tuesday evening, the atmosphere being perfectly serene, I determined to attach the pony to his apparatus, and prepare for the ascent. For this purpose, the hoop of the platform on which he was to take his stand was opened, and he was led from his stable, but was extremely annoyed by the presence of the crowd, to escape from which he took his station with apparent pleasure, and behaved rather rudely to one or two strange gentlemen who were anxious to arrange a portion of his decorations that had become misplaced. While his fetlocks were being secured, and other arrangements made, he was perfectly calm, and repeatedly licked my hands. The saddle was made fast to the hoop, to which also were attached my grappling iron, a bag of beans, and about 250 pounds of ballast in eleven bags. Soon after seven o'clock everything being in readiness, I ordered the last rope to be loosened and we ascended slowly and nearly perpendicularly. At the moment of liberation, my companion made several plunges backwards and forwards, and trembled violently, evidently alarmed at the shouts which I could distinctly hear until I had passed the Thames. He, however, in a few seconds, regained his serenity, and became quite passive, eating some buns from my hand, which by leaning forward, I could easily give him. I now hung out my grapnel to be prepared for a descent, and dismounted to arrange some ballast; but finding that my weight on one side threw the platform off its perpendicular, and considerably discomposed my little companion, I resumed my seat, and discharging a little ballast, attained the elevation of about a mile and a quarter. Here we were visited by a descent of snow of the finest texture, which from the reflection of the direct rays of the sun from above, and the oblique rays from the clouds beneath, had the appearance of a shower of silver dust. On descending a little, the snow appeared changed to rain; but on a still further descent, neither rain nor snow were to be felt or seen, a circumstance not to me unusual. During these gradations, the little animal appeared quite at home and finished his bag of beans. Having been in the air upwards of half an hour, I began to prepare for a descent; and there being scarcely a breath of air stirring, this was, with very little trouble, and without the slightest injury to the pony or myself, effected in a clover field in the parish of Beckenham, Kent. The moment my companion was liberated from his confinement, he took advantage of his situation, and enjoyed himself luxuriously among the clover, which he devoured with every appearance of a keen appetite, although he had eaten more than a pint of beans while in the air. The weight taken up on this occasion was as follows:

	lbs
The balloon and appendages (including grapnel, platform cables, ballast, etc.)	508
Weight of pony.	250
Weight of myself.	148
	906"

"Under the especial patronage of His Majesty.
Royal Gardens Vauxhall

The Proprietors respectfully acquaint the Public, that a Grand Naval Fete will be given To-Morrow Evening, in honour of His Royal Highness the Duke of Clarence. This anniversary will be celebrated with the same splendour and magnificence which characterised the brilliant illuminations and entertainments on his Majesty's Birthday with the addition of numerous superb Naval Insignia, the model of a large vessel in variegated lamps, illuminated trophies, etc. The garden will exhibit one entire blaze of splendour, and upwards of 20,000 additional lamps will occupy the Quadrangle, etc. In numerous naval devices, mottoes etc. From the time the doors open an uninterrupted succession of Amusements will be given, and on this evening THREE THEATRICAL PIECES will be performed at different periods of the night, two in the open Theatre, and one in the Rotunda. The amusing lottery wheel will again go round, and distribute 5,000 gifts, in the same proportion as before: 84 dozen of old Port wine, 8 presents of 1 dozen Champagne each, 8 presents of 1 dozen claret each, 60 presents of invitation cards for 3 to the Gardens, with supper, 200 presents of personal admission for the last 3 nights, 400 presents of personal admission, to admit 2 persons, 4,288 presents of personal admission, to admit 1 person. Doors open at 7. Admission 4/–.''

Food

''Lord Mayor's Day.
Dinner at Guildhall.
. . . 200 tureens of turtle, 60 dishes of fowls, 35 roasted capons, 35 roasted pullets, 30 pigeon pies, 10 sirloins of beef, 50 hams (ornamented) 40 tongues, 2 barons of beef, 10 rounds of beef, 50 raised French pies, 60 dishes of mince pies, 40 marrow puddings, 25 tourtes of preserves, 25 apple and damson tarts, 90 marbree jellies, 50 blanc-manges, 10 chantilly baskets, 4 fruit baskets, 36 dishes shell-fish, 4 ditto prawns, 4 lobster salads, 60 dishes of vegetables, 60 salads. Remove—50 roasted turkeys, 30 leverets, 50 pheasants, 2 dishes pea fowl, 24 geese, 30 dishes of partridges. Dessert—200 pounds of pine-apples, one hundred dishes of hot-house grapes, 200 ice creams, 60 dishes of apples, 60 dishes of pears, 50 savoy cakes (ornamented) 30 dishes walnuts, 75 dishes dried fruits and preserves, 55 ditto rout cakes, 20 ditto filberts, 20 ditto preserved ginger, 4 ditto brandy cherries.''

The law and crime

A person could be sentenced to death for forging a cheque or for stealing a horse. Public executions were popular. One thousand people watched the execution of William Corder for the murder of Maria Marten.

''Robert Taylor imprisoned for a year and to find security for his good behaviour for 5 years thereafter, himself in £500, and two sureties in £250 each. Charge: Blasphemy.''

"Yesterday morning three journeymen silk weavers named Elliot, Richards and Tatum, were publicly whipped pursuant to their sentence, for cutting the work of their employers from their looms. It appears that the practice of cutting work from the looms has latterly become so prevalent, and to such an alarming extent, as to have induced the magistrates of Worship-street office to have recourse to this mode of punishment for the purpose of checking the growing evil."

"Post-Office Robbery.—About six o'clock in the morning, the Hounslow post-office was robbed in a singular manner of about thirty bags, delivered by five of the western mails. It is customary for the guards, while the horses are changing, to throw the bags into one of the upper windows of the post-office, where a servant usually waits to receive them. This had been done, and the servant had just left the room to change her cap, when, in the interim, some fellows ascended by means of a clasp ladder, stole the bags, and made off without being perceived. A light cart had been observed, with a clasp ladder folded behind it, going through Hounslow several mornings, just as the mails were delivering their bags. The fellows in their hurry left the ladder behind them."

Letters to the editor

"Sir, I had occasion on Tuesday last to take a boat from Black-friars-Bridge to Whitehall-stairs, for which I paid 6*d*., the regular fare to Westminster-bridge, according to the list lately published in your paper. On my return, I took a boat to Hungerford-stairs, which are considerably nearer, and on tendering the same sum was treated with much abuse by the waterman, who demanded a shilling. This, of course, I refused to pay, and I was in consequence saluted with the title of 'shabby fellow,' etc., to the great amusement of the bystanders. The man had neither name nor number on his boat, or my remedy would have been simple and easy; and as I had a lady with me I did not feel disposed to incur any further trouble for the purpose of obtaining his name. I think I am right, however, to inform the public what sort of treatment they are to expect from these dissatisfied gentry, and to hint to the magistrates and commissioners the necessity of supporting with strictness the new scale of rates, which I presume has not been fixed without due consideration, and an accurate calculation of the value of the labour of the persons concerned. [signed] A Constant Reader."

Literature

"Popular novel in 3 volumes. *Ismael; or, the Kuzzilbash: a tale of Khorasan.*"

Mechanical chimney-sweeping

"The Committee of the Society for Superseding the Use of Climbing Boys in Cleansing Chimney Flues, recommend Joseph Glass, 2, Moor-lane, Fore street, Cripplegate, as a person who may effect, and who will pay immediate attention to orders transmitted by the penny post. The Committee, in giving the foregoing intimation, are reluctantly compelled to advert to the reduced state of the funds at their disposal, and earnestly and urgently to request the renewed aid of a benevolent public towards promoting an object possessing such peculiar claims on the inhabitants of this great city. A recent instance of death from climbing has taken place at Leeds, and such cases will unhappily be necessarily of occasional occurrence, so long as housekeepers will permit their chimneys to be swept by climbing boys, instead of insisting on the use of the machine."

Patent medicines, etc.

"Dr Winn's True Anticardium Paris Black and Blue Reviver for removing dirt and grease.

"The Ormskirk Medicine for bite of Mad Dogs."

"Hair, Eyebrows and Whiskers, changed from red or grey to brown or black by the Grecian Water, one application only. Neither stains skin nor clothes."

"Mr J. Paterson Clark inventor of the method of curing toothache and tender teeth, without pain or extraction. His remedy consists of an anodyne cement known only to himself, which relieves the pain and deadens the sensibility of diseased teeth previously to their being thoroughly cleaned and permanently stopped in the usual way."

"Blanch and Son's Patent Bug destroyer by steam, from water only. It can be used without taking the bedstead to pieces, and will not injure the furniture be it ever so rich. Apparatus can be used by the most inexperienced person."

"Aromatic Spirit of Vinegar. This agreeably perfumed liquor which is a well known efficacy in relieving faintness and headaches and in counteracting the effects of overheated, close, or infected air."

"Interesting to every Person—Sleep in Peace. But few of the inhabitants of crowded neighbourhoods can say they never were annoyed by those intolerable insects that hide in paper hangings. Send to the acme of stencil, near the toll-bar, Waterloo-road, to get those deadly enemies destroyed by my process of sterilising your rooms instead of papering them. It has a handsome appearance, is equally durable as paper, and, as far as I am concerned, you are warranted to sleep in peace—J. Tidmarsh."

Prices

Apartments in London, large rooms handsomely furnished on the first floor—£2 per week.
Barouche, a carriage seating four people and a driver—£115.
Beef, 8 pounds—4/–.
Board and lodgings in Dulwich for lady of retired habits—£115 per year.
Carpet bargains, best quality—3/6 a square yard.
Chemises, calico—from 1/6 to 3/–.
Encyclopaedia Britannica, 26 volumes—£31.
Hats, real Beaver—£1/1.
Mare, grey, 14½ hands high. Never inured with work—£26/5.
Mutton, 8 pounds—up to 5/–.
Newspaper, *The Times*—six pence.
Night caps—nine pence.
Night gowns—a yard and a half long—3/– to 5/6.
Piano, grand—15 guineas.
Pork, 8 pounds—up to 6/–.
Post—1d.
Suits, gentlemen's—from £2/15 to £3/10.
Sherry— 19/11d a bottle.
Tea, strong breakfast Souchong—4/6 a pound.
Trousers—£1/2 to £1/10.
Waistcoats—from 6/– to 12/–.

Situations vacant

"Wanted, in a ladies' school, a thorough Servant of All-Work, who can cook and assist in washing and ironing and household work. She must have a good character. Also a young Girl, to wait at table and make herself useful in the house. No wages will be given the first year to the latter, but she will be taught reading, writing, arithmetic, and needlework. She must belong to respectable parents."

"To Parents and Guardians—Wanted an apprentice to a Tallow-chandler. A premium is expected."

Situations wanted

"As Cuddy or Third-Mate's servant, to go to the East or West Indies, a young man who has been out before."

"As Under Housemaid, or Under Nurserymaid, a young woman, age 17, of very respectable parents, who is thoroughly disposed to make herself useful, and can work well with her needle."

Small advertisements

"To be sold, a four gallon Milk Walk."

"Quadrilles, and every other part of fashionable dancing. Private tuition. Mr. Hopkins, St. Alban's-hall, St. Alban's Church, Wood Street, Cheapside, where ladies and gentlemen may be expeditiously and privately instructed to qualify them for the first assemblies, and are respectfully informed his own family make up a complete set."

"Twenty pounds will be given, and a part of the first year's salary, to any Lady or Gentleman who will procure for a young Man, age 20, a permanent situation as Junior or Collecting Clerk, or any mercantile employment. He can write a good hand and would make himself useful."

"A Young Lady of the highest respectability and connexions, is, by the death of a beloved relative, suddenly reduced from a situation of apparent affluence to real and abject poverty, her health and spirits have fallen a prey to the secret afflictions of a wounded heart, and she is at this moment from continued illness and suffering, reduced to the necessity of appealing to a generous public to rescue her from the horrors of poverty and death. From the peculiarity of the advertiser's situation more cannot be said. Messrs Snow and Co. Bankers, Temple Bar or Messrs Hatchard and Son, Booksellers, Piccadilly, have kindly consented to receive subscriptions."

Smugglers

"During the night of the 4th, a desperate conflict took place on the coast of Sussex. between a party of the blockade Service and a numerous gang of smugglers. About midnight, a lugger, well laden, approached the shore at an almost desolate spot, between the village of Bexhill and a public house called 'Bo-peep;' and in a few moments a large party, composing the land-gang, rushed down to the beach, landed the whole of the cargo, consisting of several hundred tubs of spirits and other contraband goods. As they were making off with it in carts, the coast blockade stationed near the spot endeavoured to intercept them; but the force of the smugglers was overpowering and the blockade-men thought it prudent to retire for a time, until they could procure a reinforcement. In as short a time as possible the officers in command assembled a force of about forty men, well armed, and commenced a pursuit in the direction which the smugglers had taken. The latter, contrary to their usual custom, kept a straight course, and at Sidney Green, a small village about two miles and a half inland, the guard came up with the gang and immediately made a determined attack upon them. The armed portion of the smugglers drew themselves up in a body in regular line, and a desperate fight took place. Success was for some time doubtful. The smugglers fought with such determination and courage, that the blockade-men were repulsed, after two persons were killed, and several badly wounded. The smugglers carried off the whole of their goods. Not one of them could be secured. The greater part of the smugglers were armed with bats (ash poles, about 6 feet long, cut from the woods for the purpose), and a few of them with fire-arms. Several of the blockade men were severely bruised by the skilfully directed blows of the batsmen, and the quarter-master (Collins) had his brains literally beaten out. In the first volley fired by the blockade-men, an old smuggler, Smithurst, was killed. He was found in the morning lying dead in the road, with his bat still grasped in his hands, the weapon being almost hacked in pieces by the cutlasses and bayonets of the blockade-men. The coroner's jury, which sat on the body of Collins, the quarter-master, returned a verdict of 'wilful murder against some person or persons unknown.' In a few days the party were betrayed by one of their accomplices, and the ringleaders were apprehended. Although the informer was what is called 'foreman of the company,' he had long been an object of suspicion to his gang: but they were too much in his power to discard him."

Sport

"Pedestrianism. Sheppard, the Yorkshire pedestrian, ran 20 miles in $2\frac{3}{4}$ hours for a wager of £21."

Top of the charts

"The Tyrolese Evening Hymn."
"Twenty Thousand Tongues."
"Oh, Happy Bride."
"True Love."
"The Family Man."

Travel

"London to Cheltenham, 98 miles, in 11 hours, by the Magnet, a new fast stage coach."

"Steam Ship, Erin. 500 tons. 180 h.p. Geo M'Kibbin, Commander, will leave Union Stairs below the tower.

Reduced fares to Belfast

State Cabin	£3.
Fore Cabin	£2.
Deck	£1."

Chimney Sweepers' Slang

This has been taken from *The Last of the Climbing Boys*, George Elson, John Long.

Brieze	cinders.
Cadie	a cap.
Cant	piece.
Chif	a knife.
Chummy	a climbing boy.
Coring	cleaning out loose mortar that had fallen from bricklayers' trowels while plastering the inside of a new chimney.
Cosh	a stick.
Crib	a barn or hovel to sleep in.
Deacon	the scraper.
Deiking	looking.
Dolly	a servant.
Drag	a cart.
Feiker	a chimney sweep.
Gigar	a door.
Glim	a fire.
Greenhorn	a novice.
Jug	a shilling.
Ken	a house.
Kewtar	a sovereign.
Knullers or Queriers	sweeps who got custom by going round knocking on people's doors.
Lag	water.
Leeks or Green-uns	sweeps who have not served their time in the trade.
Mang	beg.
Meg	a halfpenny.
Mug	a face.
Ogles	eyes.
Panam	bread.
Panam and spreadham	bread and butter.
Panam and fe	bread and meat.
Panam and cas	bread and cheese.
Prod	a horse.
Queer	soot.
Querying	undercutting prices.

Switch	the sweep's brush.
Parney	rain.
Patter cant	to talk slang.
Pike the lew	clean out the top.
Puv	a field.
Rum mort	housewife.
Si	sixpence.
Snoatcher	bone.
Rag and snoatcher	a rag and bone man.
Splorger or Skufter	police or the owner of a house.
Stamps	shoes.
Thrum	twopence.
Tuggery	clothes.
Tuggy	soot cloth.
Win	a penny.

"Can you patter cant?" (can you speak slang), a sweep might ask another to see if he was genuine. "Oh, yes, I know," the other would reply, "nix is nothing, and a penny roll is a win buster."

"Now Jim, mang the splorger or the rum mort for a cant of panam and spreadham" (now Jim, beg the owner for a piece of bread and butter).

Bibliography

Annual Register, 1828.
Kellow Chesney, *The Victorian Underworld*, Pelican Books.
George Elson, *The Last of the Climbing Boys*, John Long.
J. L. and Barbara Hammond, *The Bleak Age*, Pelican Books.
—— *The Town Labourer*, Guild Books.
—— *Lord Shaftesbury*, Pelican Books.
Charles Lamb, *Essays of Elia*, MacDonald.
Henry Mayhew, *London Labour and London Poor*, Frank Cass.
George L. Phillips, *England's Climbing Boys*, Baker Library, Harvard Graduate School of Business Administration.
Brian Inglis, *Poverty and The Industrial Revolution*, Panther Books.
E. S. Turner, *Roads to Ruin*, Michael Joseph.
The Times of 1828.
Lawrence Wright, *Home Fires Burning*, Routledge & Kegan Paul.

CHAPTER 7

DRAMA AND THE DIFFICULT CLASS

Most secondary schools have one or two classes which might be termed "difficult," each containing a hard core of pupils, who, for a variety of reasons, are determined to challenge, disrupt, or even threaten any member of staff who does not resort to an effective form of corporal punishment. Such classes generally consist of third-, fourth-, or fifth-year pupils, mostly of low IQ, renowned for their truancy and a fervent desire to leave school at the first available opportunity. Disruptiveness ranges from sullen indifference on the one hand to throwing all the chairs and tables over, going to the back of the class, and challenging the teacher to do something about it, on the other.

What is in store for a drama teacher taking a typically disruptive class for the first time? The children push their way noisily into the room. They fragment into groups that display varying stages in the disruptive pecking-order. Some sit down on the chairs and tables, several with their backs to the teacher; others lounge against the windows, shouting out or whistling to other pupils who may be walking past. For a few brief moments, the teacher might manage, by raising his voice, to capture the interest of the whole class while they assess his ability to control them; but having failed the test, this hard-won concentration is quickly dispelled as one group revives their former conversation with added gusto. While the teacher is attempting to quieten them, the rest of the class see this as an opportunity to resume their own conversations, one or two of them shouting across to friends on the opposite side of the room. The chances of the teacher addressing a quiet united class are, except for the intervention of the headmaster, extremely remote. From now on, the lesson will be characterised by growing indiscipline on the part of the children and amounting frustration on the part of the teacher. A boy produces a pack of cards and a game develops. A packet of cigarettes is brought out and displayed for all to see—it is confiscated with great difficulty. A waste bin is kicked over and the contents scattered across the floor. One boy slips quietly out of the room and is discovered lurking outside the girls' toilets. . . .

The usual type of group work as outlined in Chapter Two will not work with a class such as this. The children lack the necessary self-discipline required to work together and organise a semi-polished improvisation; neither do they have the ability to sit quietly and watch other members of the form who might have a play to offer. The most one can expect from group drama with a class such as this is a perfunctory discussion, followed by a series of "happenings"— endless variations upon man's inhumanity to man. Half the group stay in the classroom while the rest disappear into the corridor. After an interminable wait—any attempt to hasten their return is always met with the plea that they are not quite ready—they explode back into the room and leap upon those left behind. Then follows a frantic few minutes of misplaced energy as they grapple with each other and fall writhing to the floor. Some members of the audience join in the fray which inevitably ends with mutual congratulations all round, honour, apparently having been satisfied. A general dusting-down of clothes follows as they wait for some show of approval from the teacher. Each play follows the same chaotic pattern. The members of the audience, if not playing cards or talking amongst themselves, laugh uproariously, especially if they think that someone is getting hurt. The members of another group begin agitating to show their play, making it impossible for the teacher to discuss the one that has just taken place. Constructive criticism is strongly resented—they have had "their bit of fun," what more is there to say? Any children interested in acting quickly become disillusioned by the lack of discipline shown and turn disruptive themselves through sheer frustration—it is a vicious circle. Questions such as, "What would you like to do a play about?" are countered with suggestions that they be allowed in the gym to play pirates on the wall bars, an idea to be discouraged at all costs. Unlike the physical education specialist, the drama teacher is not legally covered for the injuries that would inevitably result. Or, "Let's do a play about sex," aimed at embarrassing any girls who may be present.

Methods of Approach

A drama teacher with the thought of facing such a class for two lessons per week for a whole year might well despair. What is the answer?

There are two ways of dealing with a difficult class:

The authoritarian approach

The teacher achieves obedience through imposed discipline and obtains results by resorting to corporal punishment, mock severity, keeping the children in after school, giving out additional written work, or sending the ringleaders to the headmaster.

However, the drama teacher seeks, not slavish obedience, but individual co-operation from children. Worthwhile educational drama can never be achieved by authoritarian methods. There are, of course, innumerable examples where authoritarian methods in the arts have achieved admirable results: the young Beethoven was constantly rapped over the knuckles by his father whenever he played a false note on the piano. Most teachers can, against varying degrees of resistance, compel children to write essays, complete scientific experiments, solve arithmetical problems, with varying degrees of success. But a drama teacher cannot compel a child to act. To demand a child's co-operation in a drama lesson is to nullify all that educational drama stands for. A drama teacher cannot afford to alienate children through an authoritarian approach, their co-operation is vital to any type of drama work. Aside from this, drama teachers, in the main, tend to be sensitive individuals whose very nature rebels at the idea of dominating children regardless of their outlook.

The channelling approach

The teacher obtains co-operation through enjoyment, leading to self-discipline. In dealing with difficult children, it is not the authority of the teacher, but the nature of the subject which produces results.

Adolescence is a time of storm and stress, a time when the maturing teenager needs more than ever to assert his personality in order to offset the disturbing physical changes that are taking place. And, possibly, the only way a difficult adolescent child can assert himself is through physical action, often of a violent kind. The drama teacher must then seek to channel this violence into worthwhile creative endeavour. Crime and violence form the usual starting points for drama work with a difficult class.

The following methods of channelling disruptive potential towards worthwhile educational drama have all been successfully tried out with difficult children; but they are not presented as the definitive solution to the problem, only as possible starting points.

1. *Difficult children with experiences to share.* Many difficult children will have had various brushes with the law, perhaps openly boasting of

their escapades. A group of such children might be persuaded to improvise their experiences in the class room. Perhaps, by playing out anti-social roles in school, there may be less need to perpetuate them outside the class room. One reads from time to time of schools in deprived areas where a marked decrease in the juvenile crime rate can be directly attributed to the fact that the children concerned were allowed to act out their violent fantasies in the class room. There is scope here for a researcher to carry out a sociological/psychological survey to ascertain the truth of such reports. Should the results prove positive, there is obviously much that the drama teacher can do to decrease the problem of rising violence in our society. One is reminded of the native tribes of New Guinea who periodically engaged in mock battles which acted as a safety valve, and dispersed the aggressive tendencies of the young.

2. *The amenably difficult.* Children of this type seek their drama at the teacher's expense, considering it something of a triumph if they can humiliate him or cause him to lose his temper. Therefore, the teacher's first aim must be to direct attention away from himself, and on to one or two of the children concerned.

The room should be arranged beforehand: chairs set out in a circle with one or two in the centre. The teacher receives the children standing outside the circle. As soon as the children are sitting down, the teacher selects two of the noisiest children and invites them to occupy the chairs in the centre. This has the effect of focussing the attention of the class away from the teacher and on to the children in question. There is an element of surprise in this: what is going to happen now? Talking stops. The teacher capitalises on the lull in the conversation to explain briefly that the two in the circle have just robbed a bank, they are now sitting in a rented room sharing out the proceeds. As soon as the interest begins to wane, the teacher introduces another character into the plot. There is a knock on the door. One of the gang gets up and opens it. The driver of the get-away car comes in. He demands his share of the money but the other two have plans to split the proceeds fifty-fifty. They decide to dispose of him.

The teacher selects a boy to play the get-away driver and the scene continues. The driver is killed. Interest again begins to flag. There is another knock on the door. An old man living in the flat below is disturbed by the noise; he has come up to find out what is happening. He too must be taken care of. A policeman on the beat hears sounds of a scuffle coming from this first floor room and decides to investigate.... Thus, by keeping the action moving at an abnormally fast pace the teacher avoids the embarrassed pauses which inevitably result when children are given only the minimum of information concerning the roles they have been called upon to play. Also, the continual shift of emphasis from one character to another ensures the attention of the other members of the class.

As soon as this idea palls, the teacher suggests another one using each child in turn (the vociferous members, perhaps, more than once to ensure their continued co-operation). These lessons must run like clockwork, there must be no hitches allowing children time to take advantage of any temporary lull in the proceedings.

The results obtained cannot by any stretch of the imagination, be called great child drama; but the children are discovering that the subject is an enjoyable one and, by liberally praising their efforts, the teacher is implanting the idea that in a drama lesson no child is considered a failure.

3. *Utilising the class leader.* If a difficult class possesses a natural leader, one whom the children respect or fear, it is often possible to structure a scenario placing him in a key role; the assumption being that if the children do not wish to co-operate directly with the teacher, their indirect co-operation can be achieved through the enthusiasm and personality of their ring-leader who could be cast in one of the following roles:

> Al Capone, the Chicago gangster, see Kenneth Allsop, *The Boot-leggers*, Hutchinson.
> Salvatore Guiliano, see Gavin Maxwell, *God Protect me from my friends*, Longman.
> John Wesley Hardin, the Western outlaw, see James D. Horan and Paul Sann, *Pictorial History of the Wild West*, Spring Books.
> Ned Kelly, see *Ned Kelly*, Charles Osborne, Anthony Blond Ltd.; *Ned Kelly*, a play by Douglas Stewart, in *Three Australian Plays*, Penguin Books.
> Francisco Sabaté Llopart, the Spanish anarchist guerrilla, see E. J. Hobsbawm, *Bandits*, Weidenfeld & Nicolson.
> Jack Sheppard, the English highwayman, see Christopher Hibbert, *The Road to Tyburn*, Longman.

Difficult children readily identify with bandits, guerrillas, and gangsters being themselves rebels of a kind, and seem to prefer real-life lawbreakers to the villains of fiction. By dramatising the lives of bandits from a variety of countries the drama teacher is introducing difficult children to a variety of social backgrounds, thus widening their often narrow horizons.

The drama teacher might also consider the possibilities of using troublemakers with dramatic ability from the top end of the school,

where, by proving a disruptive influence, they are gaining little educa-
tionally, and giving them the responsibility of working with difficult
drama classes lower down the school. This type of alliance has proved
extremely successful and I have found a considerable improvement
in the drama work as a result. The younger children consider themselves honoured to be working with older pupils, especially if they
have a reputation for being tough and rebellious. The older children
do not, as might be expected, take advantage of the situation, but
accept the challenges involved and prove stabilising influences over
the youngsters concerned, learning in the process the satisfaction to
be gained from co-operating in a creative endeavour. They can be
cast as parents, policemen, gang leaders, etc.

4. *The vocally disruptive class.* With extremely noisy classes, the teacher
should have a tape recorder available. The children are asked where
one might possibly find a group of people outside school creating the
same amount of noise as they are making. They might suggest a football crowd. The teacher asks which football teams they support and
chooses the two most popular teams. The class is then divided into two
groups, one group supporting one team, and one the other. The
teacher asks for a volunteer to play the part of a football commentator.
He is handed a microphone and asked to do a commentary on a match
between the two teams selected. Because of the noise they will be making, the football supporters will not be able to hear the commentary,
therefore, some form of signalling process must be employed to keep
the crowd informed as to what is happening. When the commentator
points to one group, this signifies that their team is on the offensive,
and they make the appropriate noises, and vice-versa. Other signals
denote that one team or the other has scored a goal. The teacher
records the result and lets the children listen to the playback. Difficult
children are always fascinated by recordings of the noises they make
and will listen intently—here we have the beginnings of self-control—
and be pleasantly surprised by the results. This situation does produce
a surprisingly good tape, providing the commentator plays his part
well, and most boys who volunteer for the part do. By showing the
positive results that can be achieved with so little effort, the teacher
is assured of their continued co-operation in the subject. All children
want to succeed at something.

From a football commentary, the teacher can then progress to a
scenario on a football theme. Possible scenarios, preferably worked
out by the teacher, could include a British footballer kidnapped by
urban guerrillas during a South American tour, a plane crash involving a football team and their supporters, or the life story of a star
player. A suggestion from the children that they have a game of

football outside should be avoided at all costs, the game would inevitably take over from the drama, much to the distress of the head of the physical education department. The children will already have been timetabled for a games period and to pander to their wants here is to abrogate one's responsibility to teach drama. A way of overcoming this is to insist that all scenes involving football matches should take place indoors using an imaginary ball. The result can prove just as effective as the real thing, especially if the game is accompanied by a suitable piece of music such as Britten's "Moto Perpetuo" from *Matinées Musicales*.

5. *The physically disruptive class*. Movement proves an excellent introduction to drama for a physically disruptive class; those who fight their way into the room pushing over the chairs and tables. There is an obvious need for them to work off their surplus energy before any communication is possible. The teacher asks each child to find a partner, one partner becomes number One, the other number Two. They are then asked to practise, in slow motion at first, a no-holds-barred fight, taking particular care not to hurt each other. (See Chapter Nine of *Development Through Drama* by Brian Way, for a discussion on fighting and violence.) Once they have worked out a fight sequence, all the number Ones are asked to go to one end of the room, and the number Twos to the other; and then, to a suitable piece of music, *e.g.* "Skyline" and "Subway Jam" from Aaron Copland's *Music For a Great City* they are to come together, seek out their partner and go through the fight sequence they have just rehearsed; allowing plenty of time in which to tire themselves out. When exhausted, they will be in a much more receptive frame of mind for a discussion: on the motives behind gang warfare, of how such a fight would end (with one of the gang seriously injured or even killed?) and the possible outcome of such a tragedy. The teacher could then go on to discuss the ultimate futility of gang warfare and possible ways of preventing it could be explored dramatically. Useful source material can be found in the following books:

James Patrick, *A Glasgow Gang Observed*, Eyre Methuen.
Harrison Salisbury, *The Shook-up Generation*, Michael Joseph.
Lewis Yablonsky, *The Violent Gang*, Pelican Books.

6. *The inhibited class*. Perhaps the most difficult classes of all are those in which the children are too inhibited to engage in dramatic activity. Usually such children have plenty to say for themselves and will cavort about the room on their own terms, but as soon as the drama teacher attempts, however surreptitiously, to channel their responses

into creative drama, embarrassment sets in and they immediately retire to the safety of their chairs, desks or the radiators. A breakthrough with such children can often be achieved by means of the improvised tape recording. The teacher suggests a dramatic idea, preferably one requiring a wide range of sound effects that can be created vocally. To avoid misuse, materials for creating sound effects: sand, coconut shells, water, etc., should not be introduced until a standard of self-discipline has been achieved. The children are divided into two groups, one group close to the microphone improvises the story, while the rest make the appropriate sound effects. Possible scenarios might include a visit to a haunted house, a party of nineteenth-century explorers captured by a savage tribe, or an arch-criminal holding the world to ransom by threatening to blow up certain major cities unless his demands are met.

Crime, fighting and violence are useful ways into drama with difficult children, but they must be means to an end, never an end in themselves. If children are to dramatise acts of violence they should also, by means of role reversal (see Chapter 8). be given the opportunity of exploring the consequences of such criminal acts upon the victims concerned and society at large. Progression should always be from crime to social justice.

There are one or two basic points to be borne in mind when teaching drama with difficult classes. A drama lesson can be noisy. A heated confrontation between a king and his starving subjects, a group of villagers dragging a woman accused of witchcraft to be burnt at the stake, even from the best-behaved children, will inevitably generate plenty of noise. Difficult children are noisy at the best of times, therefore, one must expect the noise level to rise considerably when they are engaged in dramatic activity, particularly during the early stages before an enjoyment of the subject creates the self-discipline necessary for them to be able to move on to more sensitive areas of human experience.

It is, therefore, very important that the drama room should be out of earshot of the other classrooms where quieter work is in progress. The arrangement of the room, too, is particularly important. Everything possible should be done to ensure a prompt beginning to the lessons so that children can take their places with the minimum amount of fuss. As an aid to this, all desks should wherever possible be removed, and the chairs set out in a semi-circle in order to avoid children turning round, talking or engaging in horse-play with their friends sitting in front or behind them as they do in a normal classroom setting. This arrangement limits their conversational orbit to those sitting to right or left. If the room is permanently in use as a drama workshop, black-out facilities and rudimentary stage lighting should also be included. Difficult children whose powers of imagination tend to be less well-developed than their more fortunate neighbours, achieve considerable motivation from the rudimentary effects of light and darkness. How much easier it is, for example, to set up an escape from a prisoner-of-war camp under cover of darkness with black-out facilities and a moveable spot light. It stretches the positive suspension of disbelief of all but the most imaginative child to conceive of a night escape from a prisoner-of-war camp in a tiny room stuffed full of desks and chairs with bright sunlight streaming in through the windows. Rostrum boxes should also be provided, to create acting areas at different levels.

We have so far, in this Chapter, concentrated on difficult boys, but girls too, in their own way, can prove equally as troublesome. Material for difficult third- and fourth-year girls is harder to find than for boys of the same age. However, an interesting scenario can be built up by following the adventures of a group of girls escaping from an approved school. They make their way to London, but find that employment proves difficult without insurance cards or references from former employers. They drift into a life of crime until arrested by the police and returned to the approved school to be disciplined for their misconduct.

Encouraging girls and boys to work together in the lower half of the secondary school always poses difficulties for the drama teacher and the problem becomes more acute with a disruptive class, particularly in the third year when the interests of the two sexes are poles apart. The boys tend to be interested in war and crime while the girls, maturing earlier, are long past the age for picaresque adventures, and seek vicarious thrills in the love and fashion pages of teenage magazines. The answer to this problem with co-operative children would, of course, be group work, but, if a difficult class is not yet ready for the responsibilities of working in groups, then it is preferable that the boys and girls work together under the constant surveillance of the teacher, and some way of uniting these two disparate elements must be found. The following scenario has proved extremely popular in achieving this end.

Scenario:
The Pipeline

The time is 1943. An escape route (the Pipeline) has been organised across France to help British prisoners of war on the run from the Germans. The escapers travel by night and hide during the day. A fashion shop in Boulogne is the final stop-over before they are taken by rowing boat to rendezvous with a submarine in the English Channel which will take them home. The latest group of escapers have been flushed from their penultimate hiding place by a German search party. They manage to give the Germans the slip but it is too risky to walk the streets in broad daylight. They arrive at the shop just as a fashion show is about to begin....

CHARACTERS Manageress of a French fashion shop in Boulogne
                  Fashion models
                  Escaping British prisoners of war
                  An informer
                  A Gestapo officer
                  German guards

PREPARATION

The models describe to the manageress the clothes they would like to wear at the fashion show. It does not matter at this stage that they are anachronistic.

The manageress makes a list of the girls in order of appearance and notes down a description of the fashions they would like to wear.

The British prisoners of war decide on their characters (one is an informer) and make up a short play showing how they escaped from the prisoner-of-war camp.

The German guards practise the goose-step.

The Gestapo officer puts the guards through selected drill movements—Quick march! Halt! Fall out!, etc.

SCENE A fashion shop in Boulogne. A catwalk of rostrum boxes is placed down the classroom with chairs on either side (*see* Fig. 9)

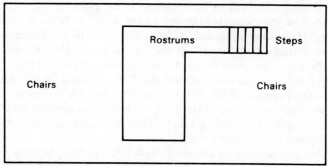

Fig. 9. Fashion show floorplan.

1. The fashion show is about to begin. The manageress is checking each girl's costume before the show starts.

2. There is a knock at the door. The manageress goes to the door and opens it. Outside are a group of escaping British prisoners of war. She tells them that they are too early, she was not to expect them until after dark. One of the escapers explains that they were flushed out of their last hiding-place by a German search party, but they have since given them the slip. They cannot walk the streets in broad daylight, they are too conspicuous. Can she hide them now? She explains that while she is quite prepared to hide them herself, she has the girls to think about. If they are captured on her premises during the fashion show the Gestapo would probably put the models before a firing squad as accomplices. She must ask them to make the decision.

3. The manageress goes back to the girls and explains the situation; she leaves the decision whether or not to hide the escapers up to them.

4. The girls argue amongst themselves. Eventually they agree that the escapers can hide at the shop during the fashion show.

5. The manageress asks the escapers to join the audience.

6. The fashion show begins. As each girl walks along the catwalk, the manageress describes the clothes she is wearing.

7. A Gestapo officer bursts into the room accompanied by a group of German guards. At a given signal the guards surround the chairs and stand with rifles at the ready.

8. The manageress complains about the interruption. The Gestapo officer tells her that he has come to watch the fashion show. He tells her to continue and sits down.

9. The fashion show continues. When the show is over the Gestapo officer asks each of the escapers in turn to show his papers. When he has checked their papers, he suddenly orders his guards to arrest them. One of the escapers panics and makes a dash for freedom. He is shot dead by one of the guards before he can reach the door. The girls scream. The officer orders them to be quiet.

10. One of the escapers (the informer) walks over to the Gestapo officer. He has been planted in the prison camp by the German authorities to find out the details of the escape route. He tells the officer that he has a complete list of details: names, stopover places, etc.— enough information to smash the pipeline once and for all. The Gestapo officer congratulates him on his initiative. He orders the guards to round up the escapers, the girls, and the manageress, and march them outside to a waiting truck. They are to be taken to Gestapo headquarters for questioning.

What happens next? Do the British soldiers and the girls manage to escape? Could members of the French resistance ambush the truck on its way to Gestapo headquarters? Or are the escapers sent back to the prison camp and the girls either shot or deported to concentration camps in Germany? What happens to the French men and women who have been helping the escapers? The class should talk about the possible outcome and improvise the rest of the story themselves in the light of their discussion.

To sum up: a drama teacher facing a difficult class for the first time must quickly assess the dramatic outlet best suited to the needs of the children concerned—fighting, tape-recording, using the class leader, etc., and structure a dramatic situation from which they can gain almost immediate satisfaction. Once they have discovered that drama is an enjoyable activity, that enjoyment and satisfaction increase with the growth of self-discipline, and that dramatic freedom is not licence to create mayhem, then they will begin to exercise their own control over their material and over those still refusing to comply.

While drama with most difficult classes will never reach a high standard, neverthheless, some disruptive classes, within certain basic areas of human experience with which they are familiar, or which they find relevant to their needs, such as crime, gang warfare, vandalism, football hooliganism, pop music, and drugs, are sometimes capable of far more interesting work than their better-behaved contemporaries. (In selecting material for difficult classes the drama teacher should, in the main, avoid work that is beyond their experience or which relies for its success upon literary source material.)

The basic social problems that cause these children to be difficult, usually a broken or deprived home background, give them experiences to draw upon fortunately denied to children from more stable and caring homes, experiences which give their drama, at best, a terrible authenticity.

CHAPTER 8

"MY BROTHER'S MOCCASINS"
Role Reversal

The aim of a role-reversal lesson can best be illustrated through an improvisation structured by Mrs. Dorothy Heathcote with a class of approved-school pupils.

On entering the classroom, Mrs. Heathcote discovered one of the boys haranguing his friends on the unfairness shown by the authorities in sentencing him to a period of detention for a misdemeanour which he considered was fully justified. While living at home he had asked his father if he could have a bicycle; his father had agreed on one condition—that he paid half the cost himself. His father would provide the rest. So, the boy took on a newspaper round, earning a pound a week, while his father gave him a further pound a week from his own wages. Twenty or so weeks went by and all the boy needed was the final pound from his father and the bicycle, which he had ordered, would be his. But when his father did eventually arrive home from work that Friday evening the final pound was not forthcoming. Someone at work had stolen his father's wages and he would be hard pressed to find the money for the rent, housekeeping, the hire-purchase commitments, let alone any extras for a bicycle. Bitterly disappointed, the boy slunk out of the house and stole the first unattended bicycle he came across. He was arrested, tried, and sentenced to a period of detention at the approved school.

"It's not fair, is it, Miss?" he said turning to Mrs. Heathcote. His question placed Mrs. Heathcote in a very difficult position. To have agreed with him would have served only to inflame his discontent still further, whereas to have agreed that the court's decision was a fair one might have alienated not only her relations with the boy concerned, but the rest of the class as well.

Such a question requires the judgment of a Solomon. However, without committing herself one way or the other, Mrs. Heathcote helped the boy to discover the answer for himself—through role reversal.

"That's an interesting story," she said, "shall we act it?" The boys

148

agreed. Mrs. Heathcote asked the boy to play himself, while the other boys in the class became members of his family, his father's work-mates, the owner of the bicycle, etc. When the improvisation was over, Mrs. Heathcote asked them if they would do it again, only this time, the boy was to play the part of his father. The other parts were also redistributed to give variety and the scenario was improvised a second time. When it was over the boy sat down in a chair, a worried frown on his face.

"You know," he said, "I've never thought about it before, but I must have been a rotten ——! There was my father, in trouble because he had lost his wages, and I had to bring more trouble on the family by stealing that bike." This boy had, no doubt, been lectured to by members of his family, by the police, by the magistrate, and all to no avail, he saw nothing wrong in what he had done. And yet, by simply taking part in a role-reversal exercise, seeing the incident for the first time from his father's point of view, rather than his own, the full effect of what he had done was tellingly brought home to him.

Role reversal then is an attempt, by means of drama, to help children to understand other people's feelings, attitudes, and points of view, in the hope that they will modify their own attitudes in the light of the knowledge thus gained. The distinct advantage of role reversal as an educative process lies in the fact that attitudes are changed from within, through self-discovery, rather than imposed from without by the teacher. In answer to a child's query regarding a particular aspect of parental authority, for example, the drama teacher does not say "You must do what your parents think best for you," rather, he suggests that the child take on a parental role and explore for himself the reasons as to why a particular stand has been adopted. When the child has seen the problem from his parents' point of view, he will then be in a better position to discuss it.

Role-reversal topics can be suggested by the teacher, but it is prefer-able, especially in the initial stages, if they stem from the children's questioning of the world around them. (Progression should be from the personal problems affecting the children to the international prob-lems affecting society at large.) If the children are concerned about a particular problem, they are much more likely to discuss it and improvise around it than they are one that is imposed by the teacher. For example, a twelve-year-old girl might say, "My mother told me I had to be in by eight o'clock last night. There was a right old fuss because I didn't come home till half past nine. Well, I wasn't doing anything wrong. We went over to Brenda's to listen to her records and I forgot the time. Now I've got to stay in for the rest of the week. Do you think that's fair, sir?" As in the case of the approved school

boy quoted earlier, if the teacher gives a straight answer, 'Yes" or
"No" he is inevitably going to alienate either the child or her parents.
The solution is to break off at this point and let the child experience,
through role reversal, something of her parents' concern when she
did not return home at the agreed time. Many of the other children
in the class will also be questioning their parents' decisions on this
point and will wish to join in. The teacher discovers other children
whose opinions coincide with those of the girl, and the class is divided
into groups, with one advocate for an open-ended approach to the
problem in each group, as far as possible. The following scenario, suit-
ably adapted to meet local variations is then improvised twice by the
children; the first time through, the children who question their
parents' right to expect them to be in by a certain time play themselves; the second time through they play the part of a parent.

**Scenario:
"What Time do you call this
to come Home?"**

CHARACTERS Mother
Father
Son or daughter (twelve years old)
Other relatives, friends of the family as required

The parents have given their permission for their son or daughter
to play out after tea on condition that he/she is home by eight o'clock.
It is now 9.25 p.m. and the child has still not returned.

SCENE The boy's/girl's home
1. Mother is watching at the window. Father comes in. He tells her
that he has searched the neighbourhood but cannot find their son/
daughter anywhere. Mother asks him to telephone the police, Father
suggests waiting a bit longer; he does not want to bother them in
case there is a natural explanation why the boy/girl has not returned
home. He suggests possible reasons. Mother suggests things that could
have happened to him/her, while father is delaying. Father decides
to wait another five minutes. He tries to read the newspaper, mother
tries to sew, but neither can concentrate.
2. Father goes to the telephone. He begins to dial the police. The
door opens and their son/daughter walks in.
How does the scene end?
Each improvisation could be presented to the remainder of the

class, but interest among the members of the audience begins to wane with repetition, and the children soon become bored and restless. But, on the other hand, there will always be those children who feel that group work which is not for presentation to the rest of the class does not require the same amount of time and effort spent upon it. Given more to a theatrical approach to the subject they fail to appreciate the value of personal discovery for its own sake. Care must be taken to ensure that such children do not sabotage the efforts of the rest of the class.

Once the children have explored the problem dramatically, the teacher calls them together to discuss their findings, throwing out a general question such as: "Well, should you stay out later than the time set by your parents?" to set them talking.

There will always be children who, either out of bravado or a distorted sense of moral values, identify with the vandal, the football hooligan, and the mugger. And there will also be those who carry their identification a stage further by actually engaging in acts of vandalism and football hooliganism themselves. How can role reversal bring home to such pupils the effect that their behaviour has upon their victims and the sometimes tragic consequences that can result from such activities?

Consider vandalism on a football special. A classroom discussion on crowd behaviour at football matches and on the special football trains provided will quickly enable the teacher to spot those children holding anti-social views. The children in the class are then divided into groups, each group containing both supporters and opponents of football hooliganism in equal numbers as far as possible. Each group creates a railway carriage interior by setting out twin rows of inward-facing chairs leaving a gangway down the centre. The following scene is then improvised.

CHARACTERS Members of the public returning home (decide
            characters)
            Football hooligans, supporters of team X
            Railway guard

SCENE A railway station adjacent to the football ground; the inside of a "Football Special"

PREPARATION Team X has been playing Team Y away and lost 3–0
1. The members of the public enter the railway carriage and settle down in their seats. The guard blows his whistle.

2. A group of football supporters race down the platform, their pockets bulging with beer bottles, rattles clacking in their hands. They jump aboard the train just as it is pulling out of the station. They crowd into the compartment deciding to vent their disapppointment on the world at large. The people in the carriage are subjected to abuse and a certain amount of manhandling. The hooligans then start to wreck the carriage: imaginary bottles and light bulbs are flung out of the windows, knives rip large holes in the seat covers.

How do the other members in the carriage react? Do they put up any resistance? Do some of the passengers manage to escape into the corridor and call the guard, or, are they powerless to do anything about the situation? How does the scene end?

The difficulty arises when the teacher asks the hooligans to reverse roles and become law-abiding members of the public, for the simple reason that those children who identify with football hooligans are not the type who would be capable of knuckling-under and accepting abuse as their opposite numbers did in the first improvisation. They are much more likely to gain the upper hand, return to their former roles and reproduce a carbon copy of the original improvisation making a nonsense of the role-reversal procedure. The only effective way of dealing with this problem is to arraign them before a superior number of children so that they are physically restrained from taking retaliatory measures by the sheer weight of numbers opposing them, thereby having to accept the same kind of abuse as they themselves were prepared to mete out to others. Does role reversal prove effective in this context? The answer must inevitably be in the negative. By forcing them to accept physically inferior roles, the teacher is only breeding resentment against the other members of the form rather than helping the children concerned to identify with those at the mercy of a wanton assault. The children holding anti-social attitudes do so from feelings of insecurity and lack of confidence; the above example will only serve to exacerbate rather than solve their problems. If placed in this position, their answers to "What did it feel like when you were the victims of football vandalism?" would be emotionally rather than rationally subjective.

Perhaps a better way of bringing home the pointlessness and futility of an act of vandalism can be achieved by means of the following scenario.

Scenario:
"He can Bleed to Death as far as we're Concerned!"

CHARACTERS A gang of vandals
Families on a housing estate
An old lady living alone

SCENE A housing estate; it is 8 p.m.

PREPARATION Those playing families go into family groups and decide upon characters. What would each be doing at this time in the evening?
1. A gang of vandals, well known in the neighbourhood, meet on a street corner, by a telephone kiosk. There is nothing to do. They are bored. They decide to break open and rob the coin box in the telephone kiosk. (Who decides this? Are they all in agreement? Does anyone try to talk the rest of them out of it? Instead, do they talk him into joining them? Or does he walk away, unwilling to be implicated?)
2. As many of the boys as possible crowd into the telephone kiosk and try to smash open the coin box, but it proves too difficult for them. They become frustrated. One of them wrenches the telephone from its connecting wires, another breaks the mirror while a third bends and twists the dial out of shape. They begin breaking the panes of glass.
3. One boy, attempting to impress the others, smashes his fist right through one of the panes of glass. A jagged piece of broken glass lacerates his arm cutting deep into a vein. Blood begins to pump out of the wound at an alarming rate. He clutches his handkerchief to the gash in an attempt to staunch the flow. The blood wells up around the edges of the handkerchief. The rest of the boys stop what they are doing and gather round him. The injured boy needs medical attention. But how to call an ambulance? The telephone is well and truly out of order.
4. Another of the boys suggests that some of the houses on the estate will have telephones. They carry the injured boy to each of the houses in turn asking if they can use the telephone. In each case they are refused, because the family concerned does not own a telephone, or because the boys have to explain what happened (or a member of the family saw them wrecking the telephone box) and the members of the family concerned are not prepared to help someone who has only himself to blame for what has happened. An old lady living on her own who has had her windows broken previously by the same gang refuses to open the door. To her, this talk of an injured boy needing hospital treatment is just an excuse to enable them to get into the house and either terrorise her or steal her savings.
How does the scene end? Does the boy literally bleed to death, or

does one of the householders relent in time to call an ambulance and save his life?

In reality, of course, the injured boy would obviously not be carried from house to house, but would be left by the telephone box in the care of a friend until help arrived. Dramatic licence has been used to avoid splitting up the group.

Role reversal is as useful in exploring areas of prejudice and intolerance as those of disobedience and disrespect. In the words of the Red Indian saying: "Let me not judge my brother until I have walked two weeks in his moccasins." Role reversal can help children to gain an understanding of, and empathy for, those against whom a parent society has erected barriers of prejudice, intolerance and suspicion. The harassment of gypsies in this country is one such example.

Before any drama work is attempted, the topic should be researched as thoroughly as time and the relevant source material obtainable will allow (*see* Bibliography, pp. 163–164).

Scenario:
The Gypsies

A number of gypsy families have recently moved on to a patch of waste ground known as Fowler's Field on the outskirts of Combringham. The local residents have complained to the council and an extraordinary council meeting has been called to discuss the problem.

CHARACTERS The chairman of the council
            Pro-gypsy members of the council
            Anti-gypsy members of the council

SCENE ONE Combringham town hall
1. The chairman tells the members of the council that he has received a number of complaints from the residents of the Albion Estate regarding the gypsies camping on Fowler's Field. What do they, as a council, propose to do about the problem?
2. A general discussion follows on the lines of the following arguments adapted from *Gypsies*, Jeremy Sandford, Secker and Warburg.

Anti-gypsy members of the council

1. These gypsies are breaking the law. The *Public Health Act* 1936, states that it is an offence to be in a tent or van "which is in such a state, or so overcrowded, as to be prejudicial to the health of the inmates." Many of the trailers on Fowler's Field are overcrowded.

2. The *Town and Country Planning Acts* 1947 and 1962 enable a local authority to forbid land to be used for a specific purpose because it is not "expedient in the interests of the proper planning of their area."

3. The *Highways Act* 1959, states that it is an offence if a gypsy "without lawful authority encamps on a highway." The *Caravan Sites and Control of Development Act* 1960, prevents a landowner from using his land as a caravan site unless he has a licence. It also enables local authorities to stop people camping on farms, commons and even their own land. Such landowners can be fined.

4. Under the *Caravan Sites Act* 1968, local authorities can provide sites for gypsies "residing in or resorting to" their area. Once a local authority has set up a site they can apply to become a designated area and fine gypsies £25 the first day and £5 every day after that that they are not on the official site.

5. Many of these Acts involve not only gypsies but also the non-gypsy caravan owner. Can one make an exception for gypsies whilst at the same time penalising the non-gypsy holiday maker?

6. Gypsies rarely licence or insure their vehicles.

7. They steal.

8. By not sending their children to school gypsy parents are breaking the law.

9. They litter the countryside with their unsightly heaps of scrap metal.

10. Gypsies should learn to conform.

11. Why should a local authority go to the expense of providing gypsies with camping sites?

Pro-gypsy members of the council

1. Overcrowding is inevitably part of the gypsy way of life. Gypsies tend to have larger families than non-gypsies and there is a limit to the size of caravan that can be pulled behind a car or lorry.

They cannot afford to buy additional vans. Boats are exempt from these Acts, more people are allowed per cubic area in a boat than they would be in a house. Why should caravans be any different from boats?

2. Showmen and circus people are exempt from these Acts. They are allowed to set up their own winter quarters. Why not gypsies?

3. Until comparatively recently gypsies have been allowed to camp on commons and by the side of the road. However, The *Commons Act*

1826, enabled local authorities to exclude gypsies from common land while The *Commons Act* 1899, allowed those non-gypsies whose right had been taken away to be compensated. Compensation should now be paid to gypsies to enable them to buy their own land while the *Caravan Site and Control of Development Act* 1960, should be amended to allow them to camp on land thus purchased.

Gypsies should have the right to camp on farmland providing they have the permission of the farmer concerned.

4. If a site is provided it should be planned with care. Many sites are completely unsuited to the gypsy way of life. Some are situated near sewer beds or rubbish tips, others do not provide facilities for the gypsies to engage in their traditional occupation of scrap-metal dealing. Some forbid outdoor fires, preventing gypsies from cooking their meals in the open air. In others the washing and toilet facilities are primitive in the extreme. Often there are restrictions on the number of dogs that can be kept on a site, and gypsies rely upon their dogs to catch the odd rabbit when funds are low. Many gypsies cannot read and therefore do not know whether they are in a designated area or not.

5. They do not knowingly break the law. Many of them cannot read or write sufficiently well to understand the procedures involved.

6. There is no evidence to suggest that the gypsy population contains a higher percentage of thieves than any other deprived section of the community. There are dishonest gypsies just as there are dishonest people in any walk of life, but it is unfair to accuse the honest majority for the misdemeanours of the few. What usually happens is that non-gypsy thieves step up their activities when there are gypsies in the area knowing full well that society will attribute the rise in the crime rate to the recent influx of travelling folk.

7. Schooling is difficult because gypsy children are always on the move. However, if winter quarters were provided, and part-time teachers made available gypsy children would be able to go to school for six months of the year.

8. Compare the damage to the countryside by non-gypsies. Gypsies assist the economy by providing industry with thousands of pounds' worth of valuable scrap metal. Local authorities should provide sites where gypsies can sort out their scrap metal hidden from public view.

9. We should allow gypsies their individuality. What right have we to ask them to conform when many non-gypsies are today questioning the values of our "rat-race" society. Society tolerates other minority groups, why should gypsies be singled out for persecution? They have a culture and way of life worth preserving.

10. They could prove an asset helping to clear away the thousands of abandoned cars that every year litter our towns and countryside.

3. The members of the council decide whether to turn a blind eye and allow the gypsies to stay on Fowler's Field, evict them by force if necessary, or provide them with an official site.

The chairman takes a vote.

If the council does decide to evict them—

The gypsies are given a twenty-four-hour eviction notice. They put up a barricade around their camping place and await further developments.

CHARACTERS   A council spokesman
             Anti-gypsy members of the council
             Gypsy leader
             Gypsies

SCENE TWO The *hatchintan* on Fowler's Field; it is evening.
1. The gypsies are sitting around an open fire on which is simmering a large tureen of *jogray*.
2. The council spokesman calls over the top of the barricade. The gypsies climb up the barricade and peer over the top. The council spokesman tells them that the twenty-four hours is up and he has come to evict them. The gypsy leader explains that one of the children is desperately ill in the local hospital and they must stay in the area in order to visit her.
3. What is the reply of the council spokesman? The gypsy explains that all they want is a piece of land, which they are willing to pay rent for, where they can break up, sort out and store their scrap metal. A place where they can come and go as they please. They are fed up with being moved on from place to place.

How does the scene end? Does the local authority allow them to stay on Fowler's Field until the child recovers, provide them with a site, or employ security men to evict them, by force if necessary?

After the first run-through, the children improvise scene Two again, the gypsies becoming members of the council and vice-versa.

Gypsy Language

This has been adapted from *Gypsies*, Jeremy Sandford, Secker & Warburg.

Chal	man.
Chavvy	child.
Chored	stolen.
Cosh	firewood.

Cushti	nice, good.
Duckering	fortune-telling.
Frashed	frightened.
Gavver	a policeman.
Gorjio	a non-gypsy.
Hatchintan	a camping place.
Hotchiwitchi	a hedgehog.
Jogray	stew.
Lifted	arrested.
Moulder	a lorry.
Mush	man, friend.
Peg	sell.
Rackley	woman or girl.
Ragging	dealing in old clothes.
Shirted	taken by the police.
Starry	prison.
Skiving	dealing in.
Tooken away	sent to prison.
Totting	dealing in scrap or junk.
Trailer	caravan pulled by motor.
Traveller	a gypsy.
Yog	an open fire.

Scenario:
The Blonde Fortress

The treatment of the coloured races in South Africa is another topic which can be explored using role-reversal techniques. The concept of apartheid, however, is so foreign to our way of thinking about race that, perhaps, we should first of all let the children explore what might happen if a similar situation occurred in this country, before moving on to events in South Africa. The colour of children's hair can provide just the parallel situation the teacher needs, especially as the length and condition of a person's hair is often an emotive subject in schools. The colour of one's hair, like the colour of one's skin, is an accident of birth over which the individual has no control. True blondes tend to be in the minority, and to place them in situations where they have considerable power over their darker-haired neighbours just because their hair is a lighter colour, effectively parallels the current situation in South Africa. If no true blondes are to be found in a class, then the children with hair of an agreed minority colouring can be selected instead. To finalise the casting, and also to give an idea of the degradation to which some coloured South Africans are subjected, these children could then inspect the hair of their own members and also of the rest of the class, rejecting members, or accepting new ones in the light of this examination.

Setting the scene

The scene is Britain sometime in the absolutely unlikely future. The government, consisting solely of blonde-haired members, has decreed that blonde-haired people are superior to those with dark hair. Most dark-haired people have been removed from the towns and cities and now live in slum conditions in overcrowded shanty towns on the outskirts. The streets are badly lit, bus services are non-existent, the crime rate soars.

Over the years a vast number of laws have been passed, enforced by a strong police force, to confirm this superiority.

A dark-haired person cannot:
1. Join an official trade union.
2. Go on strike. The penalty for doing so is a fine and three years' imprisonment.
3. Visit a public cinema without a special permit.
4. Marry a blonde-haired person.
5. Supervise blonde-haired people.
6. Vote.
7. Sit on a park bench reserved for blondes; the maximum penalty— ten strokes of the whip.
8. Hold meetings of ten or more people without permission.
9. Go anywhere without his reference book which contains his personal details. This has to be stamped by a blonde-haired employer each month. If he fails to get it stamped, he can be fined or imprisoned for a month.
10. Earn as much money as blonde-haired people who can, in some cases, earn twenty times that of a dark-haired person doing the same job. Dark-haired doctors only receive seventy per cent of the salary paid to blonde doctors. Dark-haired nurses receive only forty-five per cent of the salary paid to blonde-haired nurses.
11. Stay in a town or city for longer than seventy-two hours unless he has lived there from birth, has worked there for the same employer for fifteen years, has not been jailed for a longer period than six months, or has permission from the authorities to be there.
12. Mix with blonde-haired people in public or private places except at work and then only in a menial capacity.

The facilities for dark-haired people are always inferior to those for their blonde-haired masters. A dark-haired person cannot be carried in the same ambulance as a blonde-haired person. This could prove, quite literally, a matter of life and death in the case of an accident involving both groups.

CHARACTERS Blondes
                      Dark-haired people
                      The bus driver
                      Conductor
                      Two blonde ambulance men

PREPARATION Set out chairs creating the interior of a segregated bus: one set of seats at the front for the blondes, the other set at the back for the dark-haired people.

SCENE A segregated bus stop; interior of a segregated bus
1. The blondes queue on one side of the bus stop, the dark-haired people queue on the other.
2. A bus pulls up. The blondes get in first and sit in the seats reserved for them; the dark-haired people follow and take their seats.
3. The bus drives away. An old woman steps off the pavement right into the path of the oncoming bus. The driver swerves to avoid her and crashes into a lamp post. The passengers are flung forward out of their seats; two (one blonde- and one dark-haired female) are badly injured, the rest escape with minor cuts and bruises. One of the passengers telephones for an ambulance. In the meantime, the two groups try to do what they can for the injured.
4. While they wait for the ambulance, the dark-haired woman's condition deteriorates rapidly.
5. The ambulance arrives. The two ambulance men go straight to the blonde section of the bus. The injured blonde is carefully lifted on to a stretcher and carried to the ambulance.
6. Friends of the injured dark-haired woman beg the ambulance driver to take her with them. The ambulance driver explains that he cannot carry dark-haired people and blondes together in the same ambulance. He will come back for her later. Her friends plead with them: she desperately needs hospital treatment—delay could prove fatal. But the ambulance man is adamant. He drives away.
7. The dark-haired people go back to the injured woman. Her pulse becomes weaker.
8. Another bus arrives to take the passengers on their journey. The blondes climb aboard. The injured dark-haired woman dies. The

ambulance returns. The injured woman's friends tell the driver that she is dead.

The blonde-haired authorities have allocated one-fifth of the country to the dark-haired people and eight resettlement areas, called Homelands, have been set up in the Derbyshire Peak District, the Lincolnshire Fens, The Scottish Highlands, the North York Moors, the Lake District, Salisbury Plain, the Welsh mountains, and the moorland areas of Northumberland. Resettlement villages are in the process of being built in these areas. Accommodation is provided in two-roomed, prefabricated houses without floors or ceilings. Drainage and fresh water facilities are below standard and medical services are inefficient. Every dark-haired person has been allocated to one of these Homelands, the government's intention being to "endorse out" every dark-haired person from the blonde areas to the resettlement villages, thus creating a concentrated surplus of cheap migrant labour to be drawn upon when required. The unemployed, the redundant and their dependants, the undesirable, the idle, the recently widowed, and all those living in a dark-haired area that has been redesignated a blonde area, are being "endorsed out" of the shanty towns and resettled in the Homelands. Only those who were born in a certain area, or have worked continuously for fifteen years, or for the same employer for the past ten years in that area, are exempt. This is separate development. The two groups are parted by legislation. The dark-haired people are to set up their own communities separate from the blondes. But they are to be allowed little say in their own affairs, and none of the Homeland areas can provide enough work for the large numbers of people arriving there.

Scenario:
Endorsed Out

Cal Deriah is employed as a building worker in a blonde area. He earns twenty-five pounds a month and has a wife and four children to support. He lives in a house rented from the local authority in a shanty town just outside London.

CHARACTERS Cal Deriah, a dark-haired building worker
            Fellow workers
            A blond-haired foreman

SCENE ONE A London building site; it is a late Friday afternoon; summer
1. Cal and his fellow workers are erecting scaffolding. It is hot work and they take off their jackets, and put them to one side.
2. The foreman approaches Cal and asks him to slip across the road and bring him back an iced drink. He gives Cal the money.

CHARACTERS Cal
                 Two policemen

SCENE TWO A street
1. Cal crosses the road. Two blonde policemen approach. They stop Cal and ask to see his reference book. He tells them that he has left it in his jacket pocket on the building site just across the road. They tell him that he is committing an offence by not having it with him and that he is under arrest. Cal is taken away to the police station.
   It is a weekend. His case cannot be heard until Monday morning.

CHARACTERS Cal
                 Court officials
                 Witnesses
                 Police

SCENE THREE A courtroom
   The children should go into groups and act out Cal's trial for failing to show his reference book when asked to do so by a police officer.
   Cal is sentenced to a month's imprisonment.
   Time passes. Cal leaves prison and goes back to the building site.

CHARACTERS Cal
                 The blond foreman

SCENE FOUR The building site
1. Cal walks over to the foreman and asks for his old job back. The foreman tells him that his job has been given to someone else. He has been sacked for absenting himself from his place of work without permission. Cal tries to explain. The foreman asks him for his reference book. Cal hands it over. The foreman opens it, writes the word "sacked," and the date, across one of the pages.

CHARACTERS Lisa Deriah, Cal's wife
Cal
Dark-haired Affairs Department Official

SCENE FIVE Cal's home
1. Cal's wife is ironing. Cal returns home. He tells his wife that he is out of a job, but he will soon find another one. There is a knock at the door. Cal goes to answer it. An official from the Dark-haired Affairs Department comes in. He tells Cal that since he is unemployed he is to be evicted from his house. As his parents both came from Yorkshire (although they both died many years ago) he is to be "endorsed out" to Selehop, a resettlement village on the North York Moors. Selehop has good houses, shops and schools. Cal has three days in which to settle his affairs and leave London. Cal asks about work. The official tells him that he must apply to the labour bureau as soon as he arrives in Selehop. What is Cal's reaction to this? What does his wife say? The official leaves. Cal and Lisa discuss their plight.
2. They move to Selehop, to a damp two-roomed prefabricated house situated on high bleak moorland. Cal tries to get a labouring job on the building site, but he is informed by an official at the labour bureau that they have their full quota of workers.
3. Eventually, Cal is offered £10 a month as a cleaner in a factory thirty miles from home. Cal leaves his wife and family in Selehop and finds cheap digs nearer his work. He manages to send Lisa £8 a month for housekeeping, out of which she has to find £1·50 for the rent. Permission to go and live with her husband is refused. With four children to provide for she is hard put to make ends meet. She begins to borrow money. ...
   What happens to Cal and Lisa? The children go into groups and finish off the play in the light of their discussion.
   The situation can now be reversed, dark-haired children becoming the dominant race. Once the children have explored imaginatively the idea of an Apartheid system working within their own community they can move on through research and further improvisation to discover how such a system works out in reality in South Africa.

Bibliography

(a) GYPSIES
Marta Adler, *My Life with the Gypsies*, Souvenir Press.
Norman N. Dodds, *Didecois and Other Travellers*, Johnson Publications.
Rowena Farr, *A Time From The World*, Hutchinson.
Gratton Puxon, *On The Road*, National Council For Civil Liberties.

Jeremy Sandford, *Gypsies*, Secker & Warburg.
Olga Sinclair, *Gypsies*, Basil Blackwell.
Manfri Frederick Wood, *In The Life of a Romany Gypsy*, Routledge.
Jan Yoors, *The Gypsies*, George Allen & Unwin.
Addresses:
   Gypsy Council, 61 Blenheim Crescent, London W11.
   Journal of the Gypsy Lore Society, c/o Dora Yates, The University
   Library, Liverpool.

(b)   APARTHEID
A Place Called Dimbaza—a case study of a rural settlement township
in South Africa, Africa Publications Trust.
Colin Burnham, *Race*, B. T. Batsford.
South Africa: Apartheid Quiz, Christian Action Publications.
Trevor Huddleston, *Naught For Your Comfort*, Collins.
Bloke Modisane, *Blame Me On History*, Thames & Hudson.
Barbara Rogers, *The Bantu Homelands*, An International Defence and
Aid Fund Pamphlet.
A. Sachs, *South Africa: The Violence of Apartheid*, An International
Defence and Aid Fund Pamphlet.
South Africa: "Resettlement"—The New Violence to Africans, An Inter-
national Defence and Aid Fund Pamphlet.
A Crime Against Humanity, United Nations.
Apartheid in Practice, United Nations.
Addresses:
   International Defence and Aid Fund, 104/5 Newgate Street, Lon-
   don EC1A 7AP.
   The Africa Publications Trust, 48 Grafton Way, London W1P 5LB.
   The Anti-Apartheid Movement, 89 Charlotte Street, London W1P
   2DQ.

CHAPTER 9

ROSLA DRAMA:
Scenarios for the
Fifth-Year Leaver

The Generation Gap

CHARACTERS Susan
Her mother, father and grandmother
Other members of her family as required

SCENE ONE Susan's bedroom
1. Susan is sitting on the bed listening to a pop record played at full volume.
2. Her father comes in. He complains about the noise. He has had a hard day at work and all he wants now is peace and quiet. They argue. Susan tells him that she has just bought the record and wants to listen to it. He asks her to turn down the volume; she tells him she cannot get the true effect unless it is played with the sound full on. He threatens to pull out the plug if she does not turn it down. She refuses.
3. He pulls out the plug and storms out of the room.

SCENE TWO The lounge
1. Susan's grandmother is sitting on the settee. Susan's mother comes in and joins her. This is the first time she has sat down all day. Grandmother tells her that she should get Susan to help her. Mother explains that if she did, it would only lead to a row. Grandmother says that she shouldn't have to argue with Susan, she should tell her. Mother replies that this is easier said than done. Grandmother complains that Susan has never been the same since she started work at the factory. Her clothes . . . (grandmother makes up a list of complaints about Susan. "Now in my day . . .". Mother explains that times are no longer what they were. Grandmother says that Susan needs her backside tanned.

2. Susan comes in and catches the end of the conversation. Grandmother criticises Susan, who argues back. Mother intervenes and tells Susan not to talk to her grandmother like that.

3. Susan proudly announces that she has just been awarded a two pound a week pay rise. "In that case," says grandmother, "you can afford to pay a bit more towards your keep." Susan replies that she needs the extra money to buy clothes and records. Grandmother asks why she needs any more clothes, she has a wardrobe full as it is. Grandmother says that she will tell Susan's father about her refusal to pay more towards her keep. Her mother begs grandmother not to tell him.

4. Susan walks out in disgust.

SCENE THREE The lounge. Later that evening

1. Susan's father is watching a football match on the television. Grandmother is bored. She would have preferred to watch *Come Dancing* on the other channel.

2. A shot of the crowd shows a scuffle breaking out between two rival groups of youths. Father complains that as usual the fighting is caused by teenage hooligans with more money than sense.

3. This gives grandmother the opportunity she has been waiting for. She tells him about Susan's pay rise.

4. Susan's mother comes into the room. Father asks why he was not told before about Susan's rise. Mother tells him that he always flies off the handle whenever anything to do with Susan is mentioned. Father complains that he does not like hearing things about his daughter "at second hand."

5. Susan now comes in and asks her mother if she has ironed her skirt. She wants to wear it tonight to meet Barry, her boyfriend. Mother says that she is very sorry but she forgot all about it. She will iron it right away.

6. Father tells Susan that she is to give her two pound rise to her mother. They have both made sacrifices to bring her up decently; now it is her turn.

7. Susan says that she is fed up. She can't play her records; they don't like her boyfriends; she can't wear the clothes she wants; her grandmother is always complaining....

8. Father replies that if she doesn't like living at home, she knows what she can do. Susan goes out, slamming the door behind her.

How does the scenario end? Does Susan leave home? If so, where does she go? Does she find a room of her own, or stay with friends? Are conditions there better or worse than at home? Do circumstances force her to return home? If so, does the situation there improve? How can this family learn to live together amicably? How much give and take should there be across the generation gap?

Illegitimacy

In preparation the class should read *A Kind of Loving* by Stan Barstow. The following problems should be discussed and considered. What would you do if you discovered that you were going to be the mother/father of an illegitimate child? What would you say to your mother and father? What do you think they might say to you? Would you marry the mother/father? If your feelings towards her/him changed in the meantime, would you still want to get married?

CHARACTERS Girl's mother and father
            Other members of her family
            The girl and boy

SCENE The girl's house
1. The girl's family are watching television.
2. The girl and boy walk up to the door. They pause outside. She is seventeen and has discovered that she is going to have his child. They discuss what they will say.
3. They go into the house. The family make room for them, and they watch television.
4. Suddenly her father says, "What's wrong with you, girl, you look as if you've been crying?"
Complete the scenario in the light of class discussion.

Drugs

Caution must be exercised when dramatising aspects of drug abuse with children. Many teachers feel that by giving the subject unwarranted attention in the classroom, one is encouraging an unhealthy interest in it which may in turn lead to experimentation on the children's part where no such interest existed before. But to ignore the problem in the hope that it will go away is no answer to a younger generation eager for the facts. It is better that they learn the dangers of drug abuse within the controlled situation of the drama workshop than from the more titillating literature on the subject that is widely available; always providing that the teachers takes them beyond the glamorously defiant façade of experiences of a shared nirvana to show what can and sometimes does happen to people when they seek a solution to life's problems through chemical crutches.

Before any drama work is undertaken, children should be given an opportunity of researching the drug problem in depth (*see* Bibliography, p. 184). A superficial approach will do more harm than good. There can be no place for instant drama, and frivolity must be discouraged at all costs. Better to turn to a less harmful topic than give children the impression that the taking of hard drugs is fun. Impressions gained in educational drama are much more difficult to erase than those gained through more conventional channels.

Drugs are divided into two categories: the non-addictive (soft drugs) and the addictive (hard drugs). With non-addictive drugs the dependence is purely psychological, whereas addictive drugs produce tolerance, *i.e.* the addict needs larger and larger doses to satisfy his craving, and if the dosage is withheld, withdrawal symptoms develop.

Soft drugs

Cannabis is an example of a soft drug. Possible arguments used to persuade a novice to try cannabis might include the following:
1. Cannabis is non-addictive. It will not damage your health.
2. You're chicken if you don't try it.
3. It helps you to forget your troubles, gives you a feeling of well-being and heightens your sense of appreciation.
4. The chances of being criminally convicted are very small indeed.
5. Most cannabis users do not become heroin addicts.
   To which the following reasons for refusal might be given:
1. Because of the large profits involved, a supply of cannabis may be adulterated with other substances; consequently, you can never be sure of the strength of the dose. Cocaine, a much more dangerous drug, is sometimes added.
2. Sense impressions are altered by taking cannabis; it becomes extremely dangerous, for instance, to drive a car.
3. It might lead on to experiments with heroin.
4. It is illegal. Under the *Misuse of Drugs Act* 1971, the maximum penalty on indictment for the illegal possession of cannabis is five years' imprisonment, or a fine, or both.

Hard drugs

"Heroin is my shepherd, I shall always want." Heroin is an example of a hard drug. It takes time to become addicted. A potential addict has to overcome the queasiness that he experiences when first injecting himself with a hypodermic needle, the feelings of nausea, and the expense involved in buying larger and larger quantities of the drug to satisfy his needs.

The more heroin the addict takes, the more he builds up a

tolerance, until his body cannot function without it. The addict begins with a small dose of one-sixth of a grain—a mature dose would kill the beginner—dissolved in water and injected into the arm between the muscles. This is called "joy-popping," as the skin makes a slight popping noise as the needle is inserted. Before becoming addicted the drug-taker flatters himself that he can kick the habit any time he wants to. But soon he finds that joy-popping is not enough. He takes larger and larger doses, and still he needs more. Until one day he ties a length of cloth around his upper arm and injects the needle straight into a vein—the word for this is "mainlining." From now on he is hooked.

But the effects of mainlining, though dramatic, soon wear off and the addict has to inject himself several times a day, or withdrawal symptoms will develop. He has now become a slave to the drug. Heroin, in itself, is less harmful to the human body than alcohol, unless an addict is deprived of his supply. The danger lies in the way an addict neglects himself, once the passion for the drug becomes established. Living in filth and squalor, the addict will lie, steal, cheat, neglect home, family, work, to get his supplies. Anaesthetised against pain, addicts use unsterile needles, dissolving the white powder in water often obtained from public lavatories. And there is always the very real danger of taking an overdose, especially after a period of abstinence, for example, on release from prison.

The addict lives in a half-waking, half-sleeping state. Tough scar tissue caused by the use of blunt equipment forms on the skin, and he has to find fresh places to inject. A line of discoloured needle marks down the arm and on to the back of the hand is his badge. After repeated injections the veins collapse and are difficult to hit. Boils and abscesses form through neglect of personal hygiene. Injecting himself every hour or so, he eventually becomes a walking zombie, capable even of choking to death in his own vomit.

Drugs are not the answer. The more reliance one places upon drugs, the more difficult it is to face up to the underlying problems that caused the addiction in the first place. But no explanation has yet been found for why certain young people sometimes become addicted to hard drugs.

Possible reasons why

1. They don't believe they can become addicted.
2. They are the victims of a broken or unhappy home. Addicts are obsessed by family relationships and their jargon reflects this: a pusher is called "mother", a man is "daddy" and a girl is called "baby."

They are separated from their parents, unhappy, or in trouble, and have no one to turn to. Heroin seems to offer a way of escape.

3. Some male addicts feel that heroin sorts out the men from the boys: by taking heroin they are proving their masculinity.

4. Curiosity.

5. As a form of rebellion.

6. To find "heaven" on earth.

7. A way of opting out of society.

The following scenario takes the second of the above reasons as its starting point. The main character could, of course, be a boy, instead of a girl, and the scenario altered accordingly. To provide motivation, the class could discuss why a husband and wife might seek a separation.

SCENE ONE Jean's home
CHARACTERS Jean
             Her mother and father

1. Jean's mother is cooking the dinner. Her father comes back from work. Mother and father begin to quarrel, and bitter words are spoken. (The class should make up their own reasons for the quarrel based on their initial discussion.)

2. Jean comes in. What is her reaction on finding her parents quarrelling? Does she adopt a blasé attitude because such arguments between her parents are a commonplace occurrence? Or is she shocked because, up to this moment, her parents have rarely said an unkind word to each other? Does she take part, siding either with her mother or father, or does she remain impartial? Does she stay and try to bring the argument to an end, or does she slip away to her own room?

SCENE TWO Next evening
CHARACTERS Jean
             Bill, her boyfriend

The class goes into pairs, a girl and a boy in each pair. The girl plays the part of Jean, the boy plays the part of her boyfriend, Bill. Jean has been going out with him for the past six months. This evening, he has arranged to go with her to the cinema, but when they meet he tells her that he does not want to see her again.

Why is this, Bill?

An argument breaks out. He walks away, leaving her crying.

If there are more girls than boys, a friend could bring Jean a message from Bill that he does not want to see her again.

SCENE THREE Outside the cinema
CHARACTERS Jean
               Dave

Jean is crying. A boy, Dave, walks over to her and asks what is wrong. She tells him that her parents have split up and now her boy-friend has walked out on her. Dave tries to cheer her up. He is going to a party and invites her to come along too. They go off together.

CHARACTERS Jean
               Dave
               Jabs, a heroin addict
               Other young people

SCENE FOUR At the party; the music is "Walking in Space" from *Hair*

1. A group of young people are sitting or lying down smoking cannabis. One or two are dancing in a corner. Their talk is full of the language used by drug-takers
2. Dave and Jean join the party. He introduces her. One of the young people offers her a reefer. She refuses, giving her reasons. The rest of the group crowd round trying to persuade her to smoke it. (*See* p. 168 for the arguments that she and they might use.)
3. Jean at last accepts the reefer and smokes it. She begins to talk like the others. Dave introduces her to Jabs, a heroin addict. Jabs asks her to dance. They get on well together. By this time most of the group have fallen asleep. The party breaks up, and she goes off with Jabs.

CHARACTERS Jean
               Jabs

SCENE FIVE Jabs' flat

Jabs and Jean are sitting on the floor. She has left home and moved in with him. He has introduced her to heroin and she has begun joy-popping. Now he tells her that joy-popping is for kids. He has something that will really turn her on and make her forget her troubles. He asks her to roll up her sleeve, straps a belt round her arm, and with a hypodermic needle injects a shot of heroin straight into a vein. He takes off the belt and says that she will know what it is to live for the first time. He will give her another fix tomorrow.

SCENE SIX

CHARACTERS Jean
              Other characters as required

Jean is hooked on heroin. Following a police raid, Jabs has been arrested and sentenced to a year's imprisonment for selling cannabis. Left on her own she finds it extremely difficult to obtain an adequate supply of drugs. She has no will to work, and obtains money to "feed the monkey" by stealing from her mother's purse, begging in the streets, breaking and entering.

The class goes into groups to make up a scene showing one way in which she tries to make money.

CHARACTERS Jean
              Other characters as required

SCENE SEVEN

Almost at the end of her tether, Jean has accepted hospital treatment, has been discharged from hospital and gone back home. Her parents have come together again, united by their concern for her. Now she meets one of her old associates who sells her a quantity of heroin. In the evening, while her parents are out at the cinema, she takes a dose that turns out to be fatal.

CHARACTERS Jean
              Her mother and father

SCENE EIGHT Jean's home

1. Jean's mother and father return from the cinema. They talk about the film as they take off their coats. Mother wonders where Jean is. Father sits down to read the newspaper. "I expect she's gone to bed." "It's not like her to go to bed so early," worries mother.

2. Mother calls upstairs. No answer. She goes up to Jean's room and knocks on the door. Still no answer. She pushes open the door. Jean is lying on the floor. Mother bends over her. She is dead. Mother calls her husband. He bends down and picks up the empty syringe.
3. He goes down and telephones for a doctor. As they wait, they discuss what went wrong.

Crime

CHARACTERS Bugsy, the leader of the gang
Members of the gang
Philip Johnson

SCENE ONE A transport café just off a motorway, the time is 10.30 p.m.

1. The members of the gang are sitting round a table drinking coffee, discussing their motorbikes and telling stories of ton-ups down the motorway.
2. Philip Johnson joins them. To the rest of the gang he is something of an outsider. He tells them that he has just bought a new motorbike. He describes it to them. They make sarcastic comments. He tells them that his is the faster machine. They invite him outside to prove it.
3. Outside, they compare motorbikes. Bugsy challenges Philip to a race down the motorway. One of the gang notices that Philip's bike needs some air in the tyres. They decide to go to the nearest garage for air and to fill up with petrol before the race.

CHARACTERS Philip
Bugsy and members of the gang
The petrol pump attendant
Two policemen

SCENE TWO A garage forecourt, sound effect of motorbike engines being switched off

1. The members of the gang walk over to the office. An elderly attendant is on duty. Bugsy refers to him as grandad and asks him to fill up their tanks.
2. The attendant takes exception to Bugsy's attitude and objects to being called grandad. He tells them that it is eleven o'clock and he is closing the garage. They will have to get their petrol elsewhere. Bugsy argues with him. The attendant threatens to call the police.

Bugsy becomes annoyed. One of the gang suggests that they help themselves to petrol; the rest agree. Philip stands to one side taking no part in the events that follow.

3. While Bugsy keeps the old man penned in a corner of the office, the rest of the gang help themselves to petrol. The girls go into the kiosk and take sweets, tights, cigarettes and money.

4. After filling up their tanks, the boys open some tins of oil and pour the contents over the forecourt roadway.

5. The old man angrily tries to push his way past Bugsy. Bugsy hits him, knocking him to the floor.

6. One of the gang warns the others of the approach of a patrol car. There is a dash for the motorbikes. Philip slips on a patch of oil and falls. The others race off down the motorway. The patrol car pulls into the forecourt; two policemen get out and lay hold of Philip.

7. The old man staggers out of the office and tells the policemen what has happened. One policeman stays and questions Philip, the other drives off in pursuit of the gang. They avoid capture and Philip is left to face the consequences.

CHARACTERS A police officer
A policeman
Philip Johnson

SCENE THREE The interview room in a police station

1. A police officer is sitting at a desk. He asks the policeman to bring Philip in.

2. Philip is escorted in. The officer asks him for his side of the story. Philip tells him, but refuses to name his associates. He says that he met them in a coffee bar but does not know their names.

3. The officer tells Philip that he will take the blame if he doesn't give the names of the others. Philip refuses.

4. The officer takes a statement. Philip signs it and is led away.

An Industrial Dispute

SCENE ONE Amard's Timber Mill (*see* Fig. 10); sound effect of factory noises

PREPARATION Set out chairs and tables to represent factory floor

CHARACTERS   Three sawdust balers
             A stacker
             Circular saw operators
             Girls making packing cases
             Men supplying girls with wood for packing cases

1. The circular saw operators are cutting lengths of timber which are supplied to the girls who nail the pieces together to make packing cases. The sawdust created is sucked through pipes and deposited into a hopper above the baler. One man operates a slider situated just under the hopper which controls the supply of sawdust to the baler. The sawdust in the hopper must not be allowed to rise above a specified level indicated on a gauge which is just above the slider; otherwise, the hopper will become choked with sawdust, cutting off the supply to the baler. Should this happen, the baler has to be switched off and the hopper cleared by hand (*see* Fig. 11).

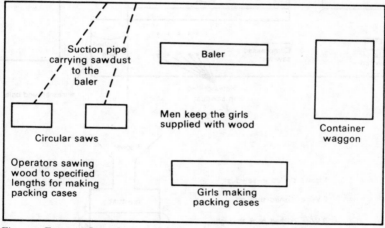

Fig. 10. Factory floorplan.

2. A man on one side of the baler drills a hole through the compressed sawdust as it moves through the baler. A man on the other side threads a length of wire through the hole. The first man drills a second hole and pushes the wire back through the compressed sawdust. The man on the side fastens the two lengths of wire together; another hole is drilled and another length of wire is threaded through. Bales of sawdust emerge from the baler and another man stacks them in a container waggon. Each waggon holds 1500 bales. The men are on piece-work rates. All the workers at Amard's are members of the Amalgamated Woodworkers Union.

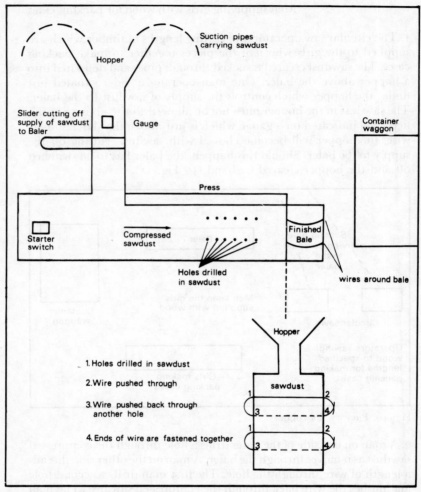

Fig. 11. Factory machinery.

SCENE TWO An office. A meeting of the Joint Negotiating Council

CHARACTERS Shop steward
Works manager
Industrial relations officer
Local official of Amalgamated Woodworkers' Union

1. Management and union representatives are sitting round a table.
2. The local official of the AWU explains that shop stewards at a union branch meeting have voted for an increase of tenpence an hour on their basic wages.
3. The shop steward gives his reasons for the wage claim.

> What are they, shop steward? Increased cost of living? Do you consider that the work is dangerous and merits the payment of danger-money? Have you increased your productivity recently? Are you asking for the rise to bring you into line with other workers in the timber industry? Did the firm make a large profit last year? Or is it a combination of reasons?

4. The works manager rejects the wage claim and gives his reasons.

> What are they, works manager? Have you recently granted a substantial wage increase? Were your profits down last year, so that you cannot afford to increase wages at the present time? Do you have a wage agreement with the union which still has some time to run? Do you agree to review the situation at a later date?

5. The meeting ends with the local official telling the management that he will put their objections to the next branch meeting. The shop steward says he will inform the men of their decision.

SCENE THREE The shop floor, Amard's Timber Mill; some time later

CHARACTERS As in Scene One

1. A group of girls finish off a packing case and find they haven't enough wood to start another. They tell the men supplying the wood to get a move on. The men explain that they are short-staffed, but doing their best. The foreman walks over and asks the girls the reason

for the hold-up. The girls say that the delay is due to the men not delivering the wood quickly enough. The men supplying the wood complain that they are short-staffed. The foreman says he will get someone else to help them.

2. He walks over to the baler and tells the man operating the slider that he is to go and help keep the girls supplied with wood. The man on the drill will have to do both jobs. The driller complains that it is as much as he can do to keep up with the drilling, let alone operate the slider as well. The foreman says he will have to manage as best he can. The man operating the slider goes to help the girls. The supply of wood begins again and the girls start work on another packing case.

3. The driller now has to work twice as hard: drilling a hole, pulling through a length of wire, drilling a further hole, pushing the wire back, operating the slider to let through a further supply of sawdust ... drilling, wiring, cutting off the supply of sawdust, drilling, wiring, letting more sawdust through; until finally it becomes too much for him. The sawdust level on the gauge rises above danger, the hopper becomes choked, and he has to switch off the baler. The foreman complains about the stoppage. Sawdust begins to pile up around the operators making sawing difficult. The balers are required to load two container vans a day; with the stoppage they will be lucky if they manage to load one. The man on the drill complains that he cannot possibly do two jobs at once. He asks the man stacking the container waggon to go for the shop steward. The other workers gather round, siding with the driller. He cannot possibly do two jobs at once. The firm will have to employ more men.

4. The shop steward arrives. The driller explains the situation to him. The shop steward asks the foreman to put the slider operator back on the baling machine. The foreman explains that he is needed to keep the girls supplied with wood. The shop steward asks the foreman to find someone else to help the girls. The foreman says there is no one else; they are short-staffed enough as it is. In that case, explains the shop steward, the men will down tools until the management come up with a satisfactory solution. The foreman says that he has no right to call a "downer;" there are procedures laid down between management and union. If they cannot agree, they are to take the matter up with the convenor; if they get no satisfaction from him, they discuss the problem with the works manager; and if he offers no solution, then the matter goes before the union.

5. The shop steward ignores his advice and leads the men off the shop floor.

CHARACTERS Shop steward
                      Local official of AWU
                      Workers
SCENE FOUR Amard's works canteen; lunchtime

1. The shop steward explains to the rest of the workers why they have downed tools.
2. One of the workers suggests that they should make this an opportunity for pushing their tenpence an hour wage claim. If their claim is refused then the whole factory should come out on strike. There are shouts of agreement from the crowd. Another worker suggests that, instead of asking for tenpence an hour, they should ask for an extra six pounds a week. Most of the workers agree. A moderate calls for a token one-day stoppage and a banning of overtime. Another warns of the difficulties of organising a strike without union backing. But they are shouted down. The shop steward tells them that, unless they are prepared to make a stand, the management will think they are weak and begin sacking the militants. If there is to be a strike, there must be one hundred per cent support. Once they are out on strike, it will only be a matter of time before they get union backing.
3. The shop steward puts it to the vote: "All those in favour of coming out on strike unless the management agree to an extra six pounds a week, please show." Those in favour raise their hands. "All those against, please show." Those against raise their hands. The vote is overwhelmingly in favour of strike action. The shop steward says he will put their proposal to the management.

> You can show his meeting with the management, or continue with the meeting in the canteen. The shop steward could walk out of the room at this point and then walk straight back in again to create the effect of the passing of time.

4. The shop steward tells the workers that the management have refused their demands. The local official of the AWU, who has just arrived in the factory, would like to talk to them. The union official tells them they must play it straight. They have the Joint Negotiating Council for negotiating wage claims. "And a fat lot of good it's done us so far," yells one of the men. The rest clap and cheer. The union official says that if they go out on strike, they will not have union backing, and will find it exceedingly difficult to reach a settlement without the help of the union. If there is going to be a strike, he is the person to call the men out, not the shop steward. There must be no "wildcatting." The steward asks him if he is going to lead the men

out, or follow on behind. "Whose side are you on, anyway?" he asks. The men begin to chant "Off! Off! Off!" The union official leaves.
5. The shop steward asks "all those in favour of calling a strike, please show." Every hand goes up. The shop steward leads the workers out of the factory.
6. A strike committee is formed.

The first week of the strike

Knowing that the men do not have the support of the union, the management send each worker a dismissal notice and his cards. An accompanying letter informs him that he will have the opportunity of re-applying for his job when the strike is eventually called off. A man who is re-employed loses all the privileges and seniority gained during his previous time with the firm.

The National Joint Negotiating Council recommends a return to work pending negotiations. The management refuses to negotiate until each individual member has been re-employed. Jobs will be available, the workers are informed, but not necessarily the same jobs as they were doing before the strike.

CHARACTERS   Picket leader
                     Picket members
                     Lorry driver
                     Police
                     Workers

SCENE FIVE Outside the factory gates; the time is 4.45 p.m.

1. Pickets are standing outside the factory gates. A group of policemen are close by.
2. A lorry with a consignment of timber draws up outside the gates. The men on picket duty walk over to the cab. They tell the driver about the strike and ask him not to deliver his load. He agrees and drives away. He comes back, after telephoning the management for advice. They have told him that the strike is unofficial.

      What do you do, driver?

3. Night-shift employees, who have returned to work, approach the gates. The members of the picket line up on each side of the roadway.

The police move in front of them, protecting the workers as they go towards the factory. The members on the picket line jeer and call out "Scabs! Blacklegs!" and other insults. A worker insults a picket member back. The man concerned pushes his way through the police line and attacks the worker. Some police move in and the attacker is dragged off. The attacked worker tells the men on picket duty that they are supposed to win support through reasoned argument, not with violence. He will never join them now, and will do all in his power to persuade those on strike to seek re-employment with the firm. The workers proceed into the factory without further mishap.
4. Those on day-shift who have continued to work are seen coming out of the factory. The members of the picket stand across their way, refusing to let them go home. The picket leader says they will only be allowed home if they promise not to turn up for work the next day.

> What happens, workers? Do you agree? Do you sit it out? Do the police intervene? Or do you try to rush the picket line?

The third week of the strike

The management sends each worker a letter, offering a two pound a week pay rise for those who seek re-employment. The management point out that by striking they have broken the procedural agreement between the management and their union. By placing their job security at risk, the strike is damaging the workers more than the firm. The members of the strike committee feel that the firm is weakening and that by holding out long enough they will achieve their original demand.

CHARACTERS Shop steward
National industrial officer of AWU
Members of strike committee
Workers

SCENE SIX A local football ground

1. The shop steward asks the workers if they are prepared to accept

the offer of two more pounds a week from the firm. Voices in the crowd yell back "No!"

2. The shop steward introduces the national industrial officer of the AWU. He appeals to the men to return to work. The union cannot support their action; it is unconstitutional and in violation of the procedures laid down. The only course open to them is to seek re-employment and accept the firm's pay offer. He says that the management will not pay a penny more. A voice from the crowd asks why the union is not supporting them. They are all union members. It should be the union's job to support its members.

3. Well-organised groups, knowing when to heckle and when to applaud, have spread themselves out among the crowd. They begin to chant "Out! Out! Out!" A group of workers by the platform drag the union officer from the stand.

4. The shop steward asks all those in favour of continuing the strike to please show. Those in favour raise their hands. "All those against, please show." There is a unanimous decision to stay out.

5. The shop steward tells them that the strike is proving expensive (postage, telephone calls, etc.). They need more money. He appeals for funds. Members of the strike committee move among the crowd collecting the donations.

6. They decide not to meet for another three weeks. One of the workers shouts back, "Let's leave it till after Christmas."

7. They carry the chairman of the strike committee off shoulder high, singing "For he's a jolly good fellow."

The fourth week of the strike

The firm asks the strikers to remove their pickets from the factory gates and let the workers decide for themselves whether they want to continue the strike or not.

The fifth week of the strike

The strike committee appeal for financial support from other unions.

CHARACTERS   Two members of strike committee
Building workers' shop steward
Building workers

SCENE SEVEN A building site

1. A group of building workers and their shop steward are sitting down to a tea-break.
2. The two members of the strike committee join them. They ask to speak to the shop steward. The shop steward introduces himself. They take him to one side and explain that they are from Amard's, and would like to make an appeal. He gives them his permission to speak to his men.
3. The shop steward introduces them to the building workers. "These lads are from Amard's. They want to talk to you, so give them some order." A building worker offers them some tea.
4. The two explain the reason for the strike at Amard's and say why they are asking for an extra six pounds a week.
5. Some of the building workers ask them questions. "Your strike isn't official, is it? Why not?"

How do you answer, strike committee members?

6. "Well, what do you want to do, lads?" asks the shop steward. A building worker moves that they help their brothers from Amard's.
7. A collection is taken. The building workers go back to work. The strikers go off to make further collections in the area.

The sixth week of the strike

The firm notifies the workers that if the strike continues, they will not be able to re-employ as many workers as they had hoped. The strikers are now beginning to feel the effects of six weeks' living off social security, tax rebates and hardship allowances. Families usually live at the standard they can afford. What happens to mortgage repayments, rent, house-keeping, hire-purchase commitments etc. when the weekly pay packet stops coming in? Consider a man earning £30 a week. On strike his money would drop to £13 consisting of £5 strike pay (if the strike has union backing), £3·50 social security, plus £4·50 tax rebate paid out by the company during the first eight weeks of the strike. After that, his money would be down to £8·50. (These are the figures for 1971. The class should find out the most recent entitlements.) It will take many months at the new rate, if the firm agrees to pay the increase, for a man to recoup the wages he has lost during the strike.

SCENE EIGHT

The class goes into groups representing a family in which the father, the only wage earner, is on strike at Amard's. He has a wife and a teenage child, still at school. What happens to the family, as the financial effects of the strike begin to hit home? Does the wife, worried that her husband may not be re-employed when the strike ends, try to persuade him to go back to work? Are they forced to break into their holiday savings? Does the wife have to take a part-time job to try to make ends meet?

———————————————

How does the strike at Amard's end?

1. Does a secret ballot, organised jointly by Amard's and the union, show that a majority of the men are willing to return to work on the firm's conditions? Does the union take a hand in some other way to organise a return to work?

2. Who can hold out longest, the management or the workers? Does financial hardship bring an end to the dispute, after the eighth week sees the end of the tax rebates? Has the firm lost many orders? Are sufficient men back at work to keep the factory ticking over?

3. Does the firm agree to the men's conditions and grant the six pound a week increase they have been asking for? When the strike is over, what concessions, if any, do the men get from the firm? What concessions, if any, does the firm get from the men?

4. Are the men reinstated or do they have to seek re-employment? Do they all get their old jobs back, or do they find that the best jobs have been given to those workers who did not support the strike? Are some men faced with redundancy? Does the shop steward go back, or does he seek employment elsewhere, believing that he would be down-graded or suffer loss of face in the eyes of the men?

Complete the scenario in the light of class discussion.

Bibliography

Books

Drugs

Anonymous, *Go Ask Alice*, Eyre Methuen.
Alan Bestic, *Turn Me On Man*, Anthony Gibbs.
George Birdwood, *The Willing Victim*, Secker & Warburg.

Max Glatt and others, *The Drug Scene in Great Britain*, Edward Arnold.
Jeremy Larner and Ralp Tefferteller, *The Addict in the Street*, Penguin Books.
Peter Laurie, *Drugs: Medical, Psychological and Social Facts*, Penguin Books.
Michael Schofield, *The Strange Case of Pot*, Pelican Books.
Dan Wakefield (ed.), *The Addict*, Gold Medal Books.
Dr. J. D. Wright, *About Drugs*, Available from Project About Drugs.

Trade Unionism

Tony Corfield and Ellen McCullough, *Trade Union Branch Officers' Manual*, Chapman & Hall Ltd.
George Cyriax and Robert Oakeshott, *The Bargainers*, A Survey of Modern Trade Unionism, Faber & Faber.
J. E. T. Eldridge, *Industrial Disputes*, Routledge & Kegan Paul.
Tony Lane and Kenneth Roberts, *Strike at Pilkingtons*, Fontana.
P. Marsh, *The Anatomy of a Strike*, The Institute of Race Relations.
John Matthews, *Ford Strike, The Workers' Story*, Panther Books.

Films and Other Source Material

Drugs

Accidents. This film shows the difficulties which can be experienced in breaking a drug habit after an accident.

The Addict Alone. A man talks about his heroin addiction.

David. David is a musician and a drug addict. The film shows him entering Syanon, a unique cure centre in the U.S.A. and shows the struggle to cure him and how he nearly leaves because he feels he cannot go through with the cure.

Drugs and The Nervous System. Explains how drugs affect the body, in particular the serious disruption of the nervous system caused by narcotics and substances taken for "kicks."

Fixed for Death. Drug addiction relating mainly to the under-twenties. Shows group discussion with registered addicts and their apathy and disgust; the effects on an addict's family. Designed for those over fifteen.

Gale is Dead. Gale became a drug addict and died by an overdose at nineteen. This BBC "Man Alive" programme asks if Gale need have died and tries to show there may be other Gales it is not too late to help.

Half A Lifetime. Shows the sordid and hopeless life of a confirmed drug addict. Thames Television.

Hooked. American youths talk freely about their experiences in drug-taking.

Narcotics: The Decision. A factual film showing how personal stress leads a teenage girl to seek refuge in tobacco, alcohol then barbiturates. At this point "hooked" companions introduce the use of marijuana and heroin. The teenager drifts into compulsive addiction and eventually arrives helplessly at the end of hope.

One Way Ticket. Dramatised documentary on drugs in modern society. Discusses the more important effects of cannabis, LSD, amphetamines, barbiturates and, to a lesser extent, heroin.

Phoenix House. A drug addiction centre in South London run by ex-addicts on a strict hierarchical basis. A record of one method of treating drug addiction. Thames Television Report Programme.

These are available from The Scottish Film Office.

Sources of Information

Association for the Prevention of Addiction, 33 Long Acre, London WC2E 9LA.

British Temperance Society, Stanborough Park, Watford, Herts, WD2 6JP.

Concord Films Council, Nacton, Ipswich, Suffolk.

Health Education Council Ltd., Middlesex House, Ealing Road, Wembley, Middlesex HAO 1HH.

Home Office Drugs Branch, Romney House, Marsham Street, London, SW1.

International Temperance Society, St. Peter's Street, St. Albans, Herts.

Medical Recording Service, Kitts Croft, Writtle, Chelmsford, Essex.

Project About Drugs, 12 Waterdale, Compton, Wolverhampton, WV3 9DY.

Scottish Film Office, 16–17 Woodside Terrace, Charing Cross, Glasgow G3 7XN.

Scottish Health Education Unit, Health Education Centre, 21 Landsdowne Crescent, Edinburgh EH12 5EH.

Tape Recordings

Drug Dependence—Are GP's on the Alert. Drug Dependence—Recent Developments in Great Britain.

Drugs in School.
A Junkie Talks.
Social Work in Relation to Drug Abuse.
Why Smoke Pot.
   These are available from the Medical Recording Service.

Film Strips

Drug Dependence, from Camera Talks Ltd., 31 North Row, Park Lane, W1R 2EN.
The Drug Problem: *LSD and Marijuana*, from Concordia Publishing House Ltd., 117–123 Golden Lane, London EC1.
Drugs in Our Society, Concordia Publishing House Ltd.
Drugs and Health, available from Encyclopaedia Britannica Int. Ltd., Dorland House, 18–20 Regent Street, London SW1.

Trade Unionism

Management and Multi-Unionism, Black and white, 25 mins.
Redundancy Agreement, Black and white, 25 mins.
Procedure Agreement, Black and white, 25 mins.
The Shop Steward's Role, Black and white, 25 mins.
The Supervisor's Role, Black and white, 25 mins.
   Available from BBC Enterprises Film Hire, 25, The Burroughs, Hendon, London NW4.

CHAPTER 10

CONCLUSION

How does one recognise good work in educational drama? This is often the question asked by outsiders. Other teachers have their yardsticks for measuring children's work and comparisons are readily available in the numerous books and publications which have appeared in recent years containing examples of children's art work and creative writing, while innumerable records have been made of children singing. All of these enable teachers of these subjects, if they so desire, to compare and contrast published material with the standards achieved by their own pupils. Unfortunately, neither the printed page nor the gramophone record can supply examples of the standards one can achieve in educational drama.

If the aim of educational drama is to help children to gain a fuller understanding of themselves and the world in which they live, and to grow in that knowledge, then external expression, in a theatrical sense, is of secondary importance. The question a drama teacher should always ask himself is not: "Is it good theatre?" but, "What are the children gaining from the experience?" For example, one class, from a theatrical point of view, might be considered good at drama, but in reality is learning virtually nothing—most children are capable of turning on a role just like a tap, but in educational terms there is little value to be gained from instant drama of that kind. A class which does not appear, on the surface, to be producing much that is viable in a theatrical sense, may be learning far more from the experience than the external showing would seem to indicate. But the fact that a subjective learning process is taking place should not blind the teacher into accepting slipshod work. Which brings us back to the question of a dramatic yardstick. An excellent BBC Enterprises film *Improvised Drama* helps bridge this gap, but many more films of this type are needed, enabling teachers to see examples of the best child drama available. But capturing a good educational drama lesson on film can prove to be a capricious undertaking, one can never be certain whether the results will justify the expense involved. A child, unlike a professional actor, is not trained to analyse and thus recapture at will the best of which he is capable. Good work in drama depends on so many imponderables: the choice of material, the stimuli, distraction both inside and outside the classroom, the time of day, the time of year, the children's relationship with their previous teacher, their current relationship with the headmaster, in fact, their attitude to the school in general. All these factors serve to assist or hinder the dramatic process.

"Great" child drama is rare, but when all the elements necessary come together in their due proportions, the effect is overpowering. One of the highlights of my professional life was seeing such work at a junior school in a working-class district of West Hartlepool. Children of eight and nine presented an improvisation based on the life of St Joan. The emotions that those small children evoked brought several of the watching adults to the verge of tears. I can recall the experience as if it were yesterday. Unfortunately, no ciné camera was on hand to record the event. When the presentation was over and the children had all returned to their classroom, a colleague asked me if I had seen the bishop recently (the boy playing the part of the bishop was magnificent: standing fully "six feet tall" he had that blend of dignity and other-worldliness one usually associates with high ecclesiastical office). I shook my head and followed him to a classroom doorway. He pointed to a small boy, slumped over his desk, his head up, gazing at the ceiling. It seemed impossible to associate this very ordinary little boy with the dignified bishop we had seen scarcely a quarter of an hour before. This awe-inspiring presentation, stimulated by Tom Stabler, has since become the yardstick against which I have measured my own work in educational drama.

A full-time drama teacher, in order to survive, must learn to conserve his energies. Drama is the most demanding subject on the school timetable, calling for reserves of imagination and powers of organisation far in excess of those required in any other subject. Headmasters can help to relieve the pressures on the drama teacher by providing him with a working area out of earshot of the other classrooms in the school. Nothing frustrates drama teaching more than having to control the noise-level in the classroom in order to consider other members of staff teaching close by. Class work should be leavened with group work in order to gain a respite from the pressures involved. While student teachers are in a school, the drama specialist should be given time off to visit other schools and colleges of education to discuss mutual problems with colleagues, enabling him to recharge his batteries with new ideas and fresh methods of approach gleaned from such exhanges.

Children involved in educational drama should never be "directed" in the theatrical sense. This, of course, is not to say that children should never be directed: when working on a text, or rehearsing the school play, they require a firm sense of direction, but educational drama is not theatre. There is no audience to criticise if the final product appears confused and lacking in unity. Educational drama requires a more subtle approach summed up in Mrs. Heathcote's phrase as "non-directed-direction."

Education is "the nurture of personal growth." A drama teacher nourishes children with stimuli as a gardener feeds his plants. Only harm can come to those plants whose stems are stretched in order to encourage faster growth. If a drama teacher attempts to stimulate dramatic growth by demonstrating to children how he thinks a part should be played, he is seeking not pupil growth but parody. A drama teacher must be an impartial chairman, never a biased autocrat. His role is to offer stimuli and a range of possibilities from which the children make the choice which is right for them at that particular stage in their development. Children must be given the opportunity to make their own decisions based upon the options open to them. They must be allowed to think out their own characters, their own moves and their own dialogue. Only then does child drama become educational drama—the most valuable tool in contemporary education.

Appendix I

PREPARING AND PLANNING A DRAMA SYLLABUS

The Layout of a Drama Lesson Plan

Subject: Drama   *Date:*
Class: 1Q   *Length of lesson:* 40 minutes

Lesson: No. 1

General aim: To improvise the story of The Goblin of Oyeyama (*see* Chapter 1).

Specific aim of Lesson No. 1:

(*a*) To arouse an interest in the story.
(*b*) To give children practice in characterisation: goblins, guards, princess, maid.
(*c*) To give children practice in controlled movement.

Apparatus:

(*a*) Rostrums.
(*b*) Record—"The Enemy God and the Dance of the Black Spirits" from the *Scythian Suite*, Prokofiev.
(*c*) Book: *The Myths and Legends of Japan*, F. Hadland Davis, Harrap.

Matter	*Method*
Introduction	
1. The Goblin of Oyeyama.	1. The teacher narrates the story.
2. *Scene One:* The princess Sanjo is	2. The teacher builds up the

out walking with her maid Kaguya in the palace garden. Shutendoji, the goblin King, and his followers descend upon the palace garden, paralyse the guards, clamber over the wall, seize the princess and her maid, and carry them off to their mountain stronghold.

scenario through class discussion.

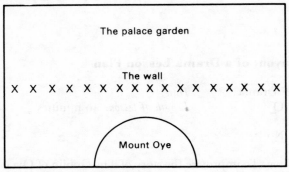

The palace garden

The wall

X X X X X X X X X X X X X X X X X X X

Mount Oye

Fig. 12. Floorplan of alternative staging.

Development

3. Members of the class are chosen to play the various characters.

3. Selected by the teacher.

4. Building the "set." The guards, princess, and her maid, build the wall around the palace garden.

4. The wall is built of rostrum boxes, chairs and tables, and stretches from one side of the classroom to the other.

5. Creating goblin roles.

5. Through discussion with the teacher, the children build up a word picture of the goblins: they are large-headed, spindly armed, short-legged, hunch-backed creatures. The children move about the room to the music discovering their own goblin characters.

6. Difficulties are overcome.

6. By further discussion.

7. Scene One.

7. The children improvise the events outlined and return to their places at the end of the scene.

De-climax

8. The children comment on the   8. Through discussion.
events in Scene One and suggest
possibilities for improvement.

Plan of activities (*see* Fig. 12)

Further reading

Alan Cohen and Norman Garner, *A Student's Guide to Teaching Practice*, University of London Press.

Drama Themes for a First-Year Secondary Class

Myths and legends provide a useful introduction to drama work with first-year secondary children. The following scheme has been designed to give pupils an insight into the varieties of human experience as represented in the myths and legends of twelve widely differing cultures.

Human error

1. *Deceit* (African). "One Hundred Slaves for a Corncob." Adapted from "The Separation of God from Man" in *African Myths and Tales*, edited Susan Feldmann, Dell Publishing Co.
2. *Greed* (Arabian). "Ma'aruf the Cobbler," from *The Thousand and One Nights*, translated N. J. Dawood, Penguin Books.
3. *Jealousy* (German). "Undine," from *Undine and Other Stories*, La Motte Fouqué, Oxford University Press. A modern work, but containing many of the elements associated with myth and legend.

The Outsider

1. *As hero* (Japanese). "The Goblin of Oyeyama" (*see* Chapter 1).
2. *As victim* (Chinese). "The injustice done to Tou Ngo," from *Six Yüan Plays* translated Liu Jung-En, Penguin Classics.
3. *As rebel* (Icelandic). "Gunnar of Hlidarend, from *Njal's Saga*, Chapters 19–77, translated Magnus Magnusson and Hermann Palsson, Penguin Classics. See also *The Burning of Njal*, Henry Treece, Bodley Head.

4. *As saviour* (Irish). W. B. Yeats, *Countess Cathleen*, from *Classic Irish Drama*, Penguin Plays.

The Struggle

1. Of conscience and for survival (Hebraic). Jonah, in the Old Testament.
2. Within a microcosm (Greek). "The Bow of Odysseus," *The Odyssey*, Chapters xx–xxii. Homer, Penguin Classics.
3. Political (Russian). "The Dragon," Yevgeny Schwartz, in *Three Soviet Plays*, Penguin Books. Also a comparatively modern work, but containing many of the elements of myth and legend.

The Search

1. For the Holy Grail (English). *The Quest of the Holy Grail*, translated P. M. Matarasso, Penguin Books.
2. For identity (Greek). "Oedipus Rex," Sophocles, in *The Theban Plays*, translated E. F. Watling, Penguin Classics. See also *Men and Gods*, Rex Warner, Penguin Books.

Possible Scenario for "One Hundred Slaves for a Corncob"

CHARACTERS Wulbari, an African god
                  Ananse, the Captain of the Guard
                  Members of Wulbari's court

SCENE ONE At the court of Wulbari
1. Wulbari and his followers enter. His subjects flatter him, offer their services, shower him with praise.
2. Wulbari turns to Ananse and asks what he has to offer. Ananse boasts that he can turn a corncob into one hundred slaves. This causes general amusement. The members of the court tell him that only Wulbari could perform such a miracle. Wulbari challenges Ananse to make good his boast. He gives Ananse a corncob. Ananse takes his leave.
    Ananse descends to earth and arrives at the village of Yendi.

CHARACTERS Ananse
                  The Chief of Yendi
                  The villagers of Yendi

SCENE TWO The village of Yendi

1. The chief and the villagers come out to greet Ananse. He tells them that he has come from the god Wulbari, and that he would like a bed for the night. They lead him to an empty hut. He tells them that he has a corncob belonging to the god. He asks the chief to place it in safe keeping overnight. The chief shows Ananse a suitable hiding place.

2. The villagers and Ananse, retire for the night. When everyone is asleep, Ananse silently makes his way to the hiding place, removes the corncob and feeds it to some chickens.

3. Early in the morning, Ananse wakes up the whole village, telling them that Wulbari's corncob has disappeared. He creates such a disturbance that the chief orders his people to fill a large basket with corn which he then gives to Ananse to appease Wulbari's wrath.

4. Ananse leaves the village taking with him the basket of corn.

He later exchanges the basket of corn for a hen. He arrives at the town of Krachi.

CHARACTERS Ananse
Merchants
Townspeople
Priestess of the temple
Ten sheep

SCENE THREE In the town of Krachi

1. Merchants are selling their wares in the marketplace.

2. Ananse arrives in the town. He shows the hen to the people, telling them that it belongs to the god Wulbari. He asks for a room for the night and a safe place for the hen. The people suggest the temple. It will be perfectly safe there along with the other hens kept by the priestess for the sacrificial rites. The townspeople introduce Ananse to the priestess. He gives her the hen and she puts it with the other birds. The people take him to a rest house where he can spend the night.

3. Night falls. The townspeople retire to their beds. When everyone is asleep, Ananse creeps into the temple, kills the hen and scatters blood and feathers over the floor.

4. In the morning, Ananse wakes the townsfolk. He tells them that Wulbari's hen was sacrificed during the night. He tells the people that Wulbari will punish them for this ghastly crime – a terrible curse will fall upon Krachi.

5. The townspeople blame the priestess. They seek her out, accuse her of killing the hen, which she hotly denies, and drive her from the town.

6. Ananse tells the townspeople that although the guilty party has been punished, Wulbari will still have to be compensated. The towns-people offer Ananse various peace offerings: a cockerel, a bale of cloth, etc. Ananse refuses each item in turn: the cockerel is sickly, the cloth is of cheap quality. Eventually someone offers a sheep. Ananse tells them that for ten sheep Wulbari might perhaps be restrained from placing a curse upon the town. Reluctantly the townspeople agree and ten sheep are rounded up and brought to Ananse. Ananse leaves Krachi driving off the ten sheep.

CHARACTERS Ananse
                       Ten sheep
                       Members of a burial party

SCENE FOUR A road
1. It is a very hot day. Ananse is resting by the roadside. The ten sheep are grazing peacefully nearby.
2. Members of a burial party walk by carrying a corpse. Ananse stops them and asks if they have far to go. They tell him that it is a ten-mile journey to the burial ground. Ananse suggests that in this heat the corpse will be rotten by the time they get there. He persuades them to exchange the corpse for his ten sheep. They agree. The mourners drive away the sheep; Ananse staggers off in the opposite direction, part-carrying, part-dragging the corpse.

CHARACTERS Ananse
                       The corpse
                       A Military Commander
                       Warriors

SCENE FIVE A military training camp
1. The warriors are practising the arts of war.
2. Ananse staggers into the camp supporting the corpse. He tells the commander that his companion is Wulbari's son. He is very tired and they would both like a hut for the night. Some of the warriors show them to a hut. They explain that a dance has been scheduled for the evening but if Wulbari's son is tired they will postpone it until a later date. Ananse insists that they hold the dance. Wulbari's son can sleep through anything. In fact, Ananse tells them, he often has to flog him to wake him up he sleeps so soundly. Ananse lays the corpse down in the hut. Food is brought for both of them; Ananse eats all of it himself.
3. The warriors dance. They sink exhausted to the floor.

4. Ananse wakes the commander. He cannot arouse his friend. Would the commander's sons come and beat him to wake him up. The sons, armed with whips and sticks, accompany Ananse to his hut. They begin to beat the corpse. "Beat him harder" yells Ananse. Eventually they give up in despair. They cannot waken him. Ananse bends over the corpse. Suddenly, he lets out a panic stricken cry. "You have killed him! You have killed Wulbari's son!" he screams. The warriors are terrified. The commander offers to kill his sons with his bare hands to appease Wulbari's wrath, but Ananse dissuades him. The only gift Wulbari would accept in the circumstances would be one hundred warriors to serve him as slaves. The commander agrees.

5. Ananse leaves with a party of warriors.

CHARACTERS Wulbari
Members of Wulbari's court
Ananse
Warriors

SCENE SIX At the court of Wulbari

1. Wulbari is holding court.
2. Ananse marches in and offers Wulbari the one hundred slaves he promised in return for the corncob. The warriors are set to work at once. Ananse explains to the court how he managed to acquire them in exchange for the corncob.
3. Wulbari is delighted and promotes Ananse to be his chief adviser.
4. The members of the court retire, envying Ananse's popularity with the god.

Suggested Outline for a Secondary School Drama Syllabus

The following outline is offered as a possible guide to the subjects suitable for dramatisation with different ages and intelligence ranges in a secondary school.

First Year

Myths and legends (*see* pp. 193–4).

Second Year
Boys
Narrative Poetry: Jean Desprez, Robert Service.

Escape Story: The Road to En-Dor, E. H. Jones.
Adventure Story: King Solomon's Mines, Rider Haggard.
Science Fiction: 2001: Space Odyssey, Arthur C. Clarke.
Biography: Lawrence of Arabia.
Historical Episode: The Slave Trade.

Girls

Escape: A group of girls escape from an approved school.
War: The Women of Troy, Euripides (improvised).
Adventure Story: A plane carrying a party of school-girls crashes on a desert island – a female *Lord of the Flies.*
Science Fiction: A planet ruled over by women.
Biography: Najmeh Najafi, see *Reveille for a Persian Village,* Helen Hinckley.
Historical Episode: The Matchgirls' Strike. See *The Matchgirls,* book and lyrics by Bill Owen.

Third Year

Boys

Unsolved mysteries.
The supernatural.
Crime.
Styles of comedy:
  Black.
  Farce.
  Slapstick.
  Situation.
  Surrealist.

Girls

Life in a women's ward.
Life in a women's prison.
Mothers in Northern Ireland, attempting to end the violence.
Supporters of Women's Liberation, trying to stop a Miss World competition.
Miners' wives waiting for news of their husbands after a pit disaster.

Fourth Year

Social situations:
  Personal relationships.

The interview.
Leaving home.
The conduct of a meeting.
A wedding.

Fifth Year

ROSLA children (*see* pp. 165–187).
For those staying on into the Sixth Form – ROSLA drama, and
researching, scripting, and performing a documentary play based
upon a local, national, or international theme.

Sixth Year
Improvisation leading to a scripted play

A great deal of class work during the first three years in the secondary school tends to be male-orientated. Traditionally, it has been
the woman's role to stay at home while the men ventured forth in
search of work or adventure. Boys are usually more vociferous than
girls in making their dramatic needs known and there is a tendency
particularly amongst male drama teachers of structuring scenarios in-
which males roles predominate, leaving the girls with "walk-on" parts
as nurses, wives, nuns, as a sop to their femininity, but giving them
little choice in dictating the course of the action. Or, worse still, they
end up in nebulous male roles as guards, soldiers, fishermen, etc. Ways
must be found of sharing the drama work more equally between the
sexes. The problem is not as acute in the first year as most girls are
still willing to accept male roles providing they are sufficiently demanding, while myths and legends offer plenty of dramatic scope for
both boys and girls.

However, from the end of the first year to the beginning of the
fourth, the fact that girls generally mature two years earlier than the
boys has to be taken into consideration, and separate work planned
for them. At first, the girls parallel the boys in their enjoyment of
adventure stories, but these must be given a female bias hence the
inclusion of such themes as The Matchgirls' Strike and The Women
of Troy; but whereas the boys continue into the third year to enjoy
action and adventure in the form of stories of the supernatural, unsolved mysteries and violent crime, the girls, in the main, prefer to
dramatise the events of everyday life.

During the fourth and fifth years, the interests of boys and girls
converge again in an exploration of the varying social situations to

be met in and out of school. Apart from the school leavers, drama at fifth- and sixth-form level, if timetabled at all, tends to be included as a respite from the pressures of examinations and the chances of performing scripted plays will depend very much upon the time that has been allotted to the subject.

Treatment of the Orpheus Theme

A drama teacher should be able to use any type of material with any age or intelligence level providing that the treatment is at the level of the children concerned. Varying treatments of the Orpheus theme can be used to illustrate this point.

The original myth tells of Orpheus, a famous poet and musician and of his great love for Eurydice. The couple had only been married a short while when Eurydice was bitten on the foot by a snake and died. Orpheus, stricken with grief, journeyed to the realm of the dead in an attempt to win back his lost love. So eloquently did he plead before King Pluto that the lord of the underworld agreed to release Eurydice on one condition: that he did not look back at his wife until they had both left Hades behind them. All went well until they reached the passage to the outer world, when, an uncontrollable impulse overcame Orpheus. He turned and looked back at his wife and in that very moment, she was snatched away from him a second time, and lost forever.

Adapted to meet the needs of a first-year secondary form, Orpheus becomes a nineteenth-century explorer. He takes Eurydice with him on an expedition in search of the source of the Nile. One evening, Eurydice wanders away from the camp and is captured by African tribesmen. Orpheus visits the chief and pleads for his wife's release. The king agrees to let Eurydice go on one condition: Orpheus must prove his superiority over the local witchdoctor. Orpheus accepts the challenge. The witchdoctor emerges from his hut, a deadly spider crawling over the back of his hand, which had previously been coated with an insect repellant to keep the creature at bay. The witchdoctor motions to Orpheus. He too must hold the spider. Orpheus quickly rummages in his pack and brings out a magnifying glass with one hand while accepting the spider on the back of the other. Orpheus holds the glass up to the sun, focusing the rays through the glass directly on to the creature's back. With a dry crackle, the spider bursts into flames, its charred body falling harmlessly to the ground. The natives fall back in awe at the white man's magic.

Orpheus tells Eurydice to follow him. They walk through the silent ranks of natives. "Don't look back" whispers Orpheus. As they near the safety of the jungle, Orpheus turns to check whether Eurydice is still following him. The spell is broken. "Kill them!" screams the dishonoured witchdoctor. Orpheus calls to Eurydice to make a dash for it and they both race towards the nearby trees. As Orpheus reaches the safety of the forest, Eurydice is struck by a volley of spears and falls dying to the ground.

With third-year pupils, Orpheus is a drummer in a pop group. Eurydice, his wife, is killed in a car crash. Stunned by grief, Orpheus visits a number of spiritualist mediums in an attempt to make contact with his dead wife, but with no success. Failure only serves to strengthen his obsession. His work suffers: he fails to turn up at the recording studios, cancels personal appearances, and lacks the inspiration to write new material. Eventually he finds a medium who convinces him beyond all doubt that she really is in touch with the spirit of his dead wife. At this point his manager steps in and warns him that unless he refrains from dabbling in the occult and devotes more time to his work, he will have no alternative but to tear up his contract and find another drummer. Orpheus heeds the warning, turns back to the group, and gives up all further thoughts of contacting Eurydice.

With sixth-form pupils, Orpheus could become a drug addict. He marries Eurydice much against her parents' wishes. Under his influence, she too becomes an addict. She takes an overdose, but her parents discover her just in time. She is rushed to hospital and makes a good recovery. They forbid her ever to see Orpheus again. To win her back, Orpheus accepts hospital treatment and is cured of his addiction. He convinces her parents of his resolve never again to take drugs and they allow the young couple to come together again. Within a month, Orpheus is back on drugs. He persuades Eurydice to have just one more fix. She agrees. She takes another overdose and dies while Orpheus, himself under the effects of the drug, attempts to summon help.

Appendix II

MUSIC AND DRAMA

Music can play an extremely important part in the drama lesson: introducing an improvisation, heightening a particular mood, acting as a stimulus, lending atmosphere to a mimed sequence, aiding character development, or ensuring a restful de-climax. The drama teacher should always have a supply of records or tapes available. The following is a list of suggestions for music related to specific situations, moods, and feelings, most commonly met with in educational drama lessons.

But school record players and tape recorders have a habit of breaking down. The teacher and the children are then thrown upon their own resources and, successful as recorded music can be in stimulating worthwhile drama work, it can never replace, in educational value, the music and sound effects created by the children themselves. The rhythmic tapping of finger tips on the seats of chairs can create a passable impression of native drumming; vocal impersonations – the chatter of howler monkeys, the squawk of parakeets – can effectively suggest the sounds of a tropical rain forest. Children should be encouraged to start a classroom collection of objects which make sounds suitable for accompanying their drama lessons. Creative music-making adds a new and exciting dimension to creative drama.

Alien worlds
Mimaroglu, *Agony*.
Stockhausen, *Kontakte*.

Birds and animals
Saint Saëns, *Le Carnaval des Animaux* – Lions, hens and cocks, wild asses, tortoises, elephants, kangaroos, fishes, birds, swans.
Prokofiev, *The Song of the Nightingale*.

Black Magic
Messiaen, *Colours of the Celestial City*.
Varèse, *Ionisation*.

Blast off
Dissevelt, "Ignition," from *Fantasy in Orbit*.

Brain-washing/Thought control.
Avni, *Vocalise*.

Chaos
Copland, "Towards the Bridge," from *Music for a Great City*.
Ives, Second and fourth sections of the *Robert Browning Overture*.
Scriabin, *Prometheus*.
Varèse, *Arcana*.
Vaughan Williams, First movement Symphony No. 6.

Circus
Meyerbeer, "Entree," from the ballet *Les Patineurs*.
Stravinsky, "Royal March," from *L'Histoire du Soldat*.

Clock
Kodály, "The Viennese Musical Clock," from the suite of Háry János.

Comic Chase
Holst, The beginning of the opera *The Perfect Fool*.
Khatchaturian, "Galop," from the suite *Masquerade*.

Computers
Mimaroglu, *Intermezzo*.

Conqueror Entering a Captured City
Mussorgsky-Ravel, "Bydlo," from *Pictures at an Exhibition*.

Cowboys
Copland, *Appalachian Spring*.
Copland, *Billy the Kid*.
Gillis, *Portrait of a Frontier Town*.
Grofé, "On the Trail," from the *Grand Canyon Suite*.

Creation
Bartók, "Andante Tranquillo," from *Music for Strings, Percussion and Celesta*.
Milhaud, The beginning of *La Création du Monde*.

Dance of Death
Saint Saëns, *Danse Macabre*.

Darting and Dodging
Britten, "Moto Perpetuo," from *Matinées Musicales*.

Death
Prokiev, "The Grave of Romeo and Juliet," from *Romeo and Juliet*.

Desolation, following a plague or a nuclear war
Messiaen, First movement, *And I Await the Resurrection of the Dead*.
Vaughan Williams, "Epilogue," *Symphony No. 6*.

Despair
Bloch, *Schelomo*.

Doom, a feeling of.
Mussorgsky-Ravel, "Catacombs," from *Pictures at an Exhibition*.

Festive
America:	Copland, *Billy the Kid*.
	Gillis, "Ranch House Party," from *Portrait of (Frontier Town.*
	Ives, "Putnam's Camp," "Redding," "Connecticut," from *Three Places in New England*.
Cuba:	Gershwin, *Cuban Overture*.
Mexico:	Copland, *El Salón México*.
The Orient:	Hindemith, Second movement of the *Symphonic Metamorphoses on a Theme by Carl Maria Von Weber*.
Persia:	Mussorgsky, "Dance of the Persian Slaves," from *Khovanshtchina*.
Russia:	Khatchaturian, Lezghinka and Gopak from *Gayaneh*.
Scotland:	Arnold, *Four Scottish Dances*.
Spain:	De Falla, "Final Dance," from *The Three-Cornered Hat; Ritual Fire Dance;* "Song of Love's Remorse," and "Dance of Terror," from *Love The Magician.*

Clog dance, maypole dance and tambourine dances. Hérold/ Lanchbery, *La Fille Mal Gardée*.
Peasants' dance: Mendelssohn, "Dance of the Clowns," from *A Midsummer Night's Dream*. Meyerbeer, "Pas de Trois," from *Les Patineurs*.

Fairies
De Falla, "The Neighbours Dance," from *The Three-Cornered Hat*.

Fanfare
Prokofiev, The Beginning of the suite *Lieutenant Kije*.
Walton, Fanfare from the Shakespeare suite *Richard III*.
Walton, Overture, "The Globe Playhouse," from the suite *Henry V*.

Fear
Varèse, *Amériques*.
Varèse, *Equatorial*.

Funeral Procession
Stravinsky, "Great Chorale" from the suite *L'Histoire du Soldat*.
Walford Davies, *Solemn Melody*.
Walton, "Funeral March," from the suite *Hamlet*.

Gang Fight
Copland, "Skyline and Subway Jam," from *Music for a Great City*.

Ghosts
Varèse, "Finale" of *Octandre*.
Varèse, *Hyperprism*.

Giant
Mussorgsky–Ravel, "Two Polish Jews," from *Pictures at an Exhibition*.

Insanity
Balakirev, *Overture to King Lear*.
Berio, *Visage*.
Cage, *Fontana Mix*.
Gerhard, *Concerto for Orchestra*.
Mimaroglu, *Le Tombeau d'Edgar Poe*.

Jollity
Walton, *Johannesburg Festival Overture*.

Laboratories
Henry, "Le Voyage," from *The Tibetan Book of the Dead*.

Levity
Prokofiev, "Juliet, the Maiden," from *Romeo and Juliet*.

Lost in Space
Blomdahl, *Aniara*.

Love, young
Prokofiev, "Romeo and Juliet," from *Romeo and Juliet*.

Meditation, religious
Brahms, *Choral Preludes.*
Vaughan Williams, *Fantasia on a Theme by Thomas Tallis.*

Meditation, secular
Barber, *Adagio for Strings* Op. II.
Delius, *A Song of Summer.*
Respighi, "Italiana," from *Antiche Danze ed Arie per Liuto – Suite III.*

Menace
Messiaen, Section five, *And I Await the Resurrection of the Dead.*
Prokofiev, "Night," from the *Scythian Suite.*
Smetana, "Tábor," from *Mà Vlast.*
Stravinsky, "Dance of King Kastchei," from *L'Oiseau de Feu.*
Vaughan Williams, Second movement, *Symphony No. 6.*

Military march
Prokofiev, "The Birth of Kije," from the suite *Lieutenant Kije.*

Mischief
Britten, "March," from *Matinées Musicales.*
Kabalevesky, "Galop," from *The Comedians.*
Milhaud, *Le Boeuf sur le Toit.*
Mussorgsky–Ravel, "Tuileries," from *Pictures at an Exhibition.*
Rossini–Respighi, Opening of the ballet *La Boutique Fantasque.*
Strauss, *Till Eulenspiegel.*
Vaughan Williams, "Overture" from *The Wasps.*
Walton: "Comedy Overture," *Scapino.*

Mischievous Spirits
Stravinsky, *Feu d'Artifice.*

Nightmare
Varèse, *Intégrales.*

Nobility
Debussy, "Incidental Music," from *Pelléas and Mélisande.*
Fauré, "Prelude," from *La Fileuse.*

Oriental Slaves
De Falla: "The Miller's Dance," from *Dances from The Three-Cornered Hat.*

Pagan rites
Stravinsky, "The Sacrifice," from *Le Sacre du Printemps.*

Pot-holing
Lewin-Richter, *Study No. 1.*

Prehistoric World
Carlos, *Variations for Flute and Electronic Sound.*
Mimaroglu, *Agony.*

Primitive Ritual
Prokofiev, "Invocation to Véles and Ala," "The Glorious Departure of Lolly," and "The Procession of the Sun," from the *Scythian Suite.*
Tippett, "Ritual Dances," from *A Midsummer Marriage.*
Varèse, *Nocturnal.*

Processions
Britten, Opening of *The Young Person's Guide to the Orchestra.*
Mussorgsky/Ravel, "Promenade," and "The Great Gate of Kiev," from *Pictures at an Exhibition.*
Tchaikovsky, *Marche Slav.*

Ancient procession:	Janáček, Opening of *Sinfonietta.*
Humorous procession:	Kodály, "Entrance of the Emperor and his Court," from the suite *Háry János.*
Medieval procession:	Walton, Prelude to suite *Richard III.*
	Vaughan Williams, *Fantasia on Greensleeves.*
Royal procession:	Bliss, *Welcome the Queen.*
	Clarke, *Trumpet Voluntary.*
	Walton, "Crown Imperial" and "Orb and Sceptre," marches.

Quarrel
Mussorgsky, "Limoges," from *Pictures at an Exhibition.*
Prokofiev, "Montagues and Capulets," from *Romeo and Juliet.*

Retreat of a Defeated Army
Honegger, "The March of The Philistines," from *Le Roi David.*

Rioting
Mussorgsky–Ravel, "The Hut on Fowl's Legs," from *Pictures at an Exhibition.*

Sadness
Elgar, "Nimrod," from the *Enigma Variations*.
Francaix, Second movement, *Concertino for Piano and Orchestra*.
Ravel, *Pavane Pour Une Infante Défunte*.
Respighi, "Arie di Corte," from *Antiche Arie e Danze per Liuto – Suite III*.
Satie, *Gymnopédies I and II*.
Walton, "Death of Falstaff," from the suite *Henry V*.

Sea
Bax, *Tintagel*.
Debussy, *La Mer*.
Khatchaturian, "Adagio of Spartacus and Phygia," from *Spartacus*.

Seasons of the Year
Glazunov, *The Seasons*.

Skipping
Prokofiev, "Pas de Chat," from the suite *Cinderella*.

Sleep
Mendelssohn, "Nocturne No. 7," from the Incidental Music to *A Midsummer Night's Dream*.
Stravinsky, "Lullaby," from *L'Oiseau de Fer*.

Soldiers, comic
Kodály, "The Battle and Defeat of Napoleon," from the suite, *Háry János*.

Soldier's March
Britten, "March," from *Soirées Musicales*.
Stravinsky, "Soldier's March," from Suite *L'Histoire du Soldat*.

Spells
Bartók, "Allegro," from *Music for Strings, Percussion and Celesta*.

Spirits, Elves and Goblins
Bartók, "Allegro," from *Music for Strings, Percussion and Celesta*.
Debussy, *Jeux*.

Space Travel
Dissevelt, *Fantasy in Orbit*.

Storm on Land
Grofé, "Cloudburst," from the *Grand Canyon Suite.*
Hérold–Lanchbery, "Storm and Finale," from *La Fille Mal Gardée.*

Storm at Sea
Britten, "Storm," from *Four Sea Interludes*, from *Peter Grimes.*

Supernatural
Arnold, *Tam o'Shanter.*
Mussorgsky, *A Night on the Bare Mountain.*
Mussorgsky–Ravel, "Gnomes," from *Pictures at an Exhibition.*
Prokofiev, "The Enemy God and The Dance of the Black Spirits, from the *Scythian Suite.*

Suspense
Prokofiev, "Russia Under the Mongolian Yoke," from *Alexander Nevsky.*

Sword Fight
Prokofiev, "Quarrel," from *Cinderella Suite.*
Prokofiev, "Tybalt's Death," from *Romeo and Juliet.*

Terror
Honegger, "Incantation of the Witch of En-Dor," from *Le Roi David.*

Times of Day

Dawn:	Britten, "Dawn," from *Four Sea Interludes*, from *Peter Grimes.*
	Mussorgsky, "Prelude," from *Khovanshtchina.*
	Ravel, "Lever du Jour," from *Daphnis et Chloé No. 2.*
Sunrise:	Grofé, "Sunrise," from the *Grand Canyon Suite.*
Sunday morning:	Britten, "Sunday Morning," from *Four Sea Interludes* from *Peter Grimes.*
Sunset:	Grofé, "Sunset," from the *Grand Canyon Suite.*
Moonlight:	Britten, "Moonlight," from *Four Sea Interludes* from *Peter Grimes.*
Midnight:	De Falla, "The Clock Strikes," from *Love the Magician.*

Triumphal ending
Stravinsky, "Finale," from the suite *L'Oiseau de Fer.*

Triumphal march
Berlioz, "March," from Les Troyens.
Bliss, "March," from the suite, *Things to Come.*
Hindemith, Fourth movement, *Symphonic Metamorphoses on Themes of Carl Maria Von Weber.*
Tchaikovsky, *Marche Slav.*
Walton, *The Spitfire Prelude and Fugue.*

Undersea City
Debussy, *La Cathédrale Engloutie.*

War
Bliss, "Attack and Machines," from the suite *Things to Come.*
Khatchaturian, "Dance of Gaditanae" and "Victory of Spartacus," from *Spartacus.*
Khatchaturian, "Sabre Dance," from *Gayaneh.*
Prokofiev, "The Battle on the Ice," from *Alexander Nevsky.*
Shostakovitch, First movement, *Seventh Symphony.*
Sibelius, *Finlandia.*
Walton, "Charge and Battle," from the suite *Henry V.*

Witchcraft
Bartok, *The Miraculous Mandarin.*
Stravinsky, "The Devil's Dance," and the "Triumphal March of the Devil" from the suite *L'Histoire du Soldat.*

Youthful high spirits
Kodály, "The Tale Begins," from the suite *Háry János.*

Round the World

An excellent two-volume set of records of the music of China, Tibet, Cambodia, Madagascar, Laos, Bali, Tahiti, Japan, India, the Jews, the ancient Greeks, and Islam, is to be found on HMV *History of Music in Sound* Vol. i, "Ancient and Oriental Music."

Africa
Music of Africa from the Malinké and the Baoulé. XTRA 1124.
Missa Luba. Philips, BL 7592.

China
Dragon Boat. Worldwide Series, China. EMI SCX 6290.

Hebraic
Hebraic Chants for the Holy Days, Marcel Lorand Trio.
Parliament Records. PLP 133–2.

India
India's Master Musician, Ravi Shankar. Fontana. TL 5253.

Japan
Classical Music of Japan. Polydor Special. 236 516.

Jivaro
Legend of the Jivaro, Yma Sumac. Capitol. T 770.

Sicily
Sicilia Bedda. Regal QRX 9020.

South America
Fuego del Ande (Fire of the Andes), Yma Sumac. Capitol. T 1169.

INDEX

213